Theone

The Old Message, A New Messenger

Theone
The Old Message, A New Messenger

Kathryn Enoch

Rowan Press

This is a work of fiction. Any similarity between a character and any real person is purely coincidental. Any similarity between a scene and a real event is strictly coincidental.

Copyright© 1998 by Rowan Press, Inc.

Published in Phoenix, Arizona 85018 U.S.A.

All rights reserved. No portion of this book may be reproduced or transmitted in any form or by any means elecronic or mechanical, including any information storage or retrieval systems, without permission in writing from the publisher, except for brief passages which may be quoted by a reviewer.

Library of Congress Catalog Card Number: 97-69183

ISBN 1-890846-00-7

Cover illustration by Erika

Printed in the United States of America

9 8 7 6 5 4 3 2 1

Glimpse of Peace™

Thanks to my editors,
especially Vince

K. E.

for spiritual seekers with open minds

Humans on the Path

Family Connections

Brigit Mane	Theone's mother
Patrick Mane	Brigit's brother
Aaron Jones	Brigit's first husband
Kristen Jones	Theone's sister
Erik Jones	Theone's brother
Sam Scougan	Patrick's childhood friend

Close Followers

Mike Zimmer	childhood friend
Mag Ingram	widowed shopkeeper
Jasper Stroud	journalist
Ian Leahy	book editor
Pilar Nuñez	widowed bookkeeper
Arela Pedersen	primary school teacher
Bobby Kolaski-Lon	beach bum
Gabriel "Spider" Giovetti	drifter

The Opposition

Glenn Chandler	minister
Vaughn Ulrich	Chandler's associate
Elliot Becker	member of Chandler's church
Judith Hutchins	member of Chandler's church

Minor, but Pivotal

Nancy Nicholson	Glenn Chandler's first wife
Tawi Shinkawa	Vaughn Ulrich's wife
Kizzie Rosen	Spider's mother
Adriano Giovetti	Spider's father
Melvin & Delora Becker	Elliot Becker's parents
Heidi, Alana, Gina, Sacha Becker	Elliot Becker's family
Don Becker	Elliot Becker's brother
Leslie Daniels	Don Becker's companion

PROLOGUE
September 22, 1968

"That's strong grass," Brigit muttered, her eyes sunk and her mind lulled. Stronger than any she had smoked before. She didn't do drugs, really. Sharing an occasional joint with a group of people you knew wasn't really doing drugs. Not really.

Brigit struggled to fix on a coherent thought. She had inhaled how much? Two puffs. Had some other substance been added to the joint? She'd heard about the psychedelic effects of acid, but also about the risk of a bad trip. LSD held no interest for her. Toking up just gave you a mellow feeling while you partied with friends and grooved on the music.

The music...Brigit giggled. Two local bands. Her younger brother played keyboard for one of them. Tonight was Paxton, Wisconsin's equivalent of a rock concert. The kids attending were townies or students from the local college. She giggled again. She was both, a townie and a student. Like, a senior student. Like, one more year and on to Real Life armed with a bachelor of arts degree in library science.

Brigit shivered, but not from being cold. Several bonfires blazed on the narrow beach, and no wind stirred the evening. She shivered again. How strange she felt. Like her whole being was opening...to possibilities.

At the fork in the county woods leading to the lake, state troopers had congregated on the service road to monitor the gathering of youth, but they had been instructed not to interfere unless the group got rowdy. Look the other way had been Chief Scougan's advice, the chief whose son, Sam, played guitar with Brigit's brother, Patrick.

The song lyrics took on clarity, and Brigit's hearing sharpened.
>*Not dreamin', it's not dreamin',*
>*It's feelin', it's believin',*
>*Listen to me.*
>*I am healin',*
>*I am worth believin',*
>*I am worth pleasin',*
>*Oh, the souls are a'grievin',*
>>*in sore need of healin',*
>>>*and beggin' to be givin' Peace.*
>
>*So I'll try again,*
>*To set your journey to its end.*
>*Set it right,*
>>*Towards the light,*
>>>*So I'll try again...*

Strange words, but soothing. And the Singer's voice...unfamiliar, eloquent, inviting...full of promise. A promise that would be kept...

The song's message, the music's sound gave Brigit peace. No, getting high gives you peace. No, peace came from the song. No, *peace came from the words* of the song...she opened her eyes to an immense moon that had risen over the lake. Its luminance commanded the sky, and Brigit was conscious that the music and the voices of the crowd had receded. She felt alone in a bath of silver light.

Ridiculous. The sweet smoke of marijuana clogged the air and the mind tended to focus inward from the drug, but the several hundred people squeezed on to blankets had not suddenly vanished.

"You have a special soul, Brigit," the Singer whispered, "a soul meant to nurture. I love you, Brigit."

This is a 'high' from grass that might not be grass, her mind warned, but she responded with complete sincerity, "I love you, too."

"Love redeems you."

"And gives you peace," she answered.

"Yes, love is the way to Peace..."

The Singer kissed Brigit, and she welcomed the love offered.

When Brigit woke, the radiance in her bedroom smarted her eyes. She had forgotten to close her shutters when she'd gone to bed. When had she gone to bed? The Singer and her behavior...that grass must have been doctored in some manner! Okay, before she panicked, she'd be logical and assess what she could remember about the previous night.

Unlike her friends, she was not casual about sex. She had been engaged to her high school sweetheart, Lyle, when she had slept with him for the first time; her freshman year in college, he had been killed in Vietnam. At twenty-one, therefore, a single involved relationship was quite old-fashioned for a generation of women taking the Pill and bent on sleeping with everybody. Yet whatever she had inhaled last night had abolished her inhibitions! A total stranger had made love to her, and if she recollected correctly, in the company of a lot of people! But at the time, there had been no people...the silver light must have acted as some sort of shield...and the singer had been familiar...more than familiar...rather, like a dear, close friend...

Brigit relaxed and stretched. No need to panic. The whole situation had been bizarre, but whatever had happened it had been good. And peaceful. During the night, and now, peace filled her. No matter what the consequences, she had totally loved the singer who had totally loved her.

At no time did it occur to Brigit that her window faced North. The sun never shone directly into her bedroom. *The room never brightened from the sun to hurt her eyes like it was doing this morning.*

Eight weeks later, an obstetrician in Chippewa Falls confirmed Brigit's pregnancy, but the singer's peaceful essence remained with her. Her supportive family respected her decision to keep the child and reinforced her calm about the future. They could be called upon for help. (Patrick affectionately teased that the solar eclipse on the 22nd had caused her wild abandon. Brigit checked the calendar expecting to attribute her wanton behavior to the full Moon. Oddly, she discovered that the 22nd had been a new Moon, not a full Moon. But it was also the Autumnal Equinox. Perhaps that condition plus the eclipse had some connection to the bright Moon she had experienced.)

Thus able to finish her education, Brigit took her last exam one month prior to a normal delivery of a healthy baby girl on June 21, 1969. She could find no logic to it, but early in her pregnancy, she had read an obscure mythical fantasy unearthed at a rummage sale and felt compelled to name the child Theone for the compassionate heroine.

The night of Theone's birth Patrick sneaked a toke on the hospital's deserted visitors' deck while he grooved on a glossy slice of waxing moon broadcasting an awesome silvery beam amid a cascade of resplendent stars.

Around the world, ordinary, but spiritually rich women dreamed of the girl child.

At Palomar Observatory, ninety miles southeast of Pasadena, California, an astronomer glanced at a calendar and noted that it was the Summer Solstice, the longest daylight hours of the year.

Adorned in flower circlets, Pagans celebrated Midsummer, a highly magickal Day of Power. In rites of purification, they leaped bonfires symbolizing the Sun, and they honored Nature, the fruitful evidence of the Goddess and God.

Astrologers already knew the times were momentous because of the orbital meeting of the outer planets of Uranus and Pluto. According to tradition, the event forecast revolution.

Six months passed. At the college library where she had found employment, Brigit met craggy, bearded Aaron Jones, a second year graduate student in social services, and they fell in love. Before she agreed to marry him the following summer, she explained to him about the unusual circumstances of Theone's conception. An empathetic man who felt his mission was to assist the less fortunate, Brigit's disclosure only served to further endear her daughter. From that point forward, Aaron considered Theone as his own.

After the wedding, the family moved to a rental in Aaron's hometown, Ashburg, a northwest suburb of Chicago. Aaron's heart arrhythmia exempted him from the Draft; having lost her first love in the war, Brigit felt thankful that this relationship would not be subject to the trauma of Vietnam.

Aaron earned his doctorate at a city university while working as a government caseworker assisting immigrants. During this period, Brigit gave birth to a daughter, Kristen, in 1971 and a son, Erik, in 1972.

Several years later, a newly funded organization set up in Chicago by a worldwide religious council to aid refugees settling in the U.S. offered Aaron a counselor position, and the Jones were able to afford their first house. They purchased one in the same established neighborhood as his parents. Near the train line, Aaron could continue walking to the station. Social work was gratifying, but not lucrative. Their used Volkswagen van required constant repair.

The Jones' sunny, red brick bungalow with a finished attic partitioned for the children's rooms became an inviting place cluttered with books and handicraft paraphernalia; the children showed no inclination to participate in competitive sports. The scents of baking cookies and freshly-cut flowers mingled. Aaron and Brigit lived their love and their children flourished.

The first three weeks of every August, the Jones spent Aaron's vacation visiting Brigit's family in Paxton near Lake Femvivant in Northwestern Wisconsin. Kristen had no interest in it, but Aaron always packed gear so that he, Theone and Erik could camp out a few nights and rise early to fish. Patrick, who had remained in Paxton, loaned them his row boat. (They fished for recreation, not survival, so Theone made sure that they caught nothing worth keeping.) Later in the day, they would hike in the woods and at night, Aaron swore the mosquitoes would eat her, but he still let Theone sleep under the stars while he and Erik retreated to the tent. She never showed any bites, and Aaron always gave credit to the smoke from the dying fire as her protection. (Theone did not mention to Aaron about the raccoons who always rested next to her or the owl who watched over her.) From earliest memory, she listed times spent in Paxton as the best.

The fall that Theone started kindergarten, the Jones decided to activate their church affiliation. They reasoned that their values had been favorably shaped by youthful attendance, and therefore important for their children to be given the same training. 'Our prayers are answered,' Aaron's parents exclaimed, when the family began attending services at the senior Jones' two-story white frame church.

Like everything else, Erik found church agreeable. A great group of guys came to his Sunday School class.

Kristen thrived on the recognition she received. She won prizes for memorized verse and always received a part as a principal player in the frequent youth pageants, or performed as a soloist in the children's choir.

Theone participated because she understood about the importance of family harmony, but she knew from the first prayer that this narrow worship was not her way...

CHAPTER ONE

Trimming the evergreen hedge by the front sidewalk, Brigit paused to watch Theone pulling her rackety white wagon down the pavement. Oscar, their Schnauzer-Cocker mix, trotted faithfully behind her and assorted butterflies frolicked around her.

"My lands! I've never seen butterflies do that!" Declared Sue, the Jones' new neighbor from next door, who was also doing yard work. "By the way, who does Theone look like?"

"A bit of me, but mostly just herself," Brigit replied. Acquaintances usually got around to asking Sue's question. Because Erik and Kristen had blond hair in varying shades and eyes in similar casts of blue like their parents, Theone's fair skin and hint of resemblance to Brigit went undetected. But Brigit burned and freckled from the sun. As many hours as Theone spent outdoors, her complexion neither reddened nor tanned.

In sunlight or moonlight the child's wavy, golden brown hair radiated with a halo. 'The rays playing', Aaron joked, 'the kid's just been blessed with a gorgeous mop.' Brigit would nod, but privately she remained unconvinced that mere illumination acted as the source of the halo. Regardless of the wattage, no artificial light produced the effect.

"She has such unusual eyes," Sue said.

Brigit smiled, but did not respond. Theone's eyes created another disconcerting issue. A person would gape at the child's translucent eyes under her unruly brows and try to determine the color. Blue, no, green, no, violet, no gray, or was it amber? Then they would shrug and conclude, hazel. Hazel eyes took on the various colors of the girl's outfits. Brigit would nod, but the truth? Her clothing had nothing to do with it. Theone's eyes actually changed color. Like the refraction in the octagonal crystal prism that the child had requested for her eighth birthday. The only request. Erik and especially, Kristen, accumulated goods. Purchased goods as opposed to the simple items that Theone assembled from nature.

"Enough of crabgrass for one day," Sue said. "I'm for the hammock and a book."

Brigit nodded absently as she stared at her barefoot daughter turning into the neighbor's yard at the dead-end of their lane. Her oldest, her tender, loving Child of Peace, as Brigit secretly viewed Theone, would not be conventionally pretty like Kristen, but she would grow up to be a striking woman...yet looks would be just a small part of her...charisma. Add the glorious smile, gently humored and charitable, never haughty. The smile, like her hair, a beacon...

Creatures found her irresistible, yet untouchable. As a baby, honeybees had hovered about Theone as if drawn to nectar; like she was a flower. On summer nights fireflies swarmed her person, setting it aglow, but they never landed on her. Wrens, robins, sparrows and other birds peacefully shared the territory of their yard. Brigit believed that every dog and cat in the vicinity had found a way to visit the Jones' home and...pay homage to Theone?

Another disturbing matter was the photographs and movies of the family. Rather, in the midst of a clear shot of others, Theone's image fuzzed repeatedly and in some cases, her image disappeared when Brigit or Aaron knew that Theone had been included in the camera's range. It seemed as if no permanent record must be kept of the child's existence...

She had received the standard childhood inoculations, but Brigit questioned their necessity. Theone had never been ill. No viruses, no allergies - she had not even contracted a mild case of the chicken pox which had felled Kristen and Erik for two weeks each. Theone did not cut herself or bruise...

Theone was ambidextrous, not uncommon except people with the ability usually favored one or the other hand for writing. Her skills were advanced and interchangeable.

Now, the latest incident with the stones...

Abruptly, Brigit whacked the bush, and a shower of pine needles and tiny branches flew about. She often wondered, but she had never worried. Theone had been conceived for a purpose greater than her understanding.

The metal wagon rumbled louder as Theone crossed from the sidewalk to the grass. She took excellent care of her custom-painted wagon, washing it often and oiling the wheels and joints; the rattle of her stones in their silver bucket made the wagon noisy. While some kids collected dolls or trucks, Theone gathered stones which she held and studied. Stones gave her answers for things. Things only she needed to understand.

She glanced at the gray frame cape-cod house on the large lot. "Hello!" She greeted to Mrs. Hagen at her kitchen window.

Mrs. Hagen never minded her presence and had assured Brigit on several occasions that Theone was very respectful of property. Oscar never barked, either. In fact, if the arthritis in her knees didn't give her such a trouble, she would join Theone in her games. (What she did was quite innocent, but Theone did not consider it a game.)

The big yard did not draw Theone, though. The woodsy area next to the lawn attracted her. Part of a forgotten quarter acre parcel owned by the town, it had been appropriated by the Hagens who had lived here for forty years. Several yards from the sidewalk, the late Mr. Hagen had cleared a section of the area to incorporate a garden design, complete with a bird bath and small fish pond. Now, neglected perennials sprouted randomly on the sunny perimeter, and grime blighted the shadowed, cracked bird bath. Mosquitoes favored the moss-filled pond as a breeding site. A rusted cast iron table had been abandoned beside a hoary oak, its gnarled, exposed roots making walking hazardous, but Theone did not find them an obstacle.

The oak sheltered two squirrels. A skunk family, rabbits, and lots of mice made homes in the undergrowth; the brush also teemed with snakes and insects. Birds abounded in the sparse branches of unkempt maples, birches and oaks.

Brambles of black raspberries, vines of wild grapes and a gaping, hulking apple tree which produced a glut of fruit augmented the creatures' diets and Theone's. The parcel was a mini-wilderness in the midst of suburbia and Theone's favorite place.

Brigit loved to garden and in early autumn, acted addicted to mail-order seed catalogues. From the earliest crocus to the last harvested pumpkin, a plethora of growth decorated the Jones' yard; this gave Brigit peace. Theone's peace came from nature unbridled, as right for her as the controlled garden was right for Brigit.

She lifted her bucket, left her wagon at the edge of the lawn and stepped into the woods. As usual, Oscar hung at her heels. Sometimes other children joined her. Across the lane a Catholic family of eight crowded into a space the size of the Jones' house. Two of the middle girls felt the draw. Next door to the Jones lived Mike Zimmer, a redhead Kristen's age whose parents were agnostics. Mike had a sensitive disposition and liked it here. Occasionally Erik came with her. He was kind and possessed a real goodness, but he had a short attention span. The corporeal world often beckoned which was part of his way. But he would mature; he would advance. Kristen was too much of the corporeal world to even come near the woods and her way saddened Theone, but she did not have the right to interfere. Perhaps someday Theone could offer Kristen Truth and she would listen. She prayed for her sister.

A sparkly, faintly green transparent stone caught Theone's attention and she squatted to investigate. She had not seen it before, but neither did its presence surprise her. As many times as she had scoured the vicinity, new stones continued to appear. It was just a part of the magick.

Aaron had been astonished at her broad assortment. (Theone called Aaron, 'Dad', because she loved him for nurturing her, but she had always known that he was not her father.) At the family's weekly trek to the library, he found a lapidary guide intending to help her identify an agate from the plain pebbles. Because, he had assured, there could not be any rock of value in the wild tangle next to the Hagens'. (Most *were* agates, and of various types, Theone conceded, most, but not entirely; nothing was plain, she protested silently.)

A citrine came from Brazil! He exclaimed. Aquamarine was a form of beryl found in New England! Jet came from Spain! Amber, this particular piece imbedded with a primordial gnat, came from the Baltic Coast! Certain of these rocks she carried about so casually were rough forms of semi-precious gems! And how on earth had they come to be in the vicinity of Hagens' yard? How on earth, indeed, Theone thought, mildly indignant. As expected, she had found the yellow quartz set to the east, the blue-green seastone to the west, the millenniums-old fossilized wood to the north and the equally-aged hardened coniferous tree resin to the south. But she did not judge another's doubt about the things she knew as right. She nurtured a hope that Aaron's continued amazement would lead to enlightenment, but it only disrupted her study because Sunday after church, he tramped the parcel of land, waving a flashlight into crevices and under dark places, agitating the inhabitants. (Fortunately, he had not disturbed any of the numerous snakes, specifically the timber rattlers who often coiled her ankles.) The mosquitoes, which did not bother her or Oscar, later drove him away. Just a freak occurrence, Aaron advised the curious family, or more plausibly, someone had thrown away a collection without realizing its value. To alleviate his turmoil, Brigit agreed that surely it was the case, then had taken Theone outside where they would not be overheard. These stones had meaning to her, Brigit stated more than inquired; they were there for a purpose. Theone smiled and said, 'I will be led to others, Mom.' Brigit touched her daughter's remarkable hair, half expecting a shock from the light. 'Keep me posted, but minimize the issue to spare Dad. He doesn't quite understand...' Brigit whispered. Theone kissed her mother to show accord.

Theone rolled the new greenish stone in her palm, thinking Brigit had to be told immediately about this one because it had to be worn on her left ring finger. A jeweler needed to cut and polish it, then fashion it into a simple setting of copper, a metal linked to the divinity since antiquity. Her twelfth birthday approached and this would be her gift. Brigit would avoid telling Aaron that the emerald was real.

As her personal beliefs crystallized, church became a burden for Theone. She participated in confirmation instruction because her refusal would have disturbed too many people, and she was not ready to defend her position. She showed care in her remarks so as not to disparage, but neither did she avow any dogma that contained blatant falsehoods. From the pulpit, Pastor Reese praised her seminary-level knowledge of the Gospels and joked that perhaps the Jones fostered a budding cleric? Aaron and Brigit smiled joyfully at their fellow members, but both knew that Theone was not what she seemed. Too many unusual occurences had convinced Aaron of her special character.

During the confirmation service, Theone's public confession of faith possessed sincerity because Jesus was a Messenger; His real words contained the authentic guide to Peace. Baptism by immersion, an act of spiritual cleansing, held a significance which preceded Christianity by thousands of years; a pledge to the church body she clearly changed to a pledge to Our Deity. (Pastor Reese frowned at her, but did not mention it later.) No Jones could get up early enough on Sunday to attend Bible study so she was spared. (Pastor Reese prayed with the family about it.) The youth program on Wednesday night mixed fun with religion so she could tolerate the lessons. Sunday sermons irked her, though. Being forced to sit attentively and listen to the lopsided tenets tried her patience, especially when the message was presented as divine guidance from a letter of Paul's. The historic perspective, the fact that these letters comprised a man's interpretation - a man's *distortion* of Truth and at such a cost to Truth - was never specified. At least the Gospels had a basis in Truth, if not a wholly accurate one. But Theone was not ready yet. Not yet. No matter how much it galled her to keep silent.

Finally, she took a rotation of duty in the church nursery department as required of youth her age. The toddlers in her care adored her and cried when their mothers came for them. And to their mothers' astonishment, they did not forget her, but babbled about 'Toni' all week, excitedly going to church the next Sunday, only to discover a new youth in Theone's place. When no one could settle the disappointed children, the adult supervisor prudently sent one of her youth helpers to retrieve Theone from worship.

Pastor Reese had grave reservations about allowing Theone to be assigned permanently because she needed his sermons; her delicate soul suffered the greatest risk during the turbulent teen years. Brigit cited to Pastor Reese Theone's exemplary behavior; she mentioned her daughter's kindness, her loving attitude, her consideration for others. Then Theone had to attend Bible study, he sternly rejoined. Brigit reminded that he himself had praised Theone's knowledge of Scripture. They compromised. Alternating Sundays, Theone worked in the nursery and if she had cared to, could have booked baby-sitting jobs every night of the week, indefinitely.

"You could sing if you wanted to," Kristen said to her older sister from the entry to her room. "Just because you haven't ever, doesn't mean you can't try now. Gee, Theone, lip sync! I sing so beautifully, I'll drown out everybody, anyway."

As part of the Christmas celebration, individual families had been asked to stand at the front of the sanctuary each Sunday in Advent and lead the opening carol. Theone did not object to the music. To the contrary, in the folderol of Christian worship this alone was the most pleasurable expression of its faith, but she did not sing, and she particularly did not wish to debut before the congregation. If she ever sang, her voice would be her weakness, and she had never felt strong enough to have her vanity tested, even in a suitable, reverential milieu such as church worship. Brigit had not asked her daughter to explain nor had she any real idea of the truth, but through the years had informed various pageant and choir directors that Theone had a soft voice. (No one would believe that she was shy.)

At her desk before her customary stone circle, Theone replied to Kristen, "I'll think about it." *'I'll visualize to seek the right course'* was the real action she would take. Perhaps now she could handle the temptation singing would present.

Hugging herself, Kristen's eyes traveled around the cold room. For a teenager on the brink of the best times, high school, Theone did not seem to be outgrowing her childhood weirdness. Her single bed, spread with a stark white comforter devoid of pillows, lay perpendicular to the royal blue east wall, and above it she had painted a metallic silver crescent. Peppercorn, their reclusive Burmese cat, lounged in the middle of the bed. A high-gloss, flaming sun filled the sky blue west wall. Glued to the ceiling a glow-in-the-dark universe of stars and planets simulated the night sky. Aside from the octagonal crystal prism spinning in the breeze from her open southern window, a brass incense burner on her pine bureau, and that small, but perfect, round emerald that she never took off, Theone possessed few items of value barring books, and those rated as valuable because of sheer bulk. Her clothing consisted of two simple knit dresses for church; otherwise, she wore generic jeans or calf-length skirts in twill or denim, unisex henley tees in earth tones, and plain cotton or wool sweaters. Even her winter jacket was denim. If she had on shoes, they were sneakers, no socks. Even in snow.

But there were stacks of books. Like in heavy-duty, Kristen thought. No fluffy novels for Theone. Kristen did not check the titles, but being in the same vehicle, she couldn't help but see that Theone hauled home virtual tomes from the library. Her mother and sister also haunted yard sales for bargains to keep permanently.

Kristen fixed on the book shelf to see the current topics interesting Theone. *"The Bible"*, that was a relief, even if it had a weird sounding section called the Apocrypha. *"Coptic Christians"* couldn't be bad. *"Digest of Greek Mythology"* consisted of pure fiction, but next to it..."*The Koran*"? *"The Egyptian Book of the Dead"*? *"Analects, The Sayings of Confucius"*?

"*The Teachings of Buddha - The Four Noble Truths*"? Whatever might be in a shabby theme-book entitled with faded purple fountain ink, "*Book of Shadows*"? She couldn't pronounce "*Bhagavad-Gita*", but mouthed, "*The Hindu Expression in...Sanskrit*"? Theone didn't speak any languages besides English. Pastor Reese taught in Confirmation Class that Hindus were cultists who believed in reincarnation! And what was Gnosticism? Who the heck was Edgar Cayce?

Kristen walked to her sister and peered over her shoulder. "How can you sit there and not shiver! It's twenty degrees outside! And what exactly do you do with those rocks? Don't you use your desk to do your homework?"

"I move them," Theone said gently, "and I'll close the window while you're in here." She made an effort to be gentle with Kristen. Her sister was so far behind and it hurt to love someone facing such a long, arduous journey.

Kristen gestured at the books. "You just read that stuff, but don't really believe any of it, do you? Except what's in the Bible, of course. Every word of the Bible was written by God through a man. It's the only True Word, Theo. You believe that, don't you? You don't want to roast in Hell. Pastor Reese says that's what happens to people who aren't in a State of Grace when they die."

Theone pushed back her chair from the desk. "I just read that stuff," she parroted, refraining from adding the truth about the New Testament. The books had been drafted by very human men who had greatly edited and fabricated, losing The Message of Jesus to foster their own vision.

"That's good!" Kristen exclaimed. "So. Unless you want Pastor Reese over here again praying with us, you'd better agree to sing with us."

"I have to set the table for dinner."

"You don't ever forget your chores, do you?"

"Being responsible is an important part of growth, Kristen."

Kristen giggled. "And you are way too serious for somebody only thirteen!" She teased. "Ryan Ikler likes you. He asked me for our phone number."

Theone considered the handsome, gregarious boy in her science and math classes. Ryan had no depth; his soul swerved way off the road. "Maybe he likes you," she suggested.

"Don't I wish! Ryan wouldn't even look at me, but to get to you." Kristen's voice lowered dramatically. "You have breasts and your period. I'm still...just a girl, but when I change, guys are going to notice me."

Theone masked a bittersweet smile. At eleven Kristen's shallow attitude could be counted as part of her immaturity. Regrettably, if her sister did not pay attention, the shallowness would remain.

Later in the evening, Theone sat in the dark, gazing from her window at the waxing moon, smiling radiantly. She had no fear of pride leading her astray because she would only be lifting her voice in homage to The Deity. And if she sang, it would be a humbling experience for Kristen, hence an opportunity for her sister's spiritual growth; therefore, she would sing because helping another was love, and love was the way to Peace.

This was right for her to sing now.

Regardless of the liturgical celebration, Pastor Reese did not permit decorations in the sanctuary with the exception of two modest brass candlesticks flanking the Bible and holding what he interpreted as seasonally-appropriate candles. He believed that decorations detracted from worship; consequently, they were frivolous. He allowed tasteful floral arrangements if left over from a wedding or funeral. Oak floors, oak paneling, oak podium, oak choir loft, dark oak pews, no cushions, no stained glass in the high narrow windows - the interior of the sanctuary was bland and austere as Pastor Reese felt befit a place of God.

Theone glanced at the familiar surroundings. She found the sanctuary especially bleak during the glad celebrations of Christmas and Easter. Nature was integral to worship. A faint, moist breeze, the sun's warm tickle, a melting snowflake on your lashes - weather belonged in the ritual just as the inclusion of indigenous flora and fauna. Jesus always preached outside. A steeple with a great bell existed on the exterior of this building, but no one ever rang it to herald the joy that Christianity purportedly represented.

Pastor Calhoun, the assistant minister, finished greeting the congregation and beckoned to the Jones. Obediently they left the front pew and came forward.

Restrained tones of *"Oh, Come All Ye Faithful"* sounded from the right side of the chancel. Mrs. Nagle, the organist, has genuine talent, Theone thought, but she is stifled by Pastor Reese's belief that austerity equals piety. With the exclusion of herself and Kristen, the family self-consciously held up their hymnals.

Kristen led the first stanza in her pleasant, but frail soprano.

O come, all ye faith-ful,
Joy-ful and tri-um-phant,
O come ye, O come ye...

Theone harmonized,

...to Beth-le-hem!
Come and be-hold Him,
Born the King of angels!
O come, let us a-dore Him, O come, let us a-dore Him,

O come, let us a-dore Him, Christ, the Lord!

O sing, choirs of an-gels, Sing in ex-ul-ta-tion...
A stanza into the second verse she realized that her family had stopped singing and were listening to her. By the third verse, the congregation had fallen silent, but Mrs. Nagle performed with a complimentary zeal to Theone's magnificent contralto. On the fourth verse, Mrs. Nagle rendered a grand, introductory embellishment, and Theone's voice soared sublimely, but she sang now without enjoyment. At the hymn's conclusion, the congregation's clapping and unprecedented cheers of 'Praise God' obliterated her 'Amen'.

"Enough!" Pastor Reese shouted from the pulpit. "This is not some performance to be applauded! This is the House of Our Lord and we are demonstrating tremendous disrespect! Theone is particularly guilty of disrespect for such a vulgar display!"

She spun around to stare at him.

He pointed accusingly at her. "You waited for this moment to draw attention away from Our Lord and to yourself and it is shameful!" He beseeched the congregation. "Here is an example of what I warn you of week after week. You cannot set yourself up higher than The Lord. It is the road to sin, never salvation." He shook his finger at Theone. "Pride goeth before destruction, Young Lady, pride is your sin!"

Theone's eyes blazed. Being born with a gifted voice was a sin and using it to exult The Deity is pride? Pastor Reese ran this church like a dictator, only HIS way was the right way, and he twisted scripture to instill guilt rather than hope so that worship served as a time of chagrined repentance, not a rejuvenation of the soul; a time of shame, not delight. He had no right to judge her and least of all on the sin of pride.

"To be born with an extraordinary ability is not a sin!" Theone proclaimed in a resonant, passionate voice. "And when lifted for the glory of Our Deity, a voice off key or one capable of four octaves is never pride! Pride is manipulating a body of believers with threats of damnation! It is a pastor who week after week self-righteously condemns his congregation for their weaknesses instead of offering them succor with a meaningful lesson to straighten their way! You cannot harangue souls into salvation! If you are going to guide a soul towards spiritual advancement, Kermit Reese, it has to be a kindly, nurturing process!"

Pastor Reese visibly quivered as he stretched his arms in supplication. "PRAY for our little lamb gone astray," he thundered in his most devout tone. "PRAY for one of our own who has strayed from the flock. God forgive this wayward soul, this young, young soul for her blasphemous insolence..."

All but a few of the congregation hastily cast down their heads.

Aaron grabbed Theone and hustled her down the aisle to the exit while the rest of the family rushed behind them.

As they passed the last pew, a woman visitor on the end lifted her head and smiled. "Why, I do believe we are in the presence of an angel. Each syllable she intoned, she spoke Truth. Just like an angel."

Aaron hesitated at the exquisite stranger's odd remark.

Theone smiled back at her. "Your soul's progress is beyond this plane," she said, "you are the angel."

The woman in white winked. "A little work on the temper, My Child, and your progress will be finished."

Aaron quickened and whisked them out.

Brigit glanced at the woman who winked at her, too. An angel? This woman was an angel! Why did the perception seem rational to her?

Pastor Reese demanded that Theone repent before the congregation. Aaron and Brigit staunchly resisted. Aaron's parents disapproved of their decision and Kristen agreed with them. The issue split church and family.

Dismayed with the minister's harsh indictment of her special child, Brigit swore she would never return to church; she decided that the Jones would establish their own spiritual traditions for Christmas. She could not bring herself to read the Bible stories, though, or pray on it without becoming furious again. Christmas was a subdued holiday.

Finally, Theone asked Aaron to approach Pastor Reese about addressing the congregation to clarify her behavior. Initially, Pastor Reese denied her request unless she kept the subject limited to an apology, but Aaron consulted with his fellow deacons who overruled the minister. Theone served as a role model for their youth and was well-liked by all ages. The members deserved to hear her side, and surely, clemency would result, thus the church would heal. Theone was allotted five minutes at the beginning of the next morning worship, the fourth Sunday in January.

The Sunday she was scheduled to speak, Theone rose early to enjoy the dawn in the frosty woods next to the Hagens' house. The discovery of a sizable milky moonstone in the bird bath gave her confidence. When she held the cabochon to the sun's first rays, a distinct profile emerged, and she offered thanks for such a clear sign from The Deity.

During the processional hymn, Pastor Reese stared coldly at Theone standing by the choir loft, and Brigit observed his intimidating tactic. Newly angered, she vowed to enter the chancel and remove her daughter the moment the song ended, but Theone smiled serenely at her mother.

Brigit lowered her eyes in acknowledgment. It was starting now, she realized. Theone's purpose...her goal, her reason for birth. Just thirteen, yet Theone's maturity was unparalleled in one so young except for another youth who had challenged religious authorities...

Brigit shut out the speculation. Since this dissension at the church she had been dreaming nightly of a white marble temple bathed in moonlight. Rationally she attributed this to the impressive picture of a temple at Pompeii in the encyclopedia. She had been helping Erik with a social studies paper on Islam and on the same page had been the topic of Isis, the Egyptian mother goddess of Nature, who, by the time of Roman rule, had absorbed Hellenistic qualities and was the most popular divinity in the Mediterranean basin. Isis was often depicted with her son, Horus, on her lap. Perusing the article, Brigit had been struck by the passage that the Isis Cult offered tremendous competition to the early Christian church until purges finally destroyed the cult in the mid-6th century AD. Purges by the Christian Church grown stronger, Brigit suspected. Curious, she had gotten a book from the library and discovered that the great enchantress, Isis, brought her mate, Osiris, the sun-god, back to life, and conceived their son, Horus; her divinity surpassed all other deities, including the sun-god. A woman goddess. A woman superior to a man...

Following her intuition, Brigit searched then for specific information that would correlate Goddess worship in historic reference to the Bible. What she found simultaneously excited and enraged her. The purge by the Christian Church in the 6th century had only been the culmination of centuries of repression and annihilation of those who had worshiped the Goddess since antiquity!

Prior to the arrival of the nomadic Hebrews in Canaan, the Goddess (known by many names, including Asherah, Astarte, Ashtoreth), was the principal deity, and women had complete societal freedom, which included sexual independence. The conflict between the patriarchal Hebrew tribes and the matriarchal Canaanites was the real beginning of the struggle later finished by the Christian Church. In the name of Elohim, to enforce their proprietary right over women, Hebrew Levite priests labeled sacred women of the temple 'whores', and they branded their ancient beliefs as wicked; they justified the carnage and defilement of those who worshiped the Queen of Heaven as ordained by their male god. One reference book Brigit read quoted passage after passage in the Bible, citing prophets such as Ezekiel, Isaiah and Jeremiah, claiming that *God* condemned women unfaithful to their husbands. In other words, the sexual freedom as expressed in Goddess worship, was a sin.

Brigit had almost choked on the apple she was eating. But it had certainly been okay for these same sanctimonious men to sleep with (and discard at will) as many women as they could buy! Considering her apple, she had a strong inkling that Adam and Eve represented just another moral Levite story meant to denigrate the Goddess as evil. Furthermore, the eventual validation of male religions in the world - Judaism, Christianity, Islam - had succeeded in squelching worship of the Goddess. Until now. Until Theone...

Deacon Mills appeared at the lectern to introduce her daughter. Brigit looked at Theone to make sure that she still wanted to do this.

Aaron leaned over and whispered, "I have no idea what she's going to say because she didn't want help, but I have this peculiar feeling that our lives are going to change..."

The old church building was poorly insulated and depending on the weather, subject to hot and cold spots. Today it was hot at the front of the sanctuary, and an usher opened a side door to let in fresh air. The flash of natural light in the dim room struck Theone's hair just as she started to speak, and the sight of the girl in the center of the chancel enthralled the muttering congregation.

"The Commandments list ten rules for us to follow, but they can be condensed into two truths," she said. "First, we are not to steal whether it be a life (#6) or a person's spouse (#7) or a person's possessions (#8) or a person's good name (#9) or from our own self-worth (#10). The second is even simpler. We are less than Our Deity and don't ever act like we are better through any form of disrespect whether it be to the souls provided to nurture us (#5) or cursing (#3) or worship of another thing (#1 and #2) or failure to worship (#4). To do any of this is to suffer pride.

"I am guilty of pride. I sang fully aware of how well I would sound..."

Amid murmurs of protest from the members, Pastor Reese cried 'Praise be to God!' He had her apology which was his due.

Theone kept talking. "...but to accuse me of pride is to suffer something worse than pride because it is a judgment, and judgment is a right reserved only for Our Deity."

Pastor Reese jumped up and exclaimed, "Why you smart aleck little..."

His words were drowned out by the members shouting at him to sit down. Enraged, he remained by his chair with his fists clenched.

Theone smiled calmly at the mixed reactions on faces. Depending on their stand, they showed encouragement because they loved her, condemnation because they sided with the pastor or thoughtfulness. The thoughtful faces were the ones she hoped to reach because they reflected a questioning of organized religion, a positive path for souls to take back to spiritual enlightenment.

"Jesus reinforced this when he stated, 'Don't judge and you won't be judged,'" she said. "'For the standard you use for judging will be the standard used against you.'" Theone descended the two steps from the chancel and walked to the open side door. Light danced around her hair, mesmerizing again both supporters and detractors. No matter what their opinion, a general impression held that this girl was special, and she had spoken the truth.

Briefly, total silence existed, then Brigit stood, declared, 'So be it!' and marched in her daughter's wake. This action triggered an instant uproar. Pastor Reese charged to the microphone and attempted to censure Theone, but Deacon Mills stepped over and tripped on the cord, cutting the power. Services were canceled.

In ensuing weeks, the church deadlocked. The deacons, desperately seeking a means to salvage the congregation, requested that Pastor Reese pursue another position, but he adamantly refused. A third of the congregation accused him of further pride and left promptly. Another third, less vocal, but impressed by Theone, left within a year.

As a result of the split, Theone was never required to attend church again. She also made her first cleric enemy.

Church had gotten to be a bore to Erik so he supported Theone wholeheartedly. He did not return to church, either.

Kristen learned that conformity won approval, and she despised Theone almost as much for her incredible vocal talent as for causing the rift, including the one in the family. Her grandparents favored the pastor's stance, and she continued to attend church with them. Everyone paid attention to her now, praising her faith and her goodness. Kristen enjoyed best the comment that she was so different from her older sister, so much better.

Brigit and Aaron eventually smoothed over the breach with his parents. At the same time to heal the family, Kristen pretended to reconcile with her sister like her grandmother recommended. It was to be expected, her grandmother had whispered, and we need to be indulgent because only God knew what kind of background Theone came from. Making Kristen promise to keep the secret, her grandmother, Edna, informed her that Aaron was not Theone's real father. No one, including Brigit, knew the man's identity.

After the church incident, Theone continued to worship as she always had in nature and no one interfered. The Jones lost their unified spiritual focus, but familial harmony was restored.

During adolescence, Theone did not develop into a social creature like Kristen and Erik who enjoyed popularity in their group of friends, but her classmates respected her because of her fairness, her honesty and her intelligence. By high school, students urged her to run for school office or tried to convince her to serve on governing boards, but making rules or enforcing rules was not her way. Her modesty merely enhanced her appeal to others, and though many claimed her as a friend, she belonged mostly to herself.

In 1985, a developer discovered the parcel next to the Hagens' house, bought it from the city, and promptly built a semi-custom, split level ranch. Theone mourned the loss of her refuge and the destruction of the wildlife, but changes - good or bad - were part of the journey.

She turned sixteen that June, and the next week she scored 100% on the behind-the-wheel driving exam. In the same period Brigit accepted a full-time position at the local library, and to ease her transition to a working mom, Aaron and Brigit decided that Theone would be in charge of the house and the family van. This responsibility included with it the chauffeuring of Erik to his guitar lessons and Kristen to her summer activities. Aaron, an executive now, traveled frequently as the refugees' organization's national director.

Sunday mornings, Theone was given permission to drive to Deer Grove Forest Preserve so that she could roam about, studying nature like she had in the woodsy area next to Hagens'. The first time, Erik and Mike Zimmer joined her. In this lush setting, on a winding, sun-dappled trail fringed with mature trees, Theone found it natural to refer to The Deity as they walked. It seemed logical to point out the gender balance in nature from simple life forms to the most complex one, humankind...

"Since this balance is symmetrical," Theone said, "and intrinsic for existence, doesn't it make sense that the Creator, Our Deity, also has a balance? If there is a male essence, isn't there also a female essence? Isn't it rather presumptuous to assume that Our Deity is 'Father'? That Our Deity consists of 'God' alone?"

"Jesus Christ was a man, and God was His Father," Erik argued. "We believe in the Holy Trinity of the Father, Son and Holy Ghost. Heck if I understand it, but it sure sounds male to me."

"The concept of a masculine multiple god-head was not a teaching of Jesus, but rather a doctrine developed by Christian church leaders," Theone said. "Even in his lifetime, The Message got distorted. Jesus was simply a Deity-ordained Messenger who used his divine powers to heal in order to gain attention, in order to be heard. But many of his followers believed that he was the Messiah prophesied in the Torah, the Hebrew Bible, a *mortal* leader who, with a miracle from God, was destined to drive out the Romans and restore a Jewish state here on Earth. The elevation to godhood would have appalled Jesus, but a *trinity* of *equal* status to God? It is preposterous! To authenticate The Message, Jesus adhered to Jewish religious law and the very First Commandment instructs that you will have no other God before me. Regardless of who Jesus really was, he remained true to Judaism and his Pharisee training which Our Deity had pre-determined for his existence.

"And the resurrection story which lifts Jesus to godhood? The sacrifice and re-birth of a god is a common theme in many religions; more specifically, at the time of Jesus, the worship of Isis, the Mother Goddess, was the most popular belief, and one part of it held that she resurrected Osiris, her husband, killed by his brother, Set, after which she conceived a son, Horus. Interestingly, five years following the law to abolish the worship of Isis, the Christian Church practically deified the Virgin Mary, which in effect replaced Isis. In Isis temples converted to churches, some of the statues of Isis holding Horus were merely repainted to represent the Virgin Mary holding Jesus. The real truth? Paul took The Message of Jesus, combined it with the ancient, adulterated Message of Isis to broaden the appeal and invented Christianity. His followers expanded on it and eventually fashioned the Bible which Christians hold as divine truth."

"You don't believe any of our religion, do you?" Thirteen year old Erik asked in an incredulous voice. He wasn't hot on church, but he didn't question what he had been taught, either. What she was saying was...sinful!

Theone smiled at him.

Erik had grown up with her; he *knew* the magical effect of her smile, but it still swayed him. "Theo, what do you believe?" Whatever it was, he would probably believe it, too.

"The Christian religion is the way for many to progress, but it isn't the only journey. It isn't the complete knowledge. There are different paths to Peace, all valid."

Confused, Erik shook his head. "Okay, I admit I'm not deep like you. What are you talking about?"

"The important thing is that you're inquiring," Theone said. "You're open now to a new way. You're unwilling to accept a doctrine just because it's all you've been exposed to so far."

Fourteen year old Mike had kept silent throughout the exchange, but he appeared pensive.

They reached a clearing with picnic tables.

"Let's sit down for awhile," Theone suggested, "I have a bag of trail mix and a water bottle in my pack."

They settled at a table, and each took a handful of the mix.

Theone continued. "Isn't it conceivable that everyone possesses a soul on a journey, and depending on reactions to the choices life offers, each soul makes different progress? Our Deity has sent Messengers again and again to facilitate progress, but humans possess a wild card in their character. It's called free will. Human interpretation always colors The Message and therefore, the various religions have evolved. It's human vanity to presume that one's religion is the only way! Each faith contains a bit of Truth because only a true Messenger can generate so much influence over so many, but *no one religion is the unique way.* Why ever do we need to belong to one particular organized religion? Why should we narrow our soul's options for spiritual fulfillment?"

"That's it!" Mike almost shouted. "My parents don't believe in anything because they say religion is a crock, but Theone's ideas make sense!"

"The Message for a soul to advance towards Peace is simple," she explained, "and the Judeo-Christian doctrines do contain the right message. Be humble, be honest and love others."

"Then being a Christian is right!" Erik exclaimed.

Theone fingered the large moonstone on her chest that she had found in the birdbath the morning she had addressed the congregation. The jeweler had fashioned a plain silver mount for the pearly oval, and she wore it on a braided silver chain. "No, Jesus' *original* Message was right," she said, "but a religion that denies the feminine essence of Our Deity and extols grace as the only means for the soul to advance to a single higher plane is again human vanity. The Mormon Church is not really a fitting example because of their past treatment of women, but their theology has always contained the *right idea* about good works being a way to achieve progress. Good works, though, must be for those less fortunate, not to benefit a chosen few who are the leaders such has so often been the case with a religious echelon. The greater the accumulation of wealth, the less your soul will progress."

"Tell that to one of those rich evangelists on TV!" Erik joked. "Or the Vatican!"

"Being Christian and being rich is an oxymoron. The truth is in their New Testament."

"So prayin' is a waste of time and breath!" Erik cracked. "All I gotta do is be a nice guy and not get real rich."

"On the contrary! Prayer, meditation," Theone paused to gaze at her brother, "...magickal spells, whatever you wish to call the link you choose to exercise, Our Deity listens. Our Deity wants us to succeed, and any sincere method will direct and inspire your soul. Erik, seeking communication with Our Deity will reveal the way best for you."

Eric drew back. "Magic? Theo, that's witchcraft! That's worshiping the Devil! I read about these mutilated sheep blamed on a satanic cult...golly, what are you into?"

Theone sighed. "The early Christian Church deliberately destroyed so much of what had been valid creed for tens of thousands of years. In order for the Church to thrive, other worship, other gods in the Roman Empire had to be eradicated. Since Judaism, the basis for Christianity, forbade magick except by the rabbis, practitioners of the Old Ways Messages - they have had many names in their long history - these practitioners were proclaimed to be barbaric, their worship superstitious and..." Theone shook her head. "And eventually the designation 'witch' became tied to evil. Now there are those who have chosen since to embrace a...a black art as a belief, but the wicked 'witch' portrayed in movies and books originated as a figment of an early Christian imagination. It was propaganda to seize authority. Today's true witches fall collectively under the religion of Wicca. They vary in their worship, but they share one thing in common. *There is absolutely no belief in or worship of the Devil. There is no ritualistic sacrifice of living beings.* Actually, witches attune with Nature; the intellect and the spirit, the body and the Earth are one with the other. Living this harmonious way is a sure path for the soul to advance."

Erik gulped from the water bottle, then retorted, "so you're always outside checking the sky, inspecting stones...I guess you're a witch, huh?"

"Do I need a label?"

For a moment the companions stayed silent.

"Uh, not to change the subject, but I did a theme-paper on reincarnation," Mike said tentatively, "uh, do you believe..."

Theone turned her attention to him. "The Christian notion of heaven is about reincarnation of the soul, and Jesus is credited with saying that in My Father's House are many mansions. His real message stated...well, it isn't important, other than to understand that the mansions are an allegory for different environments. The truth is that the soul travels more than one journey before it reaches Peace."

"Is Peace like Heaven?" Mike questioned.

"In the sense that it's the final destination."

"How many...trips does your soul have to make before it gets there? I mean, are there any who manage to find their way?"

"Oh, yes, but you would not recognize them." Theone reached across the table to clasp Mike's freckled hands in hers. She closed her eyes and concentrated. "Your progress on this current journey will be tremendous, though the journey in this environment will be difficult."

Erik laughed and got up from the table. "Next you're going to say that God is a woman who is a High Priestess re-birthed out there in the Third Dimension! I think you read too many weird books, Theo, and spend too much time alone gazing at the stars. You should hang out with some guys and get into dating."

She looked intently at Mike, then at the sky dense with cumulus clouds. "I have other plans, other things to do."

"Yeah, like start a new religion?" Erik teased.

"I don't think Theone believes in organized religion. She's not into formal rituals," Mike said. "She's concerned with the spiritual advance of the human soul. It's a very individual thing."

"Yes," she replied, "and our soul's advance should be the first concern of each of us."

The sun flared between the clouds and lit Theone's hair.

Mike's eyes widened. Theone was a Messenger! "You're going to tell the world," he exclaimed, "you're here...to tell the world."

Erik laughed hard as he turned away. "My sister, The Prophet? Get out of here!"

Theone nodded slightly at Mike, but he was already convinced. He already believed in her and wanted to embrace The Message whole. If Brigit was Theone's first supporter, then Mike was her first real convert.

Mike talked about Theone to his older cousin who in turn told her boy friend. Soon other young people gravitated to Theone until Sunday morning at Deer Grove became The Thing To Do on the weekends. For every teen who was there because it was cool, there was also one who took Theone's Message earnestly. By the end of the summer, a couple of hundred youth had coined themselves as Honest, Humble Huggers. They viewed dawn and dusk as reminders of The Deity's faithful presence. They tuned in to the phases of the moon as a focus for meditation. Lapidaries had a surge of business as the Huggers sought the four major rocks that Theone always placed in front of her when she talked. Emeralds cost too much for most of the youth, but white moonstones were inexpensive. Demand made them scarce. Huggers spoke freely of God and Goddess, of seeking Peace.

Inquisitive adults attended, too, and the local media showed mild curiosity. Generally, if they were not hooked on her Message, they rated Theone as a benign influence. She was not soliciting money nor was she promoting the joining of a cult. Her philosophy reminded many parents of their own generation's flower children except that Theone stressed a sense of responsibility to others and she abhorred drugs. They figured school would start and some new fad would catch their youths' interest.

Others, however, particularly church goers, became disturbed at Theone Jones' blasphemous appeal and their children's seeming abandonment of Christian faith for pagan worship. They were arguing with teenagers, though, a bewildering age group, so the parents prayed for divine intercession.

A secular event happened first. When one zealous boy advised his fundamentalist mother that Theone upheld the words of Jesus, but dismissed Grace as Paul's fabrication, the horrified woman took action. She sobbed her anguish to her pastor who told his trustees, one of whom was an attorney. He contacted the forestry service. For crowds to gather you needed a permit. The Jones girl violated the law.

The weekend before Labor Day six rangers in three patrol trucks appeared to notify Theone of the infringement and to break up the assembly which had spread over a big picnic area. But five of the six men got sidetracked, initially by Theone's mesmerizing appearance in the dazzling sun, and then by her speech. She stood in the center of the group on a picnic table seventy-five yards away, yet her normal pitch voice was audible.

"She's just an average kid in jeans!" The sole unimpressed ranger said. "Why the hell is she such a big deal?"

"Because if you'll listen, she is speaking the truth," the ranger next to him replied and grasped the man's shoulder with unaccustomed affection.

"God, my own partner is nuts!" The irritated ranger shrugged off the man's hand and lifted his bullhorn. "THIS IS THE FORESTRY SERVICE. YOU DO NOT HAVE A PERMIT TO USE THIS AREA. YOU WILL DISPERSE IMMEDIATELY."

Theone held up her arms as if in benediction. "The way to Peace is living with honesty and humility and love," she declared. "Tell others." She gave the crowd her fullest smile.

"YOU WILL CEASE RIGHT NOW!" The ranger barked and glanced uneasily at his relaxed companions. "Okay guys," he snapped, "get with it or am I gonna need outside backup?"

Three of the men tensed and palmed their weapons, but the kids surprised them by quietly collecting their blankets and food remnants. Theone's followers smiled at the rangers as they proceeded to their vehicles.

"What the hell is this? A love-in? Check for dope," the ranger ordered.

His partner shook his head. "Let them be, Bill. They're high all right, but it has nothing to do with drugs."

"For crissakes, have you lost your mind?"

Theone with Mike and Erik reached the skeptical ranger. "We meant no harm by our gathering," she said, "if it's against the law, we won't meet again."

The hostile ranger stared at her, perplexed. What was with this girl's eyes? She had...the same impish brown eyes as Laurie! His dear, sweet Laurie who had been a delight to everyone who had contact with her. Laurie...the only good thing to come out of a rotten marriage and killed at age fifteen by a God-damned drunk driver. His tough expression faltered. This kid, Theone, was okay. These kids were just having a good time. Like Laurie would have...a tear rolled down his cheek.

Theone gently took his hands. "Let her go, Bill. Laurie had a soul that only required a brief journey in this environment. Once here, she advanced so fast that she was ready for one near Peace. Our Deity holds souls such as Laurie's in great favor. Please, rejoice in what she achieved and get your own journey back on track."

The ranger blinked. "You knew Laurie?" He queried.

"Yes, I know every soul, including yours. You have the potential, Bill. Search your heart."

He pulled his hands from Theone's. "I'll go back to church," he said brightly.

"It's a start," Theone said and stepped away. As sad as it made her, humankind had free will, that wild card in the soul's deck, and her role was to be a Messenger only; she could not achieve a connection with everyone nor could she judge someone's decision. Oh, she could perform plenty of flashy magick to impress cynics, but outward manipulation was not the primary way The Deity wanted her to proceed.

With the deprivation of their meeting place, the Huggers Movement lost momentum because Theone refused to serve further as a focal point for any kind of formal worship. Nevertheless, genuine believers of The Message had been won. They had been given the tools to commune with The Deity on their own. They had been instructed how to live to advance their souls. Worship, then, rated less important than attitude, and in families affected by the changes in their teenagers, better relationships developed.

Adults touched by Theone's Message reacted widely. While some sincerely vowed to lead better lives for the sake of their soul's journey, many were not satisfied with the simplicity of her Message. Many thought there had to be more to it and sought additional means to sustain their recent metaphysical high. The answers came from the West Coast where adherents to an awakened spiritualism (heralded by Theone's birth in the late sixties), had already coined the term New Age. Tarot decks were consulted; astrological charts were pondered; crystals and pyramids were attributed with healing powers. A growing industry comprised of channelers, energy practitioners, colon therapists, clairvoyants, yoga masters - the varied disciplines would expand - was also emerging to assist individuals in their quest to attain a greater, more spiritual self.

Theone felt deeply the various directions her plain Message had instigated in floundering souls and realized that offering Truth was just not enough. Nothing was wrong with seeking guidance on the path, but so many humans seemed to require elaborate rituals to focus their journey. And they would squander vast sums of money to participate in these self-absorbed pursuits when to foster genuine growth in the soul, all one had to do was to share generously one's assets with those who suffered deprivation! Was this the ultimate price of free will? A presumption of the human mind:

that it had to be intricate, it had to be complicated, it had to be expensive, or it did not create positive results? How did she convey successfully that everyone had only to live with personal integrity and with a greater care for others?

She had to re-evaluate her approach, and until The Deity illuminated her as to a different means, Theone would not present Truth again in public. Surely, if she planned her course wisely, this time The Message from The Deity could withstand human distortion.

Late spring of Theone's junior year in high school, Aaron returned home discouraged from a trip to Miami where his organization was being swamped with requests to assist the latest influx of refugees from Cuba. The agency could help these people relocate to other areas of the country and funds had been apportioned to pay instructors, but a shortage existed of bilingual individuals willing to teach the basics of English to the immigrants.

"These folks are essentially middle class with decent educations," Aaron explained at the dinner table, "but things that we just take for granted, currency value, filling out job applications, understanding rental contracts... language is an enormous barrier to assimilation. Add this group to the Mexican stream into California and the Southwest. Then there are the Dominicans, the Colombians, the Salvadorians...we should be required to learn Spanish as part of our education!"

Kristen half-listened to her father, relating his topic to the hinged basket for clothing discards and foodstuffs in the church foyer. Periodically, the women's organization boxed the items and shipped them somewhere for the needy. It was as close as Kristen wished to get to poor people whom she secretly equated with all refugees. She had more important things to concern herself with, like this upcoming weekend. At the start of high school Kristen had discovered better voices than hers in the music department, and she was not willing to settle for the glee club when at church she could be a soloist in the choir. So she had devoted herself to church activities and became a leader in the church youth group. This weekend was Youth Sunday, and justifiably she had been selected to give one of the mini-sermons as well as lead the hymns. Over the years Aaron had mellowed and attended services sporadically, but Brigit never had until now. She was coming to hear Kristen speak. Kristen had prayed diligently for her mother and felt that this was a sign from The Holy Father. Pastor Calhoun, the youth advisor, had worked closely with her because Kristen wanted her message to be flawless and one that would influence her mother into returning to church permanently.

Erik stifled a yawn and reached for another scoop of lasagna from the casserole dish. Affable and of average intelligence, Erik ascribed to Theone's philosophy, but with a limited vision; therefore, he did not find his father's dilemma over communication with refugees as terribly crucial. Strumming a guitar and protesting through song whatever injustice currently interested him was Erik's way of expressing his social conscience. His general career goal was to be an environmentalist. (At fourteen, he did not have to be specific.) Saving the Earth held more importance than saving people who only polluted the Earth in the first place.

Brigit smiled tolerantly at her husband. She loved him dearly, but Aaron was a bleeding heart liberal which she respected as right for him, but her own vision for successful living had crystallized in the past year and was more practical. You nurtured your own to the best of your ability which, if necessary, included calling upon the sacred gifts of The Power. She followed The Goddess' Way; the way she truly believed was the answer to Theone's purpose for existence - to bring The Goddess back to the forefront where She belonged.

Last summer, Brigit had observed Theone carefully as she spoke at the forest preserve, incorporating it with her curious child's previous behavior. She resolved to set aside her outrage at the patriarchal religions bashing of the Goddess and, taking advantage of her job at the library, Brigit began extensive research to pinpoint Theone's spiritual core. God equated with intellect and reason whereas The Goddess equated with intuition and feelings, she determined. Both were important for the advancement of a healthy soul, but religious history stood firmly rooted. Today's conventional religions were the last place to find a complementary atmosphere. Feminism was not an issue to Brigit; Aaron had always treated her with equality in their relationship, and he had sincerely supported her decision to be a full-time homemaker. But churches remained categorically patriarchal and thus, repressive to the female spirit, an especially troublesome situation because Brigit had grown convinced that *The Great Mother came first*. Not the other way around like the Book of Genesis stated. Woman formed from a rib? Not probable! Those Levite priests *had* pulled a fast one in every respect! Stripped to its Stone Age origins, earliest religious objects were exaggerated female symbols of bellies and breasts. Repeatedly. Male symbols were almost nonexistent, suggesting that a male god had little significance. From Mesopotamia to Crete, *every* significant early civilization venerated a Goddess. Only later did gods appear in ancient history and predominantly, these gods *derived their power from a primeval female essence, The Mother, The Goddess, Gaia in the Greek interpretation*. No wonder Theone had to break away from church.

When Brigit triumphantly notified Theone of her conclusion, though, her oldest daughter smiled warmly, but she would not advocate Brigit's theory. Theone agreed that she, too, felt the greatest affinity with the Old

Ways, but it was not important unless your convictions aided the progress of your soul.

Miffed at her daughter's lack of support, Brigit returned to her research and shortly discovered Wicca or The Craft as witches referred to their practice. Blessed be! She had found herself, if not Theone. However, in a household as disparate spiritually as the Jones', Brigit realized her worship would somehow have to fit in inoffensively. On further study, she learned that the wonderful thing about Wicca was that the rules were simple and flexible. And you did not have to belong to a coven; you could be a solitary practitioner. So she adapted.

Oil-anointed candles in special colors came to have a great significance for her. On the sideboard in the dining room, she placed a round crystal bowl, the bottom embossed with a five-point star, and flanked it with a silver candle to the left and a gold candle to the right. The house often smelled of cinnamon or sandalwood incense which she burned in a conch shell packed with sea salt. During the full moon as in the previous evening, Brigit held her chunk of quartz crystal and joined Theone on the lawn chairs in the backyard where she had silently drawn the quarters, honoring earth and air, fire and water before invoking Isis to charge her imagined circle. She felt her communion with the Goddess growing stronger and had as a goal eliciting the sweet, musky scent of the sacred lotus. Perhaps Theone, who openly welcomed her mother's presence, would then be convinced of the reason for her unique birth.

Exhausted lately from traveling, Aaron was oblivious to Brigit's activities. Usually, he had already gone to bed by moonrise. Like last night.

He still looks so tired, Theone thought as she listened attentively to Aaron relate his predicament about the shortage of Spanish translators. She was seated next to him and touched his left arm. The alarm in her heart did not register on her face.

Theone glanced at her mother who wore a dreamy expression. Brigit journeyed on the right track. Isis was a terrific role model - compassionate, loyal, loving, a healer - and Brigit's intentions were well meant, even if it was not Theone's destiny to validate the revival of Goddess worship. (Her being would fuel the growing revival, nonetheless.)

She focused again on Aaron. His soul was not in peril; in fact, it had advanced slowly, but steadily all his life. A loving, enthusiastic man, he put others first, but at a detriment to his health. Aaron paid scant attention to his diet and had developed a sizable pot belly. His body was failing and sadly, his soul would have to leave it before his consciousness was ready to...

"Dad, if you have refugees settling in Chicago, I could be a teacher on Saturdays and Sundays," Theone said.

Over his half-lens glasses, Aaron fixed on her with a dubious expression. "How is your Spanish?"

"Adequate."

Brigit scrutinized Theone. Was this like the girl's singing? Possibly she spoke better Spanish than Aaron who conversed like a native in several dialects.

"You take Latin!" Kristen cried. "You've never uttered a Spanish word in your life!"

"It's similar," Theone replied. "Latin is the root of the romance languages of which Spanish is one."

Aaron smiled kindly. "Dear, it isn't quite the same..."

"HOW ARE YOU TODAY, CLASS?" Theone said in fluent Spanish. "WE WILL START BY LEARNING THE BASIC NUMBERS IN ENGLISH, THEN APPLY OUR KNOWLEDGE BY EXPLAINING HOW MANY BLOCKS WE LIVE FROM HERE."

Erik chuckled. It sure sounded like advanced Spanish to him and he loved it when Theone showed up snooty Kristen.

Nothing Theone did ever surprised Aaron anymore. Her special nature was a given. "Apparently you have done some studying on the side," he said, "and if your mother doesn't object, I'd like you to take the train in with me on Saturdays so that you can teach."

"Take it on forever, Theo! I turn sixteen, I get the van on Saturdays," Kristen said, "and I'll run errands, too." She was sure that next year when she was old enough to drive, Theone would always get first dibs on the family vehicle.

"With Theone helping out Dad, you will shoulder more of the housework, Kristen," Brigit advised.

Kristen grimaced, but kept silent. No matter what Theone did, it always exceeded her efforts. Well, someday, she'd get even with Theone for seeming to be so perfect. And she didn't know what was going on, but Brigit had been outside with Theone in the backyard again last night. It had to be some evil pagan thing because Pastor Reese had told her confidentially that Theone had been stricken from the church role for denying the Savior which was blasphemy. Theone would go to Hell because of it. This upcoming Sunday was very important, Kristen realized. Sunday she had to win her mother back to Jesus.

☙

On a chair behind the pulpit, Kristen could not see her parents seated with her proud grandparents, but she beamed just the same. At her knock this morning, Erik had mumbled some excuse and returned to sleep. Theone, of course, had not even been invited. But her siblings' absence was unimportant. Mother was here.

"New International Version, 1 Timothy 4, verse 12," Kristen recited, "'don't let anyone look down on you because you are young, but set an example for the believers in speech, in life, in love, in faith and in purity.'" Her eyes swept over the congregation before settling on Brigit. "Paul wrote these words to Timothy, but they are a timeless message for youth. Let our elders hear us loud and clear that we believe..."

Paul! Brigit thought. That chauvinist! That squasher of The Goddess! Reese, the arrogant hypocrite with his ill-fitted black toupee, had probably steered Kristen to pick a theme from Paul! Brigit scanned Aaron's worn Revised Standard Version Bible which he held open to Kristen's passage. There. In the very same letter. 1 Timothy 2, verses 11 through 14. 'Let a woman learn in silence with all submissiveness. I permit no woman to teach or to have authority over men; she is to keep silent. For Adam was formed first, then Eve; and Adam was not deceived, but the woman was deceived and became a transgressor.' Sinners, are we, huh? 'Adam and Eve' was a male-created myth to repress females! Paul served to perpetuate it!

Brigit straightened her posture and steeled herself to maintain a pleasant, alert expression, but she blocked out her daughter's cheery voice. She loved Kristen because she was her child, but her religion was totally oppressive.

CHAPTER TWO

Brigit gazed fondly at her oldest daughter in cap and gown as she crossed the stage to receive her diploma. Theone was not valedictorian of her high school class, but Brigit suspected that she could have been. In addition to a hidden intelligence, Theone possessed a rarely displayed, fine sense of humor, though once revealed, it was never at the cost of another. Many people loved Theone, or the person she chose for people to see, but there were also more than a few who did not, including Kristen. It was the cost of being...Theone.

To their disappointment, Theone had no immediate interest in attending college. Instead, she asked for help in buying a used recreational vehicle so that she could travel for a while. She explained that she needed to find other Glimpses of Peace, a comment that baffled Aaron, but made utter sense to Brigit. Neither one of them expressed any concern at the idea of her going off alone. Theone's halo protected her, Aaron joshed. Brigit attributed her own calm to the belief that Theone was of Goddess status.

As opposed to a college education, then, a recreational vehicle was certainly a reasonable request. Besides, Aaron had insisted on paying Theone the standard wage for her English teaching. She had been inclined to donate the money to any cause jamming the mailbox with solicitations, but Brigit had firmly taken her paychecks and banked them in a savings account. The sum would defray the expenses she charged on the bank card that they would guarantee for her; their financing would afford her a decent running vehicle. No one really expected her to be gone more than the summer.

Shortly after Theone made known her intentions, Erik's guitar instructor announced that he had joined the Peace Corps. Would the Jones be interested in buying at a discounted price his '81 half ton Ford pickup with a 5'x10' camper shell?

Aaron had a mechanic check it out. The three-speed manual gear, forest green truck had been well maintained, and from the snug bunk built into a cab which overhung the truck's roof to the compact kitchenette, the camper's accommodations fit Theone's requirements.

Theone left Ashburg for Paxton, June 22, 1987, the day following her eighteenth birthday. As she bade farewell to her family with promises to call often, she held Aaron closer and longer than the others. She loved him for the father he had been and knew it would be her last time to communicate her gratitude.

Pulling out of the driveway, Theone saw Mike appear, his expression dejected. She pushed in the clutch, shifted to neutral, and beckoned to him.

"I'll be back for you," she promised, "I'll be needing you a lot, but you have to grow up first."

Mike grinned, but already pined for Theone to return. Hopefully, she would not be gone very long.

Kristen did not bother to disguise her joy at Theone's departure. The goony, moony sojourns, as she considered her mother's fascination with the Earth's satellite, had increased rather than diminished. She blamed it on Theone who invariably was out there, too. Kristen remained very hurt by Brigit's nice, but vague compliments about her sermon over twelve months ago and felt further defeated by Brigit's persistent indifference to church. Theone had corrupted Mother, Kristen concluded; with Theone gone, now perhaps she would have a chance to win Brigit back to Jesus.

The trip to Paxton took four hours from Ashburg, and Theone had left in the early morning. Before going to her maternal grandparents for lunch, she drove to Lake Femvivant, and oblivious to the drizzle, walked through the woods to the shore. On the narrow beach, she shut her eyes and held her palms outward to the pewter sky. This spot is where she had been conceived, Theone comprehended, and opened her eyes to admire the rough, slate-colored water. Other passages for her would take place here, too, but not for a time yet. Not yet. First, The Deity had other things on the agenda.

⁌

Solitude had always agreed with Theone, and now being a nomad suited her, too. While traveling she turned on the radio just once a morning to hear the news because from popular rock songs to seventeenth century operas, she was free at last to sing and made the most of the opportunity to vocalize every tune stored in her comprehensive knowledge of the past. An occasional passer-by would catch a lyrical drift from her constantly open windows and marvel at the beautiful sound. Someone famous, they would determine, but what tape had that song in that voice?

By the third Monday in July, Theone had meandered south into the Ozarks. She stopped often, sometimes after only brief miles, to spend hours absorbing the Glimpse of Peace revealed in a particular river valley bounded by weathered granite bluffs. Leaving the truck-camper roadside, she rambled amid spring-fed streams of intense blue where fish darted about her, tickling her ankles, or she hiked higher ground through the stands of oaks, hickories and maples in the cliffs along wider waterways. White-tailed deer often accompanied her as did a variety of birds; occasionally, an aloof black bear moseyed behind her. Snakes entwined her arms and legs. She suffered no allergies to the poison ivy endemic to the region or any anxiety about the bats who swooped around her at dusk, vying for her attention. The area's numerous caverns did not interest her, however. Nothing made her uncomfortable except the deprivation of natural air.

Being summer, numerous vacationers filled the public areas and parks, but Theone avoided contact with people until forced to by an increasing whine from the back of the truck. From the James River in Southwestern Missouri, she accessed a county road which led directly to Bickley.

"It's your differential," the mechanic explained to Theone.

"Which is very important to safety?"

Charlie Logan operated the only full-service garage in the small town. This sexy young woman was a stranger with no automotive understanding. He could take her for plenty, including a demand for a fuck or two in the process. *But as tempting as the idea was to do both, a vague apprehension in his conscience told him it would not bode well if he did.*

"You can go a long time, Miss Theone Jones," he said, "but eventually you gotta fix it. A differential transfers power from the engine through a drive shaft which makes the rear wheels turn. You hear that whine and it means the gears are starting to wear inside the differential. The gears strip out and the wheels lock up. So when a differential goes, you got a lotta warning." Charlie was surprised at his speech. He was a damn good mechanic who didn't bother to explain anything to anybody. An auto ignoramus, as he referred to those without mechanical skill, didn't deserve to have their vehicle problems explained. (In high school somebody had called him an ignoramus once and he had looked it up in the dictionary.) This girl, though, this extraordinarily attractive girl...he felt compelled to be nice to her. And nice to Charlie meant imparting some of his area of expertise, engine workings. It was the only thing he had that set him apart; that made him special in an otherwise mediocre life.

Theone smiled at the middle-aged man's meaty, sun-leathered face. A greasy shock of brassy gray hair scrambled on his square head. He did not tell the truth very often, but his pale blue eyes mirrored that he was telling it now.

"I think you should fix it," she said, "I'm traveling alone and I'd hate to take a chance. I guess it's expensive."

"Five hundred bucks, Honey."

Theone knew she could charge it on the bank card her mother had given her, but that was not what was to happen here with Charlie. This was her sign to begin. "I don't have enough cash," she said. "Are there any jobs in town?"

Charlie snorted. "Take a look around. Does it look like there are any..." he cut short his sarcasm. What was it about this girl's eyes... "uh, my house is a mess. I mean, big time mess. My wife is, uh, an invalid. Straighten out my house and...paint it. My wife is always bugging me to do stuff like that. I'll get the paint."

"The garage, too? Sort all those magazines you haven't had a chance to read? Maybe donate them?"

"Might as well." Charlie looked puzzled. How did she know about the magazines? Because everybody stored unread magazines, he figured. She was not specific. Julie subscribed to every women's magazine in publication, but she never got around to opening half of them. Julie had good intentions, but the high-point of her life had happened twenty-six years ago when she was crowned homecoming queen and county fair queen all in the same year. She'd been a beauty, but had not a whit of talent at anything. A regular dumb blonde, but he'd loved her. Loved her even after half the fellows in their community had bedded her and a fair share from Springfield, too. Now, she drank to forget what she was never gonna be, and he stuck around because there was nothin' better to be had.

"Then you're agreeing that if I clean up your house, you'll replace my differential in exchange," Theone said, "and if you have no objections, I'll sleep outside in your back yard until the truck is fixed."

"No need. We got extra rooms."

"I wouldn't impose and I genuinely prefer to be outdoors."

Charlie smiled at her smile. "Where ya' from in Illinois?"

"A suburb northwest of Chicago."

"You're kinda young to be out on your own."

"I have indulgent parents, Charlie."

"Well, let's go tell Julie that I found a handy,...gal. It's just a coupla blocks from here."

Theone lifted her backpack from the concrete floor.

Something bothered Charlie; she had known his name without being told, but he shrugged it off. Probably somebody in town had given it when directing her to the garage.

Just inside the Logan's screened porch, Theone stood by Charlie and formed a cursory impression of Julie: thin and eyes. Huge blue eyes that seemed even larger because of her gaunt face framed by sparse gray-blonde hair. Her skimpy nylon slip emphasized her emaciation, and the papery skin on her spindly limbs had reddish-blue bruises. From touching, Theone surmised, touch Julie with the slightest pressure, and a mark would be left. No remnant of beauty remained because the luster was gone in her lovely eyes. A diet of cheap scotch had wasted her body and her soul.

Slumped on the glider, Julie glared at the stranger. Did Charlie think her in too much of a stupor not to recognize a hooker when she saw one? Did he feel he could bring one right into their home and she wouldn't notice?

"I don't need help with my house," she slurred, "and you don't look like you ever painted anything in your life. Get lost."

Charlie smiled apologetically at Theone. "She's doing it in exchange for some work on her truck, Jul. It's the only way she can afford to get it fixed. She'll do exactly as you tell her to, okay? She won't disturb anything or change anything without your permission."

"Where you staying in town?" Julie lit a new cigarette from a smoldering butt and took a long drink from her metal tumbler.

"Charlie has agreed to let me sleep in the backyard."

Julie sputtered, "Our yard? Well, how convenient for you two! I suppose I should be grateful you're not planning on fucking under my roof."

"God, Julie! You bitch and bitch that I never do anything and here I bring you a nice, strong girl who's willing to help and how do you act?"

"Fuck you, Charlie."

"Not with you, you sodden bag of bones! Lay off the booze, will you?"

As they argued, Theone moved closer to Julie. She knelt in front of her and before Julie could recoil, Theone clasped her hands in hers. "I really need the work to pay off my debt," she said softly, "please give me a chance."

Julie focused on Theone. Her eyes had been that same color as this girl's! Like pansies with a velvet sheen. Dillard Beechum had called them that. Her first lover. The town's rich boy. The one who had made all sorts of promises which she had believed. These were beautiful eyes like hers had been when she'd been queen of the world. Clear, healthy eyes, not weary, veiny-red ones that she now saw in mirrors. There was no intent to deceive in these eyes, either. These eyes, like the soul, were...pure.

"Start in the kitchen," Julie said. "Goddamn flies are having a party 'cause the screen is ripped in the door. Charlie don't do dishes and I sure as hell ain't doing dishes I had no part in dirtying."

"Thank you," Theone replied and got up to go inside the house.

Charlie watched her disappear into the murky interior.

Suddenly, a beam of light hit him from the screen door, still open to the concrete steps to the front walk, and it bounced to Julie, startled by the brightness. They stared at one another in perplexity. Then, their expressions changed to a chary regard. They had not really looked at each other in ages, and found it not as unpleasant as they thought it should have been.

By the end of two weeks, Charlie had long since gotten in the new differential he'd ordered from Springfield, but he procrastinated in fixing Theone's truck. His wife, his house - *his life* - had changed wonderfully, and he had to give full credit to Theone. He wanted to keep her around permanently.

Charlie had been amazed. Come that first dusk, Theone not only cleared the kitchen surfaces, but she also cleaned the oven, did a load of laundry and organized enough magazines in the garage to find his tool shelf in order to dig out his plumbing kit to fix the leaky faucet. She apologized for not having supper ready, but there wasn't much of a selection other than snack items. Charlie sprung for burgers from the local Dairy Depot.

The next day, Julie roused herself to accompany Theone to the grocery. Then, Wonder Girl went right back to her steady tidying - shoveling refuse in a few cases - *plus* had a tasty chicken casserole ready for supper. Julie actually ate a decent portion with her scotch. The following night, Julie ate the pancakes, applesauce and ham slices without washing down the meal with scotch.

When Julie remarked that the place belonged in a magazine layout, Charlie told Theone that she had more than paid off the differential, but she smiled in her radiant way and reminded him that they had a deal. Provide the materials and she'd paint the house. Okay, he'd said, the weather was iffy so to get it done before a rain, they'd paint it together. Maybe get Julie to do some of the lower trim on the porch. Julie took the idea seriously! Her hands trembled and she had to have a couple drinks, but the rails were white and the drips were hidden in the bushes.

First Friday, Charlie took them out to the local VFW for the all-you-can-eat fish fry. By now, everybody in town had heard about Theone, and everybody was at that fish fry. Funny how Theone dimmed, and Julie had taken on a shine. In their bedroom later, he kissed Julie and she'd been very responsive to his advances. Now, he had to fix the truck. There was nothing to detain Theone; in fact, he'd not kept his end of their agreement, but he loved the girl. Julie loved the girl. If she would just stay...

"Super!" Charlie declared. "You got real talent as a cook, Theone. I've always been a bean man and nothing hits right like a warm soup on a cool, rainy night."

"Oh, Charlie, remember the time we ate those terrible bean burgers at that health food spot in..." Julie's voice faded when she realized that she hadn't been with Charlie, but another guy. There were so many other guys, but Charlie had been proud to marry her, no matter what her reputation, and he had been the one who had stuck with her.

"I don't recall, Julie," he said kindly, "but it must have been something."

"Uh, Patty Thurman mentioned she goes to AA in Springfield on Tuesday nights. I didn't even know she had a problem!" Julie flushed. "I might catch a ride with her next time."

"I could take you. I always need to shop parts for stock," Charlie offered.

"I think I should go with Patty, but another night we could do that."

"Maybe see a movie," Charlie said hopefully.

Julie smiled affectionately at her husband, and he saw the beauty he had married.

Theone placed her spoon by her bowl. "I have to be on my way," she said. "Is the truck ready, Charlie?"

Charlie blinked guiltily. "I'll finish it up tomorrow. Painting the house kind a took time away from business."

"It's okay. I've enjoyed staying with you."

"I can't believe you've been comfortable on that hard, wet ground, Theone. You're going to catch something sleeping outside like that," Julie admonished.

"My pup tent and sleeping bag have kept me snug and dry."

"Just the same...you could come inside and stay on a spell. We'd like that, Theone." Julie shyly patted the younger woman's hand.

Theone turned up her palm to clasp Julie's.

"Like having our own kid," Charlie joshed, half-serious.

A bit teary, Julie nodded.

Theone reached for Charlie's hand with her free one. "Promise me you'll stay honest with one another," she said, "that in spite of the other's weaknesses, you'll swallow your pride and love each other. It's the way to Peace."

"You've sure given us peace," Julie said.

Theone smiled. "I've helped you find your way back on to the road. Now it's up to you to care about staying on it. Your souls' progress is dependent on your mutual efforts."

"We're not church people," Charlie said. "I'm not sure..."

"Church is not the answer for you. Growth for you both will come from nurturing the other, and in so doing, those around you will be influenced. Share what you've discovered so that they might find Peace, too."

Julie grinned at their guest. "Well, you're not pushing church which is truly a relief, but I still believe you are a gift from God."

Theone laughed. "I just care about you like any messenger of love."

Charlie and Julie exchanged looks. This girl had restored their self-worth; she had re-shaped their very existence. Theone might dismiss the miracle she had performed, but they wouldn't. And if sharing with others what she had done was her request, then they would.

Charlie and Julie Logan were Theone's first disciples.

∽

From Bickley, Theone drove east to Kentucky then south to Tennessee and due east again into the Appalachian region. She stopped often to hike and Glimpse Peace. In the bald-topped Great Smoky Mountains, cast with their bluish haze, she enchanted the local wildlife; white-tailed deer and black bears, ruffled grouse and turkeys routinely accompanied her as she wandered the virgin forests of spruce, hemlock, buckeye and birch. Wading through streams and into lakes, trout and bass danced in escort. Although she preferred the local roads, she traveled the interstate highways when The Deity wanted her to be there. At a truck stop, a pregnant runaway, the same age as Theone, was touched by the words that the baby she carried was an important soul, one who could achieve greatness as a peacemaker if this soul had a caring mother and a nurturing environment. Theone drove the young woman to a bus station and gave her the money to get home.

Off the interstate to appreciate the Shenandoah Mountain range in Virginia, Theone found an angry Korean-American tailor. He'd had a tire go flat, but could not get anyone in the remote town ahead to come help him change it. Theone calmed him, then assisted him. The man lauded her Christianity and interspersed pleas to Jesus for forgiveness with harsh condemnation of the local heathens. Christians were not the only people who showed kindness to others, she told him, and contrary to Christian notion, not loving those who hurt us was okay as long as it did not consume us or destroy our reason. Souls suffered enough trials without that extra, impossible burden of trying to love everybody. More important was to be peaceful about conflict. Harming others never advanced your soul's progress.

He stared at Theone and saw the forgotten eyes of his real mother. The man confessed to being a war orphan and raised in a Protestant church by adoptive parents, yet felt drawn to his roots, particularly to shamanism, his birth family's beliefs.

An intermediary, a shaman, was not necessary to commune with The Deity, but wishing to attune to natural spirits is right, Theone thought. Return to it, she urged, your soul is trying very hard to get you to recognize your way to Truth.

The tailor was so exhilarated at having his own longings verbalized, that he fell to his knees before Theone, praising her. Share with others what you feel, she counseled, and recommended that he bow only to The Deity. Theone had changed his life! He wanted her name.

She smiled and walked to her truck, claiming to be just a messenger of love.

He wrote down her license number, but soon lost it.

Theone came into contact with many people (not all with success). Some were influenced with words while others she reached through a combination of aid and The Message. Whatever her technique, she employed no splashy magick, yet she altered lives tremendously, and those she touched remembered her with reverence.

The people Theone uplifted shared in common a bereft spirit; additionally, their circumstances were mundane; their finances tended towards meager. Until she met the Shaws in early November, she had not touched the soul of one affluent human.

North of Harrisburg, Pennsylvania, Highway 443 ran parallel to Interstate 81 through the Blue Mountains. On a remote stretch of the highway, Walton Shaw and Claire Healy-Shaw traveled east at a leisurely pace in Walton's BMW. The couple was on their honeymoon, but they had discussed the merits of taking such a motor trip longer than their recent decision to marry. Walton, a corporate attorney and the first African-American hired at a prestigious law firm in St. Louis, Missouri, allowed little time for a personal life. Claire, shift-chief nurse for a twenty-four hour emergency care facility in the city was equally as committed to her career. Their mothers attended the same Pentecostal church and had connived for six months before finally getting the two introduced at the Christmas Eve service three years ago. Whether it was an attraction or a convenience, they began calling upon one another when in need of an escort. Gratifying sex followed. Then, Claire's apartment lease had expired and it made sense to move into Walton's condominium. Their relationship was steady, but superficial until Walton's father's heart attack prompted Walton to review his fast track life. His first conclusion was to vacation by auto through pastoral areas, meaning the cellular phone would be kept stashed in a suitcase, and he'd attune with nature. His second conclusion was to propose to Claire because they had mentioned a general interest in having a child. The two decisions seemed to go together. Claire planned a wedding at the church to please their mothers and a chic reception at an exclusive restaurant to please their prominent acquaintances.

They had been sole company for the past five days and discovered just exactly how much they really did like each other. Privately, they both felt relieved, but they were also getting bored with the bucolic scenery. Mile after mile of green valleys and gentle hills just did not fascinate them, yet neither was willing to admit it, either. They still had nine days left, and this idyllic trek was something they should be enjoying.

"Want footage of this field we're passing?" Walton asked Claire who had been videotaping their trip.

Claire looked at the churned soil, stripped of its harvest. "I've done plenty of farms," she answered mildly sarcastic, "you'd think we'd never left the Corn Belt."

"Well, I'm going to pull off by that big tree ahead. We've seen one car in the last fifteen minutes and zero gas stations with none anticipated."

"Three cups of coffee does that to you," she said absently.

A corroded Buick Electra with a loose muffler approached due west. The passengers, Del and Ernie, were two locals with misdemeanor records for vandalism. They had just been fired from their laborer jobs on an overpass construction project for the interstate. Everybody on site sniffed or snorted or nipped something, they carped. They'd been singled out because their black-ass boss hadn't liked them from the start. The further they drove, the surlier they got. Ernie washed down two amphetamines with a swallow of whiskey from a pint and offered the bottle to Del.

"Don't hog 'em. Gimme a popper," Del demanded.

Ernie dug a couple from his unzipped quilted vest pocket. "You still got that 45 in the glove compartment?"

Del took a swig with the pills and replied, "Hell, yes! You never know when you might meet a nigger who needs a fucking education."

Ernie howled as he fumbled open the knob and pulled out the automatic. "Hefty sonabitch, ain't it?"

"And loaded, asshole. Give it to me so's you don't blows your dick off."

"Shit and you won't?"

Del grabbed the barrel and took the weapon from his companion. "I had a class 'fore I could get a permit."

"Since when does an ex-con get t' own a gun?"

"Ever hear'a fake id's?"

Ernie was impressed.

Two miles behind the Buick, Theone in her vehicle had neared the finish of singing every score from a musical popular in the forties. She smiled at the blanched sun outside her open window. It was about nine a.m. and the air nippy.

Walton heard the noisy Buick just as he zipped his pants. Good timing, he thought, turning from the tree to walk back to the BMW parked on the shoulder.

"Holy motherfuckers!" Ernie yelled. "Nigger to the north! Gimme the gun!"

Del peered out the dirty front windshield as he rolled down his window. "Fuck you! It's my gun! It's my nigger!"

In front of the BMW, Walton paused because the sedan had slowed. Probably a local seeing if we have car trouble, he figured. People were friendly in rural areas. They were yelling something unintelligible because the vehicle's muffler made too much of a racket.

With Ernie screeching in his ear about niggers, Del lifted the 45 and emptied the clip in the direction of the bespectacled man. The impact of firing the weapon caused Del to lose control of the steering wheel, and the automobile swerved on to the opposite shoulder of the BMW's position. Del dropped the pistol in his lap, though, and got hold of the Buick before it slid into the irrigation ditch.

"I surprised the fuck-ing shit outta that nigger!" Del cried as he regained the black top and floored the gas pedal. The Buick fish-tailed before righting.

"Jesus H. Christ! You shot him! Ha! Ha! You shot him!" Ernie shouted. "We gotta watch the news tonight! We're gonna be on the fuck-ing news!"

"Damn right!" Del said. "Gimme the bottle. This here calls for a fuck-ing celebration!"

Slow motion.

The horror only lasted seconds as did Claire's paralysis at viewing Walton's chest explode, but it seemed to happen in excruciatingly slow motion. Suddenly she realized that she was screaming and it brought her into focus. She stumbled from the vehicle, wrenching her ankle, but mindless of the pain, she got to her husband. He was not breathing.

"CPR," she muttered, "he needs CPR, but his chest...oh, God, I can't press on his chest because of the...bullets...oh, God...I might make it worse..." With little hope, Claire lifted Walton's chin and administered mouth-to-mouth resuscitation, trying to inflate his lungs by applying pressure on his upper breast bone.

The clear air carried the sound of the rapid gunfire and Theone abruptly quit singing. She spied the BMW and concentrated on the area in front of it. The sight of a woman hunched over a body did not surprise her, and she increased her speed.

"...out of nowhere...a car...uh, they just...shot him! Oh, God..." Claire gasped to Theone between breaths into Walton's still lungs. She gripped his wrist and shook her head. "I can't get a pulse...oh, God."

Kneeling beside the couple, Theone could see the man's soul hovering above him. If his body was not dead, it would be soon, unless... "You have a phone in your car," she said, "I'll take over while you call."

Claire's pupils had widely dilated and her nostrils flared, but she kept control of herself. "It's locked up...it's been a joke...Walton has been testing...his will power! Oh, God, he might never make a call on it again..."

"Let me take over so that you can get it," Theone suggested.

"Oh, God...I can't leave him! I'm medically trained!"

Theone placed her hand over Claire's on Walton's breast bone. "You have to call for help," she said.

Claire gaped at the stranger. This girl had the same eyes as Dr. Voecker! Dr. Voecker was the coolest, most competent doctor on staff. Everyone agreed that he was the best physician in an emergency situation. She puffed into Walton once more and moved out of the way.

Without missing the woman's rhythm, Theone blew into Walton's mouth. "Go get the phone first, Claire," she ordered, "then anything to keep him warm."

"Yes, yes!" Claire hoisted herself on the bumper and hobbled to the rear of the BMW. The suitcase was at the bottom of their gear to boost Walton's resolve; he figured it would be too much trouble to access. But even if the phone was in the front seat, it was not going to make any difference, she thought numbly. At the clinic, she had witnessed serious gunshot wounds that even Dr. Voecker could not fix. If a bullet had not struck Walton's heart, major damage had still been inflicted. His blood loss was substantial.

Theone bent over Walton, but instead of breathing into his mouth again, she placed her hands on his chest. Bullets had missed the heart, but had lethally injured the left lung and shattered an upper vertebrae. Interfering with the Natural Course was not her right; saving him was not her decision. Yet she could feel the potential for growth that would be destroyed in this soul and in Claire's. For the Shaws to survive this tragedy would favorably advance not just their spiritual journeys, but also the two souls that had been allocated to be born to them. The renewed Shaws would give wonderful guidance to offspring. They had so much unfulfilled love to be shared with so many others...Theone petitioned The Deity.

The trauma team on the med-vac helicopter from Harrisburg found a situation less serious than the wife's original evaluation of her husband's injuries. They expected to transport a corpse. The gunshot victim was unconscious, but breathing regularly; his pulse low, but stable. The wife was in extreme shock and kept babbling about some angel who called herself a messenger of love.

◈

Concealing his excitement, Jasper Stroud said to Walton, "An acute, healing white light is a classic scenario for this type of experience. Tell me about the rest of it."

Jasper considered himself a truth seeker rather than a standard investigative journalist because he specialized in free-lance reporting of religious phenomena - debunking it or if deserving, corroborating it. From a home base in San Antonio, Texas, he maintained a country-wide network of informants who kept him apprised of any such events. News about a brutal attack on a stranger would not normally have interested him as a subject to be probed, but the wife's insistence that an angel had saved her husband qualified; now, as a bonus, the husband seemed to have undergone an unprecedented near death episode.

In a hospital bed, Walton grinned at Claire as he spoke. "Well, while I was suspended in that light, Mr. Stroud, a melodious feminine voice quarreled with a rich masculine voice. The female asserted, *'I'm letting her do this!'* The male countered, *'She isn't to perform flashy miracles! We agreed that, invariably, it invites the wrong kind of response!'* The female asserted, *'Love is her essence!'* The male countered, *'That isn't logical!'* The female asserted, *'Logic does not rule here.'* There was a moment of silence. The male conceded, *'You're right.'*" Walton chuckled. "Like most females, she won the argument. Immediately, the light receded and I was rushing towards my body."

"She was a real angel arguing with God for Walton's life," Claire said with fervor.

"You heard the conversation?" Jasper asked politely.

Claire gazed at him. "No, I was frantically trying to reach the cell phone! But the only reason Walton is alive is because the angel convinced God to perform a miracle." She patted her husband's right shoulder and leaned to Jasper. "Walton was not breathing. He had no pulse! He was...dead."

"So, you got 911, but couldn't describe your location. This..."

"Angel."

"Yes, this 'angel' spoke as if she were standing next to you and gave very accurate coordinates which you repeated without hesitation to the operator." Jasper stopped writing to look at her. "Then you went to Walton who now didn't seem as bad as you had thought. What did she do?"

Claire smiled at Walton who winked at her. "The angel took my hands in hers and told me how precious our souls were to The Deity. We were meant for great progress which we would achieve by living honestly, humbly and with love." She kissed her husband's forehead. "So I gushed that we'd be in church every Sunday from now on." Claire chuckled. "The angel advised me that having faith in Our Deity didn't require church worship unless this truly inspired our souls."

"Did you defend church?"

Walton answered. "Claire admitted that church would not inspire her and I can tell you, it wouldn't me, either. But each day I watch the sun rise from this window and I praise God that I'm still around to see it. When I'm released from here, I'm going to continue watching it rise and set as well, every day. That's my sermon and my inspiration."

Tears filled Claire's eyes. "Mine, too," she said. "Also, we're quitting our jobs and moving to a community in Missouri desperate for a medical person. No town ever needs another lawyer..." She paused to smile at her husband, "but we'll find something for Walton to do."

"Raise kids. Why, I might just turn into a househusband and dispense with legal advice."

Jasper hid his impatience. Their reaction to the miracle was typical. Chances were the every day world would intrude and they would revert to their old attitudes. "I appreciate your comments, but we've digressed a bit," he said. "After the angel's advice about church, she did what?"

"She got up," Claire said. "I stuttered, 'Are you an angel?' She smiled this incredible angel smile and said, 'No, but I am a messenger of love.' I don't remember thanking her, but she said, 'Claire, you and Walton "thank The Deity."' How did she know our names if she wasn't an angel?"

"Then she got into her car," Jasper prompted.

Claire concentrated. "It was a...camper. No, a truck with the kind of camper that just slides onto the truck bed." She stared at Jasper. "We were both covered with Walton's blood. Within five minutes of my call, the road was crawling with patrol cars and a helicopter buzzed overhead! Those two losers in their crappy Buick were spotted right off the bat and she drove in their direction. How come no one could find her? Or even remember her? She had to stop somewhere to clean up. My clothes were so bad, I threw them away." Claire nodded with assurance. "She was definitely an angel."

"Can you describe her physically?" Jasper questioned.

"Beautiful."

Jasper waited for details.
Claire smiled complacently.
"That's it?" He asked.

Claire had thought that the angel's image would leave a lasting impression, but she retained little memory other than a general sense of incredible beauty. "She was not of this world, so there's no point," Claire said as she stood up and held out her hand in dismissal. "It's been nice chatting with you, Mr. Stroud."

The writer shrugged and rose. "I believe you," he said sincerely, "and I also believe that she might appear again. I was hoping for a description to have comparative data."

"Why don't you worry less about the source of our inspiration and apply what we've learned to rejuvenate your own soul," Claire recommended. "She spoke the truth."

Jasper smiled agreeably. Walton's experience was genuine, but Claire's story was off. He trusted his intuition which told him strongly that their savior existed in corporeal form. Dubbing her the Roadway Angel, he vowed to search for a pattern and find her.

◌

From Pennsylvania, Theone veered southeast to meet the ocean, then angled up the coast, tracing the Atlantic Flyway. From North Carolina to Massachusetts numerous national wildlife refuges beckoned her and by mid-December, she arrived at Brigantine NWR, another sanctuary for migratory birds just north of Atlantic City, New Jersey. Webbed with man-maintained channels, the twenty thousand acres of salt marsh drained at low tide and turned into mud flats which provided plentiful food for waterfowl and shore birds.

Since 1958 when six of their predecessors had their wings clipped by refuge authorities, a particular gaggle of Canadian geese nested permanently at Brigantine. They made a big fuss over Theone.

CHAPTER THREE

Mag

During his life, Frank O'Hennessey attended six am Mass daily and always sat in the back row by the south side aisle. At that time on clear mornings in Day Light Savings months, the angled sun would fire the stained glass scene of the Crucifixion at the front of the century old Queens, New York cathedral, and the icons of the saints paneling the walls of the sanctuary seemed alive from being imbued with the same natural light. Frank never took communion, although he faithfully went to confession. No matter how many ardent Hail Marys he mumbled, he never felt worthy to come forward to receive Christ's Body from the priest or to be anywhere near the chalice of plain wine, transmuted into Christ's Blood, which rested majestically on the altar.

As a youth Frank entertained the idea about becoming a priest, but a strong obsession with sex hobbled his spiritual quest and created the dilemma about his unworthiness. The more he tried to think pure thoughts, the more he seemed driven to masturbate. Finally, at age nineteen he met seventeen year old Avis working at the drug store near the high-rise in Manhattan where he was employed as an apprentice ironworker. (O'Hennesseys had been ironworkers since construction of the first skyscraper.) Avis suffered as much dual guilt and repressed sexual passion as Frank. In four months, they had to get married, and at regular intervals in the next five years, they produced three babies.

On the day of Frank's fatal fall from a twenty-second story iron beam, he was riveting absently and thinking about sex. The hung-over ironworker above him missed his step and on his way down clipped Frank who was thrown to a beam ten feet below. Before he died from a broken neck, he made his last confession to a petrified city inspector clinging to a secured vertical beam, and part of it was to extract a promise that his children be educated at the parish school.

Newly-rich from the construction's company's insurance settlement, Avis promptly married the slick financial consultant who culled the obituaries for potential clients. In less than a year, the money and her husband were gone. Avis lost her trust and gained a permanently sour expression; her youthful prettiness disappeared. At twenty-five she resolved, no more men.

Marguerite, Frank's youngest born in 1954, had just turned two when her mother made her decision about men, and from that point on, Marguerite and her two older brothers were at the mercy of the Roman Catholic educational system. While Avis drudged on the assembly line at a local bakery, her kids went to the nursery sponsored by the parish and run by the nuns. As each reached kindergarten age, they were enrolled on scholarships in the parochial school. Charity cases, Marguerite-nicknamed-Mag once overheard a nun comment about the O'Hennessey children. Her brothers, Frank Jr. and Anthony, detested the rigid program, and Avis was always having to beg for another chance. But until she reached twelve, cute, chubby Mag liked school, often volunteering to help teachers afterwards or assisting the scorekeeper during intramural sports. Her brothers were nice to her, but seldom home, so being with kids her own age was better than being around her grim mother.

The first time Roland nailed her, Mag's breasts were still more puffy from baby fat than puberty. She'd had one period. Since she was excellent at denying negative experiences, she managed to convince herself that she'd only imagined what Roland had done to her until it happened again three weeks later. And again two weeks after that.

Roland, of lank, stringy hair and spongy lips that gaped due to a severe overbite, drove a school bus and was the school's janitor. He was also the brother of Father John, the monsignor. Mag was the last student to be dropped off, which was a block from the apartment where the O'Hennesseys lived, and because of her after school activities, it was often dusk. Roland swore she'd never get a ride to school again if she did not lay down in the aisle and let him do it to her. She could not walk to school; it was too far. What would she tell her mother? Avis worshiped Frank's memory. Being educated in the parish school was an absolute. Mag tearfully endured Roland's assault and lied about the blood on her uniform, claiming it was her period.

The fourth time Roland made his demand, seventeen year old Frank Jr., in his '56 two-tone Fairlane, spied the parish bus shadowed in the alley between the deaf optometrist's and the shoe repair shop, both owners Roman Catholic. Rumors about Roland's deeds had circulated for years among the students, but no girl had ever made a public confession; no concrete proof had ever been established. Finding the bus location fishy, Frank Jr. had a hunch. He pulled into the alley nose to nose with the bus and laid on his horn.

When Roland appeared unkempt to peer through the windshield, Frank Jr. got out of his Fairlane because of curiosity; he went berserk at the sight of his sister trying to straighten her clothes. He vaulted the steps to the bus, but Roland refused to release the door lever. Mag resorted to screams which intimidated Roland. He grabbed Mag and pulled the lever, using the girl as a shield. Frank had no qualms about removing the obstacle. He cuffed Mag on the side of the head and she tumbled into the front passenger seat.

Unlike his late father, scrappy, caustic Frank Jr. held no reverence for the Church. He lifted weights regularly and had developed a sinewy, muscular body. Roland was several inches taller and heavier by sixty pounds, but his defense reflexes were nonexistent. Frank Jr.'s right punch flattened the older man's nose and a left one to his abdomen doubled him over. Frank Jr. finished the man by shoving him into the driver's seat where his head bounced off the window, cracking it.

By now the shoe repair owner had turned off his buffing wheel to investigate the noise. He shook his head as he ducked back into his shop to call the parish office before a police cruiser happened by. Perhaps this time Father John would let Roland hang in the breeze, he thought.

Avis settled for cash, enough to make an ample down payment on a row house in a better neighborhood. Disgusted with his mother for not prosecuting the asshole and suing the Church, Frank Jr., who had already quit school, now moved out.

Mag's morning sickness upped the stakes for Avis to remain silent. With this settlement she bought a new Oldsmobile and negotiated for Mag to be sent far away. (Avis reasoned falsely that distance would minimize the gossip.) Mag spent her pregnancy at San Pedro Monastery in the Jemez Mountains north of Albuquerque, New Mexico. The monastery was known primarily as a retreat center for priests with drinking problems, but in the local vicinity it was common knowledge that nuns and other victims impregnated by priests went there to have their babies.

At the monastery, Mag suffered only briefly from homesickness and actually enjoyed her stay. Youngest by many years, the sympathetic, confined women pampered her. Childbirth was another disaster. Her pelvis was too small to deliver, yet the monastery physician procrastinated in transferring her to a hospital until fetal distress made it an emergency. The baby died; Mag's uterus was damaged. The diocese anted plenty for the loss, but this time Avis did not benefit from Mag's misfortune. While Mag was in New Mexico, Frank Jr. had contacted the family brain, Aunt Eloise, Frank Sr.'s older sister, who lived in Dana, New Jersey.

Competent, sensible Eloise O'Hennessey headed the physical education department at the high school and unbeknownst to her family, espoused a gay lifestyle. A kind, stable person who loved her niece, Eloise agreed with Frank Jr. that Avis' behavior was deplorable and suggested to her sister-in-law that after the baby's birth, Mag would be better off living in New Jersey. Shrewdly, Eloise took legal steps to be named guardian, and thus Mag returned East to her aunt's. Since she had been well tutored at the monastery, she was promoted to eighth grade on schedule.

Dana was a small, quiet homogeneous town where everything was in walking distance. Mostly upper class whites, the high school graduating class averaged two hundred fifty with eighty percent college bound. Mag had not gotten street tough like her brothers, so she blended into Dana, yet too many adult things had happened to her. She never quite felt like she belonged in a place where football was the main enthusiasm and players and cheerleaders ranked as gods.

Other than severe acne for approximately two years and a penchant for donut binges, Mag seemed to recover her physical health. Her gouged emotions healed slowly, though, and she never had any desire to return to Queens or to Catholicism.

Eloise had no use, either, for a religion that venerated a virgin, yet denied females in the priesthood; for a hypocritical faith that advocated celibacy, yet condoned men like Roland around children.

In Eloise's tidy house, then, the niece and aunt proved compatible.

When Mag turned sixteen, a friend of Eloise's offered her a counter job at the Italian delicatessen she owned. The friend's cousin, Herb Ingram, worked for her, too. Ten years Mag's senior, Herb was a shy, scrawny man with a prematurely balding pate who came alive slicing salami; he could cleave deli meat as thin as the machine could. Herb was so accomplished that he had a reputation, and matrons expressly requested for their cold cuts to be hand-carved by him. His knife collection was Herb's pride, and he had a display rack for them on the wall behind the meat case. The set was never completely arrayed, however. If he wasn't slicing with one of his knives, he was cleaning a stainless steel blade or honing it or oiling a wooden handle.

Mag was shyer than Herb was, and it made him bold. They both flushed with pleasure when he stammered that her knobby brown eyes were like raisins, and he really liked raisins. Then he admired the way the sun had lightened her hair, mentioning that he found blondes attractive. On the way home from work, Mag bought a bleaching-kit and had Eloise strip the color from her brown pixie. Ensuing mutual flattery led to coffee after work at the O'Hennessey house where Herb soon became a fixture every free moment. Herb's gentle kisses and lack of interest in sex made them a perfect match because Mag's interest was also nil. His impotence suited them.

The summer Mag graduated, Eloise's steady companion, a justice of the peace, married the couple. Years before, Eloise had invested the church hush money in a college trust fund for Mag. Since further education did not interest Mag, she and Herb decided to keep the money reserved for the day when their horoscopes indicated the auspiciousness for them to open their own deli. Herb was very serious about astrology and carefully charted their forecasts. Mag figured it was as good a belief as anything offered by an indifferent cosmos.

In 1976, a state referendum approved legalized gambling in Atlantic City and by 1978, the first casino opened. Herb and Mag vacationed at the community undergoing rehabilitation, then consulted the stars. Their horoscopes confirmed what they both felt - open an upscale deli on the famous boardwalk. Expensive rent, but from all indications, an advantageous move. Mag had already proven that she had a knack for putting together fancy party trays, and living with Eloise, she had gotten to be a fanatic for cleanliness. Board of health inspectors often spoke of her in glowing terms to the less hygienically concerned. Thus, in the spring of 1979 in Atlantic City, the Ingrams unveiled The Clever Cleaver which was an instant success, and Herb's slicing skills soon earned him the same eminence that he had enjoyed in Dana. Mag's last memories of her early traumas faded, and for a brief period she was unconditonally happy.

Legalized gambling created jobs and the general economy improved, but it did little to better the poorer neighborhoods which fringed the glitzy casino area. In 1986, a drug-crazed punk with an automatic pistol held up the deli for seven hundred fifty-seven dollars and odd cents. He emptied his clip at Herb, Mag and a customer just for the hell of it. Herb did not survive.

Meanwhile, Frank Jr. had been incarcerated for involuntary manslaughter. He'd killed a man accidentally during a fist fight. His parole and Herb's death coincided, and a grieving, convalescing Mag invited her brother to move in with her.

⁓

Brigantine was a controlled environment, but in view of the hundreds of thousands of birds that gathered on the eleven mile area, the refuge was as successful as any natural habitat designated as a winter bird haven. Bundled in a heavy parka, Mag walked along a section of the marsh where the Fish and Wildlife Service mingled fresh and salt water to foster the growth of the plants and small marine animals which whetted water fowl appetites.

Herb had been fascinated by Canadian geese and when he heard the honking overhead, he always stopped slicing to smile at Mag. Being so close to Brigantine, they had visited the refuge many times, especially during the seasonal migrations when swarms of flocks continuously ascended and descended.

Mag repressed the urge to weep. She would never stop yearning for him. Herb had been her refuge and now being close to the geese he had admired helped her temporarily to feel closer to him.

She walked slowly because the punk's spray of bullets had punctured her abdomen; after eight months, it still hurt to move, but every day the pain receded. Her therapist was pleased with her progress. Physical progress, Mag thought, as she slogged through a brackish pool in her Wellington boots. Mentally, she remained stagnant, mired in an abyss of spiritual nothingness. Herb's horoscope had predicted a big change, a new way of life. The idea had perplexed them. They were so content with their shop and with each other. How could a change be beneficial to them or even interest them? Mag understood now the danger of knowing the future. No concept of interpretation occurred until the ax fell. Hindsight especially vexed because there was no way of going back and avoiding that ax.

She stopped to watch a disjointed formation of brants land. Other varieties of geese were quite disciplined in their flight formations, instinctively organizing their mass into V and Y patterns. She remembered Herb commenting that these dark birds were so small and their flight so disorderly that they were often confused with ducks.

"Brants are special, aren't they?" Theone said.

Mag glanced at the young woman who had joined her. She was of similar, average height. Was she wearing only a nylon windbreaker?

"Yes," Mag answered, "my husband studies...studied their habits because there are so many here in the winter. They feed on the eelgrass and sea lettuce. Imagine in the spring, they fly all the way back to the extreme northern part of the continent just to nest."

The two women inspected each other. The afternoon was misty and overcast, and the hood on Mag's jacket partially shadowed her face while Theone's tousled hair hid hers, but their eyes connected.

Mag trembled. This young woman had the same eyes as Herb! A drab hazel-brown with uneven pupils. Very kind, loving eyes. Eyes at peace...a soul at peace.

"I'm sorry for you he's gone," Theone said, "we can't control other's choices and so often it involves hurting the innocent, but Herb's soul advanced on this journey." She brushed back her hair so that Mag could see her smile. "It may not seem important now, but because of your tragedies and how you deal with them, your soul, too, will make great progress in this existence."

Mag stepped closer to Theone. "Who are you?" She whispered.

Theone held out her hands, palms up.

Mag reached, then noticed her gloves. Quickly she peeled them off, and the moment she touched Theone, she was engulfed with the sense of peace that she had seen for Herb in the young woman's eyes. Tonight she would sleep well, Mag thought confidently, and tomorrow she would be less depressed. Frank Jr. was trying awfully hard to run the shop, but he wasn't one who liked being confined long to the same spot. She either had to throw herself into it or...sell the deli. But what would she do? Cold cuts, cheese and salads were all she knew besides keeping a house clean and orderly. At thirty-three, she could hardly retire. Mag stared at Theone. This young woman was going to need someone to take care of her because she had more important things to do than fix dinner or do laundry.

"Do you need a companion?" She asked Theone, surprised that she had uttered such an audacious remark.

Theone squeezed Mag's soft hands. This pudgy bleached blonde with a doughy complexion pitted with acne scars was the most genuine person she had met in her travels. Mag Ingram had suffered tremendously in her life, yet love gushed from her, seeking a target. The Deity was very pleased with this soul.

"I will need you," Theone said, "but not for quite a while yet. You must determine how you wish to settle your affairs and I have to return home shortly to help my mother. We do have time to talk. Shall we start?"

Mag nodded earnestly, inattentive to the squawking brants hoping to be noticed by Theone.

As the women walked the marsh trails and in subsequent days together, Theone shared The Message with Mag. At first, Mag believed that Theone was an angel, but soon realized that what she was went beyond that. Not that it mattered. Theone had given back her life and gotten her soul on the right track. As long as she lived, Mag would honor The Deity and serve Theone. It was the winter of 1987.

In Bickley, Missouri, Jasper Stroud unwound his wool scarf and settled into the floral patterned easy chair that Julie Logan had indicated before she had left him to make coffee. Paydirt, he thought with elation. Oh, he'd found a number of folks who venerated an unknown young woman with some sort of insight into recognizing your problem and helping you solve it, but nothing substantial enough to follow as a lead until the tip from the AA member in Springfield. A new member had spoken before the group, claiming with conviction that her life had been changed by a miracle in the form of a mere girl. The woman had sworn that this girl, who must have been a disguised angel, had just shown up one day in her truck which required repair work.

Angel.
Truck.
Roadway Angel.
Jasper had called his travel agent.

Julie spoke over her coffee cup. "Theone was quite real, but out of this world at the same time. I don't mean like goofy or crazy, but, you know..." She looked at Jasper.

"Ethereal?" He supplied.
"Does that mean angelic?"
"Yes, or celestial, heavenly."
Julie smiled. "Heavenly. That sure fits Theone Jones. How we loved that girl and how we learned to love each other!"
"She really had a tremendous effect on your life."
Julie chuckled. "You don't know the half of it!"
"Is there any chance you got a picture of her?"
"There was never no reason to."
"Did she give you a permanent address?"
"Midwest somewhere. We never got no details 'cause like I told you, she and Charlie did a trade. You planning on writing her up for a magazine or newspaper? She'll be famous one day, whether you do or not, you know. People are gonna listen to her and go away changed for the good. Word will spread. Guess it has already, huh, since you're here."
Jasper laughed pleasantly. "I'd like to find her so that I can experience personally what she is. Did she give you any other clues as to her identity?"
Julie's expression was baffled, but calm. "I'm a recovering alcoholic and take each day at a time. I've learned not to beat myself up when I realize how many brain cells I've destroyed and with it, my ability to recall information."
Jasper smiled with encouragement.
Her face brightened. "I joined her one night when she was sitting in the grass, staring at the moon. It was just a bitty sliver, but Theone acted like it was the most beautiful thing in the whole world. She mentioned that her middle name was her mother's maiden name which was Mane."
"'Moon' in Norwegian," Jasper mumbled.
"That's what she said! How'd you know?" Julie said, astonished.
"I have an interest in languages," he explained.
Julie got up from the sofa. "I can ring Charlie at the shop. He might have some things to add."

In Springfield's airport, Jasper was too excited to wait. He cashed a ten dollar bill for change and settled in a telephone booth. Theone Jones came from a suburb of Chicago, Charlie Logan had remembered, but she'd never offered any details as to its exact location. It was enough for Jasper, though. All he needed was her name. Having the state narrowed the search of motor vehicle records.

༄

At the Jones' kitchen table, Brigit gazed at Theone who had appeared suddenly a few hours ago, right after Kristen and Erik had left for the first day of school following the holidays. But her return was not a surprise. Theone would have *known* Aaron had died and that her mother was in need.

"You were gone six months," Brigit chided. "We never thought you'd stay away for so long! Aaron never had a chance to say 'goodbye' to you." Her voice broke and she sobbed.

Theone leaned over and embraced her mother. "He never had a chance to say 'goodbye' to anyone, but he felt you there in spirit. He felt me there, too, and that's what mattered to him. For those souls who have made progress, Our Deity provides this loving sensation to ease the transition."

Brigit withdrew and wiped her face with a tissue. "Aaron couldn't give away the love fast enough and his great big loving heart just burst, didn't it? I could never keep him home when he was sick. Getting him to a doctor was impossible. He just kept going until...the off duty paramedic on the train couldn't even revive him a minute after the attack. Well, Christmas has been a strain since you told off that old phony Reese. Now, with Aaron's death three days before the holiday, I won't ever want to think joy in December..." Brigit cleared her throat. "Pastor Calhoun gave the service on the 27th. I wasn't thrilled about the church setting, but it was important to Grandma and Grampa. They didn't dare suggest Kermit Reese's involvement. If I'd any idea how to contact you, we would have waited for you to get here."

"It's okay, Mom. My presence might not have been...good for everyone. And you and I understand the reincarnation of a progressive soul. Dad's physical self is gone, but his soul has reached a higher level."

"The Goddess has been a source of comfort," Brigit said frankly, "of course, I can't share this with Kristen who swallows whole the patriarchal swill that Reese preaches. We are so far apart spiritually."

"It's her way," Theone said gently, "is she coping all right?"

"She and her grandparents are sustaining each other."

"I expect that Erik hurts a lot," Theone said.

"He's trying so hard to be brave..." Brigit paused to get control of her voice. "You were always close, and he'll be glad you're home. Only fifteen and losing his father...how am I supposed to deal with my loss and his? Aaron's life insurance was adequate and the house is automatically paid off with the mortgage insurance we carried, but I can't put kids through college on a librarian's salary."

Theone took her mother's hands in hers. "I'm here for you, Mom. We'll handle it together."

Brigit felt her daughter's strength and the love flowing from her and was tempted to rely on her, but it would be wrong to shackle Theone. Her Child of Peace must be free to enlighten the world. "I can't ask that of you," Brigit said. "You're here for a greater purpose."

Theone smiled. "There's time for every purpose. Presently, it's this one."

"You won't go to college yourself, will you?"

"Further knowledge isn't available for me. I'll just get a job for a spell."

Brigit catalogued the 'beyond education comment' in her mental file, *She Is of The Goddess. Her Knowledge Is Innate. Don't Pursue This.* And she could pretty much narrow down the type of job her daughter would choose to hold - it would be out of doors and she would have plenty of people contact.

Within the month, Theone achieved a perfect score on the civil service exam for postal workers. By late February, 1988, she was taken off rotation and assigned a permanent mail route in nearby Rolling Meadows.

◡⁀

Mike Zimmer was thrilled by Theone's return. He could not remember a time when he was not attracted to his older neighbor. Well, he considered, attracted was too strong a term...or it was the wrong term to describe his feelings for Theone. Attracted implied some base emotion. He was drawn to her like metal to a magnet; there was no control over the pull, yet it was not physical. (Beyond simple hugs, physical contact mildly repelled him.) It was a cosmic connection, he deemed, during moments of reflection on what bound him to Theone.

As a youth she once commented on Mike's profundity, and because of it she felt she could be more open with him than others. Next to her mother he represented the most comfortable relationship she had. Of slight build and a fastidious temperament Mike did not enjoy extracurricular activities and developed few friends by choice. He never forgot what he valued as his highest compliment from the most respected person he knew.

Theone's Truth frequently awed Mike, but it did not intimidate him. Although his response was often 'wow', he did not feel tongue-tied, but enlightened, and always in total agreement. He simply felt right around her.

Mike's introspective nature did not mesh with his acerbic, money-obsessed parents whose pressure to excel was only slightly veiled. Just do your best, they trilled. As long as best was A's, he speculated. Once, to test his suspicions, he purposely let his quarter grade average fall to C+. His parents' reactions ranged from 'you'll have to attend junior college' (horrifying for any decent scholar) to 'you'll end up a food worker at the very high school you attend now.'

Fortunately Mike's perfectionism made for an industrious student. (It had long since stopped embarrassing him when his parents bragged about his superior grades to virtual strangers.) Yet high marks were an end in themselves rather than a ticket to an impressive college. Mike was quite content to apply to the state university closest to home, Northern Illinois in Dekalb. While his bureaucratic parents envisioned their son as a doctor or an attorney, Mike wished to study sociology and entertained vague plans to teach, but only if he had nothing else to do. In his heart he admitted that he'd bide his time studying an enjoyable subject while he waited for Theone to become...whatever The Deity had destined her to be. She was THE source of spiritual power, and therefore should be freed from the mundane. She would need an organizer, a guy to clear the way, someone with an attention for details, an advance man to smooth the path for her ministry. Mike wanted the job to start now - high school was a bore - but there was no hurrying Theone who kept encouraging him to keep up his fine scholastic work. It wasn't time yet.

But at least she was back. Mike had missed her terribly.

⁓

"Why don't you go be weird somewhere else!" Kristen cried at Theone who knelt in front of her open bedroom window gazing at the early evening sky. How she resented her sister's return! Brigit's prime attention riveted on Theone, just like in the past, and she'd made no gains in winning Brigit's soul for Jesus. Her mother's disinterest in church may have remained, but at least Theone's absence had guaranteed that there would be no dark influence to create an endangerment. When Brigit died someday, Kristen wanted her mother in Heaven with her father.

Theone's job choice embarrassed her, too. A mail carrier, of all stupid things! Theone had absolutely no ambition, no desire to improve herself! And for a best friend she chose ugly Mike Zimmer with his glaring red hair, bulging green eyes and big Jewish nose. Geeky Mike was as peculiar as Theone was!

Ignoring Kristen's rudeness, Theone got up and quietly closed her door. Her sister's determination to drive her away backfired. She simply treated Kristen with kindness, which only served to aggravate her further.

It was easy to end an exchange by closing the door, but not so simple when the conflict involved more than the two of them. In the church youth group, Kristen paired off with Pastor Reese's youngest son, Kevin, a handsome, wise-mouthed kid who often hung out at the Jones'. He encouraged Kristen's negative feelings by making fun of Theone, usually within hearing, but only during Brigit's absence. Theone counseled Erik to disregard the insults, but the vicious remarks about her job, her clothes, her rocks, whatever, incensed Erik. Aaron's death had hurt him deeply, and he needed Theone's caring presence at home; he did not want awful Kristen to force her to leave again.

Theone

More than once Theone had been forced against her nature to intervene with mind tricks to temper the heat in the exchanges. Theone also made sure that memories blurred so that none of the siblings mentioned the fights to Brigit, struggling to adjust to widowhood. She had lost both her loves early in life and her present grief at Aaron's death abated slowly.

Five years of this ordeal, Theone pondered each time she mentally diffused Kristen, Kevin and Erik's deplorable conduct. This was manipulation of their souls' paths, but justifiable for her mother's sake because Theone could not break her promise and leave. Would it be necessary to live in a scrappy atmosphere for five years? Because five years minimum would pass before Erik finished his education, and she would be free again to share The Message. Theone often suffered from restlessness, but The Deity controlled her being, and continually, The Deity answered her queries that this was Their Desire for the present. *Heed The Deity,* Theone reminded herself over and over as she quelled her impatience. *Trust The Deity.* The Deity knew best.

༄

From his rented sub-compact car parked in the next block, Jasper used binoculars to view Theone's passage from house to house. He'd varied his times and locations, but generally, Jasper had been observing her for several weeks. She had shown no sign that she was aware of his presence, and surprisingly, despite the wintry weather lingering into spring, she appeared comfortable in only a white nylon windbreaker over her blue cotton uniform.

He sharpened his focus. A Doberman Pinscher tore across the shallow lawns of the tract houses. "Nasty dog," Jasper murmured, "mean eyes often typical of the breed, but if the pattern holds and I wholly expect it to..." the fierce Doberman halted abruptly a foot in front of Theone walking up a driveway. With a yelp, the animal crouched and rolled on to its back. Theone shifted her mailbag and bent to scratch the dog's belly, then straightened. The Doberman stood and docilely permitted Theone to leash him.

She always carried a leash, Jasper had discovered, so that she could return whatever dog she had attracted to its owner. He suspected that the leash was merely for show because 'attracted' was a mild term for the animals' behavior. This unique young woman enchanted animals, domestic and wild. Noisy birds spiraled about her; chattering squirrels scampered by her; mewling cats followed her; exuberant dogs hurdled at her. Her return attention was sincere, but brief, and apparently it satisfied the animals who would return to their prior activities. (It did not dawn on Jasper that the season was too early to see ants marching in columns for her review or other insects - bees, grasshoppers, flies and so forth - whizzing round her.)

Theone stepped on to a concrete stoop, but before she could lift the mailbox lid, the front door opened. People, also, were attracted to her, Jasper had found, yet she lost no time on her route. As with the animals, her greetings were sincere, but brief.

Jasper watched Theone cross the lawn to the next house where a tabby sauntered in her path. Neither the leashed dog nor the cat exhibited any belligerent behavior. No messages, no miracles these days in her contacts, but she still possessed an irresistible power to mesmerize. Why had she ceased? Had her father's premature death forced her to consider family and put her evangelizing on hold?

He'd narrowed her journey to a six month period of remarkable encounters. Each story had been verified as much as a mystical event could be; its narrator checked for soundness of mind. The lasting effects of her influence boggled him, although the Shaws had been by far the most dramatic. They had proved him wrong. The former Yuppie couple was already happily relocated to a small community mid-state, and Walton had recovered sufficiently to impregnate Claire. One of the final people affected had been a recent widow in Atlantic City who had stated that she was waiting for Theone to summon her. Theone. Pronounced with a soft 'th' and long vowels, THEE-O-NEE. Translated as "Name of God". Jasper had checked his Greek dictionary.

No mysteries had surfaced in her middle class background. A cursory examination of her parents' histories seemed normal; their liberal sentiments had been seeded presumably by the sixties activism of their youth. But perhaps he should check family more closely, since unusual events had occurred in Theone's short life. At age thirteen, there had been a major controversy over some accurate Bible-based comments she'd made at her conservative church which had split the congregation. A few summers later she had gained quite a following of teens who had gathered for her simplistic preaching at a forest preserve, but she had abandoned the mission when confronted by authorities. Like others touched by her, many of these Honest, Humble Huggers still practiced what she had taught them. That perplexed him. Why were followers not inundating her? How could she remain so...anonymous? Somehow, part of her gift was a knack for fading in importance without weakening the impact of her message. This was further supported by the conclusion that she had no interest in personal gain. Purportedly, she possessed valuable stones, but according to reports, she had nothing else of worth.

So who was Theone? She referred constantly to The Deity, yet she never claimed to be one or born of one. She referred to herself as a messenger of love, not an angel, yet it was the perception of many who had experienced her that she was indeed an angel. 'Angel' translated as messenger.

Theone disappeared around the corner, a sparrow sailing by her. Jasper lowered his binoculars. Without a bit of personal contact, he had accumulated more than sufficient evidence to write a convincing book about her, a book that would be a best seller, yet he hesitated to tap out even a sentence on the computer keyboard. (He did not dwell on the film he had wasted trying to capture a sharp picture of her. Even with a sophisticated camera and a telephoto lens, every single print had blurred.) Theone just wasn't ready for publicity, he kept thinking. When she was ready, she'd let him know. *She'd let him know.* Why did that make sense? And in fairness, he must do a direct interview to authenticate that she was real; however, thus far he had failed to approach her.

Jasper's breath became shallow, and he swallowed hard. *Because the idea of approaching her frightened him.* Why? Would she have such a profound effect on him that his intellectual control would disintegrate? *Was he truly prepared to have what he had always believed to be a bedrock Christian faith challenged and possibly altered by her message for his soul?*

He started the car. Perhaps hire a detective to watch for signs that she was activating her ministry, Jasper decided as he drove towards his motel. Meanwhile, he was going home to San Antonio to write the book. He intended to be as ready as possible to publish when she was ready to spread her message again. A meeting between them could wait until then.

CHAPTER FOUR

Glenn

Glenn Chandler was an unplanned, mid-life baby and as a youth, he had one incessant, fervent wish - that he'd grow to be as tall in stature as his two much older brothers. The eldest at 6'2 played on the football and basketball teams in high school and won a full scholarship to Marquette in Milwaukee where eventually he attained a degree in pulmonary medicine. The next eldest at 6'1½ did almost as well in the same two sports. In his early thirties, he achieved tenure as a bio-chemistry professor at the University of Kentucky.

By age sixteen, his parents' assurances that Glenn would gain more inches had not happened, but he was not surprised that he had stopped at a mere 5'6. In his heart, he'd known all along and had grown inured to other children making fun of his puniness. Unlike his brothers, he favored his mother from her fine blonde hair to her stumpy legs. Glenn required eye glasses to correct astigmatism. To add to his stress, he secretly worried that a correlation existed between height and measure of intelligence. His brothers were brilliant; he had to work relentlessly for every grade.

Glenn learned early to compensate, though, just in case he stayed short. The first time grade school offered band lessons, he insisted on taking up the most-attention getting instrument, the drums, and he stuck with his choice, dreaming of becoming a virtuoso. The band director did not have the heart to tell him that he was tone-deaf. In high school he auditioned for the award winning jazz band, and this director was blunt about his talent. Yet Glenn refused to quit, and he played four years in the marching band where he diligently read the music to stay on key. Besides, the idea behind a marching band drums was noise, not rhythm.

He practiced until hoarse to develop a superb speaking voice and outwardly, he projected a lot of presence; aqua-colored contact lenses favorably dramatized his watery blue eyes, but it was not the same as being a handsome star athlete. His mother supported his efforts in debate, but his father never attended any of the contests. He was disappointed in having a short son, or so Glenn concluded. In fact, his father was a neurological surgeon at a prominent Chicago hospital who found his work more absorbing than any of his offspring.

Since Glenn's father earned an enormous income, his mother was a professional volunteer who served on various charity boards and chaired fund raisers for affluent donors who liked to enjoy themselves while they were giving. In their wealthy North Shore community and at broader levels, the Chandlers were lauded for their contributions to society, only Glenn always felt that people did not include him in their appraisal.

Freshman year at a downstate university a great thing happened. His roommate played an electric guitar and he invited Glenn to jam with a couple of other guys he knew. They formed a heavy metal band, which required no particular rhythm talent on Glenn's part, and by sophomore year they sounded fairly good to local hangouts. Glenn was not crazy about smoky bars, and there was no money in it, but he thrived on the recognition with one exception. He shied away from the jaded groupies who would surely eye his small genitals and make unflattering comparisons.

Second semester sophomore year, two great things happened. In biology lab, Glenn met freshman Nancy Nicholson whose father was the senior pastor at a thousand member Inspiration of Grace (IOG) church in a Chicago suburb.

Initially, her background was not as important as her stature. Virtuous Nancy was a petite 5'2 and had a round, sweet face. She was also easy to dominate since she was accustomed to her autocratic father giving orders. Glenn felt he had met the girl of his dreams.

The next great thing hinged on the first. The Chandlers professed no religious ideology and therefore, they had not seen any reason to provide such training for their sons. But Glenn had gone to church on occasion with a Baptist friend whose parents claimed that they were concerned for Glenn's salvation. The preacher had mesmerized Glenn with his booming sermons about the powerful Almighty, and as a result, Glenn equated God with his all-powerful father who controlled life when he excised a patient's brain tumor.

Nancy took Glenn home and to church. Doctor Nicholson, a striking man with silvery good looks, preached of love and forgiveness in a compelling voice. The message, however, did not make as much of an impression as the man's marvelous delivery. Spellbound, Glenn realized that everyone in the crowded sanctuary was, too. The glorious choir added to his pleasant feelings about church. He had determined communications to be a good career choice with a minor in psychology, but after one sermon, he was convinced he should join the church and study theology.

Pleased with the young man's zeal and proud that he had effected Glenn's conversion, Nancy's father personally supervised his instruction in the fundamentalist IOG faith, but recommended that Glenn proceed with his original course of studies. Keep your present major, the reverend advised, a successful ministry depended as much on the words as the articulation of those words; behavior training learned in psychology courses would come in handy during counseling sessions, an added source of income. Glenn would get plenty of textbook theology in seminary.

Doctor Nicholson pointed to his own accomplishments with open vanity. As senior pastor, his major job requirements were to preach at two services weekly and to lead a Bible study quarterly. Additionally, he supervised the other three pastors (associate, youth and music) and a lay staff of seven. Because of a manageable work load, he was free to participate at higher levels of church government such as chairing the district's powerful minister review board, one which assisted the bishop in addressing cleric conduct. Edgar Nicholson was accorded a lot of respect and he took full advantage of it. If the church was his fiefdom, then the district council was the House of Lords at which he also served as vice-moderator.

The reverend became Glenn's ideal, except that Glenn's ambition was greater. He would not be satisfied with a small sphere of power. His ministry would make him famous the world over. Glenn set aside the drums, redoubled his study efforts and chastely devoted himself to Nancy. He did not wish to exhibit any conduct that might mar a stellar ecclesiastical future.

Following Glenn's college graduation, Nancy's father married the couple before they moved East. Excellent grades and Edgar Nicholson's recommendation insured Glenn's acceptance at the prestigious IOG seminary in upstate New York. Nancy, her education abandoned, dutifully found employment as an administrative assistant in the dean's office. A school endowment fund paid Glenn's tuition and his father continued a generous allowance. The young Chandlers were quite comfortable, although in later years, Glenn alluded to his student days as austere as he felt befitting for a true man of God training to be a spiritual leader. At seminary, he espoused a repentant persona, like that of IOG founder, Hosea Elrod, and would mention in awe the vision of Christ that supposedly had inspired his conversion, one similar to the Apostle Paul's on the road to Damascus. Glenn so wholly identified with the early Christian master, that he came to judge his best sermons as those which reflected not on the Gospels, but on the example of Paul's life and his interpretations of Jesus' teachings.

Glenn's first pastoral call was painstakingly sought and his campaign to win it, carefully plotted. He was as grateful for his father-in-law's influence as he was for the man's suggestion that he study what he had, especially the psychology courses. (By virtue of his profession, he would have control over others' lives, but understanding the dynamics behind behavior was a useful tool in manipulation.)

Lead the youth, assist with pastoral care, preach monthly - the moment Edgar Nicholson gave him to read the Church Search Form [CSF] forwarded by the senior pastor, Tom MacDougall, Edgar's friend at seminary, Glenn wanted to be the new associate pastor at the Carmel By the Sea IOG Church, and he tailored his Personal Application Form [PAF] suitably. Other than preach, he had no interest in working with youth or providing succor to the sick and elderly as the CSF stated, but the coastal location on the Monterey Peninsula was ideal. Just north of spectacular Big Sur, Carmel By the Sea was so exclusive, there were no street addresses, and he presumed the congregation would be very wealthy. The experience on his resume, then, and the contacts he would make, would outweigh the distasteful aspects; he'd simply set his mind to building an impressive track record and move on as soon as possible to a call like his father-in-law's. (His ego prevented him from recognizing that plum calls like Edgar's had to be earned through years of service supported by well established credentials.)

He got the job at Carmel, which he deserved, but Glenn rejoiced in private. In public, he modestly praised God for the position which he believed as divinely directed to him.

A year after Glenn's arrival in Carmel, Tom MacDougall was diagnosed with advanced lymph cancer. The situation was grave for the man, but an unexpected opportunity for Glenn whose false sincerity in dealing with the youth and the infirm had revealed flaws. (During an overnight lock-in at the church, he let the senior high group into his office so they would leave him alone to sleep. The subsequent phone bill listed a series of calls to a pornographic 900 number. He swore to the bookkeeper that he was with them the entire night and nothing of the sort had happened. After the episode, he designated a young adult as leader and rarely showed up for gatherings. The church secretary's husband, who owned a jewelry shop in Carmel, frequently saw Glenn lunching or golfing with big donor members when he had told the secretary he was going on hospital calls.)

Now, he certainly could not be expected to handle everything while his superior fought death with chemotherapy in a San Francisco hospital. Except for his committee involvement with the district, Glenn proceeded to perform church functions a maximum of eight hours in any given twenty-four and minimized his on the job availability by seeing people by appointment only. He often treated the administrative staff with condescension and in one-on-one sessions with members, he would make spiteful remarks about other members, later denying it. Within another four months, his dazzling sermons impressed a lot of people who had no other exposure to him, but also a sufficient number in greater need of pastoral services were complaining about him to board trustees, the governing body of the church. Yet Glenn had prudently befriended select trustees, those who additionally functioned as commissioners to the district. Furthermore, he had ingratiated himself with the district's bishop, an obstinate man with a power complex, who surrounded himself with sycophants. Glenn fit right in. Perhaps Glenn was less than adequate in some areas, but he was inexperienced and entitled to mistakes, the bishop reasoned to the minister review board. He would learn from them and thus grow in faith. The district needed to support one of their brothers. The commissioner trustees from the church concurred, but Carmel's board as a whole felt the district board should arbitrate.

Meanwhile, Tom succumbed to cancer and the split minister review board could not entice another minister to serve as interim until a church search committee could find a new pastor. (Under IOG by-laws, Glenn could not apply for the senior's position.)

Just short of two years had passed since Glenn's call. He had garnered enough support to keep his job, but the church was in turmoil. Nancy provided a way out.

In six years of marriage she had failed to conceive. Her gynecologist recommended that she see an associate practicing in San Diego who specialized in fertility problems, and the program involved an extensive time commitment. Fortuitously, a long standing senior pastor call was open at a declining urban church in San Diego, and the district bishop advised Glenn to submit his PAF; he would be given impeccable references. It was Glenn's least desire to apply; the pay was substantially less, the staff small, but he needed a fast, graceful exit. Nancy's sterility was a good excuse.

The Chandlers' stay in San Diego was bleak in every respect. Glenn disliked the elderly, fixed income congregation who showed no appreciation for his flamboyant sermons. He avoided their potlucks, their piddly craft fair, their sickbeds. Unlike his previous district bishop, however, this one was not susceptible to Glenn's flattery. Eleven months into his service, the ministry review board strongly counseled Glenn to seek a position elsewhere. His references would not reflect the difficulties that his current position had engendered. Nancy was too depressed to show sympathy for her husband's career problems. She had finally conceived and promptly miscarried.

Glenn appealed to his mother to speak to his father. Would they fund more education? If he attained his doctorate in theology his PAF would be greatly enhanced, and he could achieve the important position he dreamed was his destiny.

His father assented to financing tuition, but Glenn would have to work for living expenses. Edgar Nicholson talked to a colleague on staff at Foley College, a denomination-affiliated liberal arts school in central Illinois. Glenn could fill an instructor's position in comparative religion while he worked on his thesis which he would write under the doctoral of divinity program offered at the IOG seminary in Kansas City. Nancy would work again, too, as a secretary in the music department.

It was 1989. On the brink of thirty, his fine blonde hair thinning, Glenn felt trodden by bad breaks. Teaching was a poor substitute for the pulpit and his dull wife could not even give him a child which would be proof of the virility he suspected others doubted. But he promised himself that these conditions would only be temporary. He would overcome these obstacles and rise to greatness. He was born to be renowned.

CHAPTER FIVE

In 1911, Foley College had been constructed in the midst of picturesque woods willed by a loyal IOG member of the same name who had owned them as part of a vast farm on the Illinois River in Grundy County. The campus and the town which had grown up around it lay directly west of Starved Rock State Park and approximately 100 miles southwest of Ashburg. Grants from the Foley family also endowed the school, but attendance was costly even with a scholarship such as Kristen Jones had received.

Money issues did not perturb Kristen, though. Her father's death had not changed the Jones' lifestyle and she inferred that Aaron's insurance must have paid off generously. She still got new clothes and pocket money for snacks, makeup, entertainment, whatever. So had Erik until his sixteenth birthday when he started earning his own cash working part-time at a big discount store on Northwest Highway.

It did not occur to Kristen like it had to Erik that Theone's income supplemented Brigit's, thereby protecting their security. Theone brushed off Erik's questions about it; Brigit told him straight out the truth. He did not bother enlightening selfish Kristen for whom the truth would make no difference.

Brigit felt a lot of guilt over her inability to communicate with Kristen and the deprivation of a father in her children's lives. Foley College would be a burden, but it meant so much to Kristen to be able to accept the block scholarship.

As customary, Theone offered no opinion, but cheerfully went about delivering the mail entrusted to her. Now and again, Brigit wished her eldest would make a judgment about something. The only injustice that upset Theone was when it was to others and then, with forbearance, she attributed free will.

∽

Outside Kristen's new dormitory, Theone studied the surroundings while she waited for Erik to finish stacking a load of their sister's belongings from Brigit's minivan. The maples, oaks and walnuts on the campus were ancient, and the trees had been sacred to past inhabitants because she could feel the vibrations of spiritual ceremonies. Whoever had designed the campus had shown a great regard for the forest setting and had cleared only what was necessary for the buildings. The Deity favored this place. Would Kristen find enlightenment here? Theone never ceased hoping.

"Isn't this wonderful?" Kristen exclaimed. "There's ivy all over the red brick and I adore the white trim! It's the perfect college campus just like in back-to-school fashion layouts!"

Brigit smiled faintly. Pious, self-centered Kristen who had done little to deserve this opportunity was the one getting it! She looked at Theone who seemed intent on the trees with no care for what people considered important, only with an appreciation for Nature, the Earth Mother Gaia's Creation.

In a passing convertible, several male students yelled a greeting at them. Kristen laughed and waved. Oblivious, Theone contemplated a burnished copper leaf.

Standard reactions, Brigit thought as she gripped a heavy suitcase. Of course, when boys discovered smart, pretty Kristen's rigidity, what she referred to as a purity of faith, they found other companions. Including Kevin Reese who last heard was in a detox program for teens. In Theone's case, boys liked her, yet they seemed to understand intrinsically that she was not for them. She was very maternal while simultaneously exuding sexuality. An intimidating combination.

Brigit looked again at Theone. Her blazing hair flowed wildly around her heart-shaped face dominated by those thick, unmanageable brows which no tweezers had ever touched. The eyes that were everyone's eyes and instantly endearing or disturbing. Odd that tee shirts and jeans concealed so thoroughly the lush, curvaceous body Brigit knew her daughter possessed. A perfect woman. Theone, The Goddess...the embodiment of motherly love and carnal desire...in previous incarnations, The Goddess had always had one or more consorts. Well, perhaps Theone's perfect essence had evolved beyond a need for men.

"What's funny, Mom?" Theone stood by the minivan holding a box. Kristen had led an over-laden Erik inside the dormitory.

She must have been chuckling aloud! Brigit fibbed, "Oh, the memory of my first day at college."

Theone stepped closer to her. Fondling the moonstone on her chest, she said, "Sex is supposed to be irresistible because Our Deity desires for us to mate so that other souls will have an opportunity to advance. When it is time for it, there will be a man who is right for me."

Brigit dropped the suitcase and stared at her. "How often do you read minds?"

Theone shrugged. "I don't consciously. I see things in eyes and... understand. The truth shows a distinct clarity whereas a lie appears as a shadow."

"You are meant to be in love with someone?" Brigit's comment was wistful. She felt that she was the closest person to Theone and wanted to keep it that way. Brigit did not rule out another marriage, but did not expect to find anyone, either. Other men just did not compare to Aaron. Wherever Theone was going, Brigit planned to be there with her.

Theone turned her face skyward and closed her eyes for a moment. Then she regarded Brigit. "Mom, it might be hard to imagine, but you will meet someone again. Someone who has suffered as much as you have. He will be...an old acquaintance."

Brigit bowed her head and fought an urge to fall at her daughter's feet in supplication. Why? Why had she of all women been chosen to renew the spirit of The Goddess? No matter how much she meditated and sought, she was never given an answer!

A gust of wind rustled the trees and Brigit experienced the same sense of solitude that had come upon her the night she had conceived Theone...the sense of Peace...

You were chosen as a surrogate because of your wondrous soul, The Singer said. *Theone is Our Child, but your love gave her life.*

Brigit's eyes opened and she gaped at Theone watching her. "Did you do that...telepathically?"

"No, Our Deity spoke to you."

"Just like that? I've been praying for years!"

"The aura here is highly inviting and I just...petitioned on your behalf." Theone clasped Brigit's hands. "The important thing is that whoever is chosen by Our Deity to nurture a Messenger, has foremost the capacity to love. You have it."

"This is not the time for one of your weirdo conversations," Kristen exclaimed. "I have a lot of stuff to move in and Erik shouldn't have to do it all."

Brigit tensed, and Theone tightened her grip. "Everyone in your life is there to present choices for your soul," Theone whispered, "good or bad, happy or sad...it's your choice."

Brigit's awe and desire for further explanation faded. She stepped away from her eldest and smiled tolerantly at Kristen and Erik who stood side by side. Theone was the child of her soul, but these two blue-eyed, ash blondes connected her biologically to humankind. Dainty Kristen sported an outdated bouffant hairstyle favored by country singers, but it helped soften a sharp chin and thin nose. She used a heavy hand to apply makeup to her sensitive complexion and picked at blemishes, delaying the healing. (Erik teased that it was her nastiness erupting.) Thoroughly feminine, she favored soft colors and fabrics with ruffles and bows.

Erik was built like his burly dad. He had also inherited Aaron's grin and infectious giggle. The siblings had dissimilar personalities. Kristen shared a judgmental, pragmatic, demanding nature with her Grandmother Jones. Erik was like Brigit - affectionate, loyal, idealistic.

Choices, Brigit thought. We are given choices for our soul. Eric did not concern her. His soul, like Aaron's, was good. Erik would naturally make good choices, but Kristen had always given her pause. *Kristen would cause trouble for Theone...real big trouble someday...*where had that idea come from? Past experience, Brigit concluded, and there was no changing it.

"Mother, hello? Are you in a trance?" Kristen's tone was impatient.

Brigit sighed and glanced at Theone whose eyes were currently Aaron's. It no longer disconcerted Brigit when this happened. If anything, she appreciated the chance to feel his love again and to be comforted by his metaphysical presence.

⁓

Kristen waited inside the glass door of the music department office by the secretary's desk. She had auditioned for campus choir and was here to improve her chances by asking the director for some career guidance. Truthfully, her goal was already set. If she couldn't find the right man to marry, she would earn a music education degree and teach at a preschool or on the primary level. Little children were okay to work with because, generally, they behaved.

Nancy Chandler glanced resentfully at the pretty student who had asked politely for her to buzz Dr. Rybki. She hadn't started out life mean-natured, but circumstances had ebbed her optimism. Like her mother, Nancy had chosen to be subservient to her husband. If she had dreams, they were secondary to Glenn's. The doctorate was important for him, but working as a secretary again was a difficult step backwards for a childless woman who felt that one of her narrow options for fulfillment involved motherhood.

Nancy punched Dr. Rybki's button and spoke into the intercom when he responded. She mumbled the directions to the professor's office at Kristen, then slumped in her steno chair.

Last night she and Glenn had gotten into a rare quarrel. She had confronted the fact that she was barren, but he refused, and by so doing, would not consider adoption. He would not consider her needs. For once. Just once. She always agreed with him, with his choices, with the directions they took. Little in her life gave her joy, but a baby would change that.

Nancy stared with hostility at the letter displayed on her computer monitor. It was part of a four-page master for a mailing to alumni soliciting donations for program support. She still had to set up the merge containing the names and addresses. The ease of word processing made no difference -

she hated to type! Sometimes she just wanted to kill herself to end the futility. Sometimes, it seemed more than an idle, self-pitying thought.

⁓

Midcenter in the lecture hall, Kristen gazed at Reverend Chandler, mesmerized by his voice. He had the most dynamic delivery of anyone she had ever listened to in a live setting. (Certain preachers on television stirred her spirit.) Reverend Chandler was just giving an introductory lecture on the course outline. What was he like in the pulpit preaching the Gospel?

She had scoffed at taking Comparative Religion, a required subject for her curriculum, because she felt that learning more about other creeds would be of no use to her. Her beliefs did not need bolstering or illumination. She already accepted whole heartedly that Jesus was The Savior and she could defend The Gospel with numerous memorized verses. But having Reverend Chandler as a teacher would make any class exciting.

Her sight lingered on the speaker's left hand. Naturally, he was married. Kevin had told her that ministers always married young to circumvent the sin of premarital sex. And from what she had seen, ministers stayed married because they lived righteously. They invited Jesus into their lives and He was on their side. Marrying a minister appealed to her, if she could find one who had not already found a mate.

Kristen glanced at the students around her. Minister material or not, the boys looked so immature! She focused again on Glenn Chandler and decided to inquire after class if he ever gave sermons because she wanted to attend the service. Someone like him had to be important here on campus and he would be a good mentor.

Glenn smiled with pleasure at Kristen. She was a pretty girl who without the poofed hair would be shorter than him and clearly she was a good Christian. Kristen was dressed in a nice pair of tailored slacks and a plaid jacket, a soft blouse, too. Not the sloppy, sagged pants and baggy tee shirts so common among the young. Lovely co-eds on the campus were plentiful, but Kristen was the first one to show such regard for him. Glenn had never entertained any notion of being unfaithful to Nancy, but her sour attitude lately had not encouraged him to seek intimate relations. It was easy to be attracted to Kristen.

"There is a Chapel service every morning at 7, Kristen," Glenn advised, "and the clergy on staff preach on a rotating basis. I haven't checked yet when I'm scheduled, but I can let you know."

"I can't say that I'm really great about getting up early," Kristen replied, "but I will if you're giving the sermon. Which church do you attend for worship on Sunday?"

"First Inspiration of Grace."

"Oh, of course, like our college. I was raised in a Shepherd church. We didn't have anything holy roller, but it was very Bible-based."

Glenn had never heard of a Shepherd church, but there were so many splinter groups even in the IOG denomination. "I'm very Bible-based," he said. "It has nothing to do with denomination, but with your personal commitment to live according to Scripture. The Word of God rules my life and I can see that It rules yours as well."

Kristen shook her head in wonder. "Yes, that is exactly true! You are so...wise." Forthright Kristen blushed. Handsome, erudite, religious - Reverend Chandler was such a perfect man!

"Perhaps you'd like to try worship the IOG way," Glenn suggested, "I'd watch for you if I knew you were attending." It was as close as he could come to flirting and surprised himself at how easy it was to talk to Kristen in this manner.

"I'm not locked into any particular church," Kristen said. "I mean, I'm at college now. I should spread my wings." Uncharacteristically, she giggled. "What time on Sunday?"

He smiled at her. Her girlish adoration alone qualified her, but she also seemed prettier the longer they talked. Kristen Jones was very appealing, but even if it was disagreeable to remark on it, he was married; the gold band on his finger was plain enough. Glenn said, "My wife and I attend the second service at 11:00 a.m. She will be pleased to make the acquaintance of such a charming and devout young woman as yourself."

"Do you ever need a sitter?" Kristen inquired. She bet his children were just precious and it would be neat to be around his house. It would also earn her brownie points.

"We haven't been blessed," Glenn said curtly.

Kristen sensed what she determined was sorrow. "I'm so sorry for... mentioning something that must be...painful."

Glenn nodded. Kristen Jones was warmhearted, too. He wished he had a kid so that she could baby-sit. Having her around would be...tempting... better they kept their relationship in a classroom setting. An affair could taint his future.

൭

Nancy was not so self-absorbed that she would miss changes in her husband's behavior and these were particularly obvious ones. Something or someone had him whistling, checking his appearance in mirrors and refusing dessert because of his weight. During conception binges, they had coupled perfunctorily nightly, but otherwise made love every week or so. The pattern had altered. For the past two months, Glenn had not shown any desire for sex. But it did not make sense! She knew her husband and he would not dare cheat on her! Glenn was insensitive and he tended to ignore her, but he was also dogmatic and would not break the 7th Commandment. That Kristen who had joined their church mooned over him, but Glenn treated her like any tolerant minister would. There was not a girl Nancy could think of who she felt could induce rigid Glenn to stray.

At the music department file cabinets, Nancy stopped sorting correspondence and qualified what motivated her husband to be faithful. He was more superstitious than pious. The idea of going to Hell scared him. In that respect Glenn had a lot of conviction in his faith, she thought cynically.

To add to her melancholy, the Advent Season approached and Nancy felt terribly depressed at the idea of celebrating Jesus' Birth when her own womb remained woefully empty. She slammed shut the drawer she was at and rested her head against it. Everything about her life was detestable.

∽

Kristen sighed and plunged into the difficult subject. "Pastor Glenn, this is embarrassing to talk about, but you're a man and one I consider to be my personal minister." She looked at him with uncertainty. "I hope you don't mind that. Being my sort of personal minister?"

"I'm honored," Glenn said with sincerity, "and I'm glad you feel so comfortable with our friendship." Kristen had gotten into the habit of accompanying him to his office after class, and he planned his schedule to allow time for her 'little chats' as she called them. Her adulation fed his ego in more ways than one.

Kristen sat back in the chair next to his desk. "Do you think here is...a discreet enough place for me to discuss...uh...something personal about my social life?"

Glenn scanned the glass partitions which divided the large room into separate office cubicles like his. Several were occupied, but none nearby. "I think it would be all right," he said. "What's upsetting you?" He refrained from patting her. As a pastor, he shared in congregants' joys and grief; he was accustomed to offering and accepting benign hugs. But even holding Kristen's hand would constitute a carnal act because in his heart he lusted for her. He should be bothered by his thoughts about Kristen, but they were harmless; it was not like he intended to act on them.

He glanced at a photograph of Nancy on his desk. She had turned out to be a big failure as a wife. His sperm count went off the boards so why should he have to compromise his expectations of marriage because of her infertility? His wife would have an influence on his best opportunities, too. Why should his career potential be hindered because mousy, timid Nancy was less than adequate? Now, Kristen would be an asset as a pastor's wife.

She had a sparkling presence and the right views which she expressed with effectiveness. Her lady-like appearance was pleasing and she achieved the maximum from her thin soprano. She was a virgin and he would be her only lover. There would be no unflattering comparisons to bigger men...

"...I am really in this quandary about how to, you know, make these boys understand that what they want should be saved for marriage." Kristen looked at Glenn expectantly.

Marriage. Boys wanted...sex. God. Some pimply boys were trying to screw his Kristen! Glenn had not been listening, but bluffed, "Are you telling me that these are fellows on this campus?"

"Oh, yes. I'd rather not name them because I don't want to get anyone in trouble, but...yes. I can't go out more than a few times before...I have this conversation!"

"Your high standards are commendable and how sad that there isn't more respect from today's young men, especially Christian men. This might not be easy, but perhaps you shouldn't date until you're positive that a boy is more...morally attuned to your ideals."

Kristen innocently batted her eyes at him. "I just wish I could meet a boy like you. I mean, a boy with your personality. I'll bet you were very respectful when you were going with your wife."

Not because of any moral convictions, Glenn thought. He had kept from screwing Nancy because he had not wanted to jeopardize Edgar Nicholson's patronage. "We waited until marriage," he said, adding casually, "but I don't condemn premarital sex if a couple is very serious about each other. Sometimes your love overwhelms you, and God understands our frailties. We ask forgiveness and He grants us His Grace."

Kristen gathered her wool coat and fuzzy tam. "At the rate I attract creeps, I don't suppose I'll ever know what that's like," she exclaimed dramatically.

Glenn laughed kindly. "You will find a special man, Kristen. You will. Pray about it and I will, too."

She gave him a keen look. "I already do. Constantly."

Glenn had the strongest hunch that their prayers were specific and the same. Kristen wanted him as much as he wanted her, but Nancy was an immovable obstacle.

⁓

Since Aaron's death, Brigit had saved a week's vacation and gone to her parents' in Paxton the week between Christmas and New Year's. It was the busiest season for the post office, so Theone could not take any time off, but Kristen and Erik had school breaks and usually joined her.

This year Brigit was on her own. Kristen had assignments to finish because semester finals occurred right after the holidays and Erik had his job. Theone would keep order and share her truck.

As she passed the sign indicating the miles left to Lake Femvivant, the words of the Singer rushed through her. *Love can redeem you. Love is the way to Peace.* The Deity may have chosen her as a vessel for a Messenger, Brigit thought, but the honor had not entitled her to an easy life emotionally and certainly more tragedy would come. Only The Deity knew what was in store for Theone, but Brigit imagined the worst. History was one cruel human act after another and the indoctrination of the Crucifixion served as a stark case. Mankind killed its prophets.

Brigit shrugged off the image. Theone had promised to be around as long as her mother needed her which in Brigit's mind extended to Erik's graduation from college. She had a long respite from the strife that surely would beset Theone when her ministry started in earnest.

With a pleasant farewell, Brigit turned from the couple she had known since childhood. She had spent enough time in her brother's vast wood-paneled recreation room and intended to go upstairs to see who was in the living room of the new English Tudor house. Her little brother, Patrick, the rebel, had finished law school, established a thriving practice in Paxton, gotten active in politics and as a reward, had been appointed recently to the federal district court in Madison. His younger, second wife did not foresee a problem with his plans to commute. They wanted their two children to continue their schooling in a wholesome environment which did not include the state capital.

Brigit reached the landing crowded with guests and smiled vaguely as she moved among them. What she should do is go outside on the patio for some fresh air. Nobody dared smoke inside, but the air was stagnant and she blamed it for her headache.

Sam Scougan got a glimpse of Brigit between people's waists, a common view for him due to his permanent position in a wheelchair. He and Patrick had been friends since kindergarten, but until last month, Sam had been living in Minneapolis. Near the scene of the accident, he thought. Near the hospital, near the therapist, near the trade school which had finally made him realize that he could have some hope for a future.

Ten years ago a drunken dive off a pier into three feet of water had broken his neck, paralyzing him from the chest down. In some ways, the stupid act had salvaged his life. He had been a bum, eking enough money from gigs to rent a furnished studio and to buy tequila for himself and whatever girl liked sleeping with the band's rhythm guitarist. Now, tequila wreaked havoc on his kidneys already prone to infection because of his sedentary situation. Sex was not a casual proposition for a paraplegic grateful to have recovered minimal use of his hands. (Thankfully, bed's main event was a reflex that had not been impaired by his disability, but it would take a special lady to get him to try it.) And what rock band could handle the restrictive travel arrangements required of a cripple who had to carry a rechargeable battery pack to power his wheels?

His immobility was not a major issue to operating a computer, though. A keyboard was quite accommodating to the slightest tap. And despite his weak muscles, he had retained strength in the index and middle fingers on his left hand. Being a southpaw and strumming a guitar had been training for something worthwhile.

Once the booze had burned off, he had discovered he possessed a logical brain with a genuine aptitude for programming. It was why he had been successful in building a consulting business; because of modems, he had the freedom to live wherever he wanted. Last month, the house he had built on property inherited from his parents had been ready finally for occupancy and he had settled back in his hometown vicinity.

Sam craned his neck to keep Brigit in sight. She was a few years older than he, but even in her forties, she was a babe. And a widow, Patrick had remarked. Sam recalled that Brigit's fiance had been a Vietnam casualty. Then, some fly-by-night had knocked her up at one of the gigs he and Patrick had put on at the lake. Like him, life had been tough on her, but maybe he could have a hand in changing that. Sam chuckled softly. Before his physical self-destruction, he'd been tall and good-looking. Well, nothing had happened to his face, but things weren't quite the same, Pal, not even in the slightest...still, he touched the power activator on his wheels and started excusing his way to the patio where she had gone. Brigit had been a tender, compassionate girl. In her sorrows over the years, had she lost those traits?

"Sam, I admire you," Brigit said, "and I would expect that your soul is very advanced because of your choices." She smiled sweetly at him.

"My soul? Okay, I guess getting my act straight relates to the soul." He wheeled closer to her. "You're cold. Why don't we go inside?"

Brigit's silver lamé tunic and black leggings offered little protection from the wintry air, but reminiscing with Sam had warmed her heart. The outside temperature was irrelevant. However, he had mentioned his susceptibility to viruses. He probably had to be careful not to get a chill.

"Would you like to go...for a drive?" She bit her lip. "I have a minivan, but do you have to ride in a special car?"

Sam grinned. Brigit was even more terrific than he remembered. "I got dropped off and if you're willing to help me, your van will be fine."

"Oh, certainly I'll help." As Brigit led the way back into the house, Theone's prediction occurred to her. Sam was an old acquaintance...he had suffered as much as she had...she would have to tell Sam everything, but it would be okay. He would understand and accept.

Later at sunrise, a tired, happy Brigit crawled into her childhood bed and considered something else. She and Sam had gone to his house and spent the night talking non-stop; they had already expressed a mutual wonder at their love. The issue of Theone had made him adamant that obligations with the children were part of the package. If she was who Brigit claimed, then Theone should be freed from family responsibilities to get on with her mission. He also hoped to meet this Child of Peace soon. His soul could use a jumpstart. Brigit had laughed with assurance and kissed him. Sam had no idea just how much of an impact an encounter with Theone could have on his soul.

CHAPTER SIX

"I find this whole thing with my mother to be such a...distress," Kristen complained to Glenn who sat across from her in the booth. "Why does she want to marry a man confined to a wheelchair? She'll just be his nurse."

Glenn signaled the waitress for more coffee. Since semester break, they were no longer teacher-student and had grown bolder in their friendship. Glenn was careful to advise Nancy when he met with Kristen, although his wife acted so remote these days that he was not sure she heard him. Nonetheless, he had explained that Kristen was having problems, and he was counseling her. He had also been prudent to advise his faculty superior who was a minister and supplemented his own income with counseling. A public place such as this off campus cafe served as a perfectly above-board setting to conduct what others would perceive as a relaxed client session. Kristen did not compensate Glenn, but he always made a show of keeping notes in a black binder.

"Your father is gone, you and your siblings are leaving the nest," Glenn said. "Brigit has a strong need to care for someone and this Sam, limited by his wheelchair, has a strong need for care. It's a classic co-dependency situation." He smiled at Kristen who looked petulant. "Does it feel like Sam is trying to take your father's place?"

"He wouldn't dare! I just met him that one weekend and he was nice, but I had no idea what was going on between them. He's an old friend of my uncle's and I assumed that he was in town visiting. Why is Mother acting so juvenile? She's...middle-aged!"

Glenn refrained from saying that Kristen's mother had a smidgen more than ten years on him. "Has it occurred to you that Brigit needs financial assistance and Sam offers a solution? You mentioned that he writes business software which could be quite profitable."

Kristen gazed at him. If Glenn was not married, he would date her. She could tell in his eyes that he...*liked* her, the age difference was as inconsequential to him as it was to her. Glenn was perfect, other than the wife issue. He did not discuss Nancy except in general, neutral terms, but the woman was the barrier. Marriage was sacred and Glenn's respect for his was one of the reasons Kristen loved him. She would never consider instigating a more personal relationship, but if he was ever free...totally implausible. She sighed.

"Money has never seemed an issue at our house, but I suppose paying for my education could be a factor. The scholarship doesn't cover everything. How awful to think my mother might have to marry for money! Couldn't she at least find a man who was...healthy?"

Privately, Glenn agreed, but it was not Christian to express such sentiment. "How do your brother and sister feel?"

"Erik plays a rhythm guitar and likes Sam because he did, too, professionally, before he had his accident. Mom's moving to Paxton because Sam has a custom house he built for his handicap needs, but that's great with Erik who wasn't sure about leaving home for college. Now he can commute to Mom's Alma Mater which is in town about ten or so miles south of Sam's. It's a good situation for him." Kristen sipped from her cup.

"And your sister's opinion of this marriage?" Glenn was curious about Theone who Kristen disliked with such intensity, but would never discuss in detail.

Kristen set her cup hard on the table and coffee splashed over the rim. "She thinks it's wonderful, but why would she care? Aaron wasn't her dad. Nobody knows who her dad was. My mom doesn't even know!" Horrified, she gaped at a mildly surprised Glenn. "I didn't mean to tell you that. It's just that I feel so relaxed with you and, and...please don't think less of me or less of my mother for what surely was just one transgression. God has to forgive her. I pray about it all the time, but my mother is so influenced by Theone."

Glenn clasped Kristen's hand which he had started doing and justified for the purpose of comfort. "Does your mother accept Jesus as her Savior?"

Her face anguished, Kristen enfolded his hand with her free one. She might as well confess the secrets she harbored and then maybe Glenn could give her some guidance on insuring her mother's salvation. "I don't know about Mom. Theone has some weird beliefs which Mom has no objection to, but whether she believes herself in this stuff..."

"Weird? Like cult?"

"Theone fools with rocks and meditates."

"Crystals," Glenn said with scorn. "New Age malarkey, Kristen, and it's unfortunate that your sister has been suckered by this phony philosophy."

"Theone has been this way forever. She got kicked out of church because of it."

"Really?" Glenn was very intrigued. He'd never heard of a Protestant church expelling a member. It must have been for dire reasons and confirmed his assessment that the Jones family was dysfunctional. Kristen was lucky to be normal.

Kristen changed the subject. "I wish I could ask you to attend the wedding with me so that there would be a Christian minister present. It's being held in July in Paxton at my uncle's big new house which has a gazebo in the backyard. He's the one who's been recently appointed a judge."

"I would like to be a part, but you know I can't." Glenn smoothly withdrew his hand from hers. They hovered on impropriety and as much as he desired Kristen, his future still meant more to him.

Kristen was frustrated to be stymied again, but this time she was also relieved. Glenn seemed to be just as fond of her, in spite of her disclosure about Theone, and it was important to her that Glenn liked her no matter what.

~

The regular school term ended and summer loomed. The college departments operated part time and Nancy would have even more empty hours to fill. As a last attempt to combat despair, she timidly proposed to Glenn that they take a vacation anywhere but to visit their families. Before he had finished his list of objections relating to cost, Nancy had tuned him out. She'd take her own getaway.

Theone's twenty-first birthday coincided with significant passages for her family. On June nineteenth, Erik graduated from high school. Due to a sudden, important project offer, the twenty-third was the only Saturday for weeks that Sam would have free, and Brigit rescheduled the wedding from a date at the beginning of July. They postponed a honeymoon.

Kristen would not learn about major news affecting her life until June 30th when she received Glenn's letter dated June 24th, eleven p.m. (The Ashburg post office had forwarded it with other mail.) Glenn had gone to the college computer center right after church that day to compile notes and access research sources on the school's database. At six thirty, he returned to the town house they rented and noticed water seeping from under the locked bathroom door. He could not get a response from Nancy and called 911. By the time the fire department removed the door, Nancy had been dead for several hours. Empty prescription bottles for sleeping pills from her gynecologist and their internist were in the sink, and she was submerged in the overflowing bathtub, the faucet left running. Glenn's last line to Kristen read, I HAVE SO MUCH ON MY LIST THAT IT IS DIFFICULT TO FOCUS, BUT AT THE TOP IS, 'WHEN WILL YOU BE BACK IN FOLEY?' He closed with LOVE.

Sam financed Kristen's expensive commuter flight connections so that she could get to Glenn immediately. The cab delivered Kristen directly to the town house and neither Glenn nor Kristen considered their behavior unseemly when Glenn kissed her passionately in greeting. Glenn's marriage proposal was quite natural, and they suffered no guilt when inside an hour they fell on to the bed to make love nor did they have any problem with the fact that the site of Nancy's suicide was only a few feet away.

Kristen discovered that sex was super, and Glenn's suppressed lust for her exploded, but after a couple of days, they reluctantly decided that she should return to Paxton for the summer. Foley was a small community and they did not want to create any gossip. He needed to show bereavement for a period, but the clergy was a tolerant, condoning type. Request forgiveness, accept Jesus, and the soul was redeemed - it was the guarantee of the Resurrection. Behavior had little to do with salvation. By the start of the school term, any remarks on campus would relate to the appropriateness of their dating because of their educational ranks, not Glenn's widower status.

During their separation, Glenn would expedite his thesis preparation. Kristen's education would continue only to the extent of time Glenn needed to finish his doctorate.

~

To Mike Zimmer's chagrin, Theone had given notice to the post office when Brigit gave hers to the library, and she had moved with her mother and brother to Sam's. Yet her stay like Kristen's was only temporary. (She placated Mike with this promise.) With her family obligations ended, Theone spent hours at Lake Femvivant, acknowledging the wildlife who paid homage to her as she wandered, waiting for a sign.

Sam's jagged, two-acre wooded lot was approximately a mile north of the state park perimeter at Lake Femvivant, and his house, built on the highest elevation, was U-shaped with a courtyard central to the design. Brigit set to gardening the barren enclosure and shortly, the surrounding glass reflected a riot of colorful flowers.

The doorways of the house were extra wide to accommodate a wheelchair and not even the shallowest stair had been constructed in the 2000 square foot residence. On one of the western tips of the U, Sam had placed his office, two long built-in counters split by an aisle. Sam had only to spin in either direction to reach any of the four computers, a dot matrix printer, a laser printer, a scanner, plastic cases of software and reference books arranged in assembly line fashion. The office had muted illumination, and equipment lights gleamed in various shades. Incongruous with the control-room appearance of the work area was a picture window which banked the furthest wall and offered a sweep of the sky above the treetops.

Soon after Sam and Brigit's small, family wedding, Theone sought out her new stepfather. Because Brigit had loved him instantly, Theone had presumed that Sam's soul would be in an advanced state; upon meeting him several months ago, her expectations had been confirmed. An issue between them needed clarification, though.

"This is a favorite time of day for me," Sam said when he noticed Theone in the entry. He brushed the SAVE sequence on the keyboard and steered his wheelchair to the picture window which had been set far enough away from his equipment so that it would not create a glare on his monitor screens. "You're drawn to the sunset, too, aren't you? Come watch what's left of it with me."

Theone joined Sam at the window, and they studied the display in silence. Against the orange remnant on the horizon, the trees patterned a crooked, forest-green silhouette, and chunky gray clouds hung over the setting like a canopy.

Sam glanced at his stepdaughter and his attention riveted. Her irises were transparent as she stared at the scene, and her face glowed with its own light. Brigit had been candid about Theone and who she was, but until now he had not really believed...

"Miracles get fast notice, but it's too easy," she said without looking at him. "The soul's advance is without much substance. For your soul to make real progress, you have to ponder and make deliberate choices. You have to live with the consequences of your actions and by so doing, forge a better path for your soul."

He sagged in his wheelchair and replied, "Your powers can't heal me." From Brigit's comments, Sam had gathered that Theone was capable of telepathy and would discern his obsessive desire to be whole again, but she could not perform miracles. The fact reinforced his doubt about Brigit's beliefs in her daughter's supernatural presence.

Theone turned and gripped his wrists dangling from the arm-rests of the wheelchair. "Restoring your ability to walk will not enhance your progress!" She exclaimed.

"I've dealt with very real demons and I feel pretty comfortable that my soul has ended up in okay shape. Its condition isn't that important to me, Theone. What is important is trying to keep up with my brain. I think so quick and with only two functioning fingers, I can't get out the information. I have to concentrate on the labor of input and my ideas fragment. It's so frustrating and time consuming to re-capture whatever I formulated..."

She held his wrists, knelt in front of him and grasped his hands. Her gaze locked with his, and Sam saw khaki brown eyes fringed with thick dark lashes. These clever, affectionate eyes were unlike anyone's he knew, yet strangely, they were familiar. Instinctively he comprehended that the person who possessed these eyes was special to Theone...and would be special to him. Very special, but whose eyes were they...

"Our Deity has followed your struggles and is pleased with your journey," Theone said. "You aren't conscious of your soul because you no longer need to be. What you are and what you will continue to be is intrinsic now."

"So my Hell is here."

"It is gone." She released him and stood up.

Sam smiled hesitantly.

"You will share your technical knowledge with one who will prove more gifted than you, but who is undisciplined," she said. "Teaching self-control will be part of your role."

"I've got a lot of experience with that!" Without thinking, Sam lifted his left wrist and squeezed Theone's right palm held open to him. He gaped at his hand and flexed his fingers, then he tried his right hand for strength. Full sensation had been restored as high as his elbows! He still would not be able to wheel his chair without power, but he could work all ten fingers at a computer. He could feed himself with a fork, and with practice, use a knife to cut meat. He could strum a guitar and make music again. He could caress Brigit...tears flowed down his cheeks. "My God, Theone, My God. You are the Daughter..."

"I am a messenger of love from Our Deity, and if my request is valid, powers are granted to me." She regarded him kindly. "I don't make many requests because I was not sent to dazzle with Our Deity's energy, but to instigate a re-focus on the soul's journey."

Sam bent his head forward and was able to wipe his eyes. He looked with wonder at his functioning hands, then rubbed his suddenly agile fingers on the stainless steel wheels of his chair. "You could heal all of me, but you won't," he said matter of fact. "You restored my hands to prove a point."

Theone stepped away from the window and smiled at her stepfather. "Physical therapy has been a great benefit to you, hasn't it? It's amazing how much you can accomplish when you try."

"Amazing," he echoed. Her eyes were hazel now and she appeared...like herself. Whoever that was, he thought. And what had just happened here? It was already vague. His hands! He had his hands. Theone was right about the therapy and how hard he had worked to rehabilitate himself.

Sam grinned at the dove gray hue left on the horizon. Every day he would seek a moment such as this one to praise The Deity for Brigit, for his talents, and for Theone, for enhancing his abilities to lead a productive life.

∽

It turned out to be auspicious that Glenn channeled his energies towards completion of his doctoral dissertation because exactly eight days after Nancy's funeral, Kristen had conceived during their marathon bed session. Brigit offered Kristen the same support her family had given her, but in the course of an extended, early September phone call, Glenn assured Brigit and Sam that in a distraught moment he had been weak. He had overwhelmed the innocent Kristen and prayed mightily for pardon, but the baby meant that it was God's Plan. Marrying Kristen would give him the greatest joy next to the praise he felt for the Lord. Brigit thought, another sanctimonious minister using God to justify his irresponsible behavior! Kristen clearly adored the older man, though, and Brigit swallowed her objections.

Following the start of the fall semester in late September, Glenn orchestrated an astute move. He brought Kristen to meet his former father-in-law and asked for his blessing. Edgar Nicholson appreciated Glenn's gesture. Nancy, God forgive her, had abandoned her husband and her faith rather than seek professional help for her apparent depression. Depression was assumed because she had left no note. Kristen Jones was an exemplary young woman and Edgar understood how a man, particularly a minister, needed a helpmate. Glenn was extremely fortunate to have found the right girl so soon after his loss. (When Edgar insisted on marrying them, he was unaware that Kristen was almost three months pregnant.)

Nancy's distressed mother defied Edgar and did not attend the nuptials, but the majority of Glenn's colleagues at Foley College showed up as did most of the members of Kristen's Ashburg church from which three served as her bridesmaids, and the entire Jones family celebrated with the couple, including Aaron's parents. Patrick Mane and other relatives came from Wisconsin. Glenn's brothers, along with Erik, stood up for him, and no emergencies set off his father's pager, but several others beeped among the numerous associates of the stellar Chandler family.

Standing by a cracked-open window, Theone observed the scene in the church's fellowship hall. A heavy duty, curtain-type partition could be pulled to divide the big tiled room, but Kristen's non-alcohol, finger-food buffet reception had attracted quite a crowd. The whole area was packed with well-wishers.

If it had been Kristen's decision, she would not have invited her older sister, but Brigit had insisted that Theone come to the wedding. Being inside a church stifled Theone, physically because stained glass filtered the natural light and mentally because the original significance of Jesus had been so adulterated. Why could not the honest souls who avowed faith in this Messenger see through the hyperbole that had resulted? It was difficult for her to keep silent!

"Gee, here you are," Erik said as he handed Theone a cup of punch. "Some of us finally got released, but Kristen is still with the photographer, trying to break the camera. But it might be Glenn dragging it out. He seems to enjoy having his pic taken a lot, too."

Theone smiled tolerantly at her brother, ill-at-ease in a black tuxedo. Brigit and Sam had met Glenn, but she and Erik had been introduced to him for the first time last night at the rehearsal dinner which had been hosted by the groom's family at a fancy Greek restaurant. The Chandler men had supercilious attitudes. Possibly it was because of their advanced educations or perhaps their upper class background, but Erik had labeled them snobs, including the soon to be brother-in-law. She had experienced a different sensation upon meeting Glenn.

Theone stood an inch taller than Glenn, but he had not been intimidated by her height. Rather, he had looked into her eyes and seen the melancholic ones of Nancy which he had failed to recognize as very ill. The sudden enormity of his negligence jolted him, and Theone had been inundated with his thoughts. *He could have saved Nancy, he could have listened to her, he could have paid heed, he could have gotten her help, yet he would still have been stuck with her...he wouldn't have been able to marry Kristen and Kristen was 100% better...Kristen who could lead a prayer or quote the right scripture or sing a sweet solo...Kristen who liked sex...Kristen who was very fertile...*Glenn also got an inkling of who Theone was and spoke harshly which broke the psychic connection. He had admonished her to seek repentance because whatever she was doing endangered her salvation. His expression revealed his temptation to make the sign of the Cross, as if to ward off evil.

She had not tried to touch Glenn's hands because she already knew this man's soul. What saddened Theone was that Kristen would be lost now to Truth. She would be swept up in Glenn's ministry and her soul, like her husband's, would stray from a progressive path.

CHAPTER SEVEN

Vaughn

Intellectual conceit resulted in Vaughn Ulrich's failure to achieve the accreditation requirements for a college degree and because of it, he could not pursue a seminary education. Yet a lack of formal theological training did not stop him from finding a niche in the multi-million dollar Christian services industry, and he accomplished it without resorting to a mail order diploma or an off-the-wall ordination.

It did not take a degree to market God, he always stated in his motivational seminars aimed at congregations wanting to increase attendance and stewardship. All it required was a sincere belief in the product, which, in this case, was the promise of salvation.

Vaughn had a short, beaked nose and a weak chin; he frowned constantly which cast his mouth in a downward curve, and under knit brows, he blinked repeatedly from his contact lenses. Frequently he posed with arms crossed over his chest, but his rather defensive, stern appearance did not detract from his success. A serious, cautious man generated trust.

At age forty-one, Vaughn finally gave up the profitable travel circuit for several interacting reasons. First, he received a lucrative job offer to run a church. A common enough occurrence - church leaders frequently enticed him. (Many fine ministers had no business sense, and one of Vaughn's key points in a seminar was that a smart church hired a manager.) This particular church, however, was in Sedona, Arizona, an area of gorgeous red rock and terra cotta earth one hundred fourteen miles north of Phoenix. Purportedly, Sedona had energy vortexes or power points, captivating to New Agers who believed that by visiting, their personal psychic energy would be heightened. The leaders at Calvary Inspiration Of Grace Church thoroughly supported their pastor who felt challenged to halt the encroachment. Vaughn took particular exception to New Age bunk himself. 'Cult crap' was his precise definition.

The reason with the most weight was Tawi Shinkawa, the attractive daughter of the only Japanese family in the congregation. In the early seventies, Dickie Shinkawa, Tawi's father, had sold his flower farm on Baseline Road in Phoenix to land developers and had reinvested in Sedona real estate. Now a millionaire Dickie leased his prime property like he was playing a game of Monopoly which he always won. The twenty acre church site had been a gift, though, as had a major portion of the building fund. Despite what the Bible said about Grace being the sole ticket, Dickie felt salvation had its price tag. If he gave generously of his largess to the institution, it would help pave the road to Heaven.

Tawi worked sometimes for her widowed father with whom she lived, but mostly, she volunteered at the church. She taught Sunday school; she served as a trustee on the governing board; she chaired the annual Christmas bazaar; she organized a monthly food distribution to the poor; she held title as Treasurer; her life was Calvary, and she had reached thirty-eight without involvement in a serious romance. Men had always shown an interest, but Tawi was very picky. He had to be a good Christian, preferably IOG; he must have financial independence; he could not be divorced or have children; he had to relate to her culturally. She was ripe for glib Vaughn Ulrich whose parents had been part of a mission team sent to Japan right after World War II. With mutual satisfaction, they negotiated and merged.

Under Vaughn's direction, Calvary IOG changed in size and focus. For starters, he cleaned house. The financial secretary objected to Vaughn's handling of short term investments because he did not secure trustee approval. She also had a problem with his sole signature on checks. Soon, subtle rumors circulated about the woman's ability and she felt forced to resign. The associate pastor for administrative affairs who had supported the financial secretary quickly realized that his position was tenuous and updated his PAF. Yet Vaughn was a master at keeping himself above reproach. He knew about church people and a group of sycophants always existed who liked to attach themselves to the power base. Vaughn counted on them to do his dirty work.

By the end of his first year, membership had dropped from eight hundred to five hundred as the truly spiritual core of the church sought worship elsewhere, but by the third year, the rolls had gained seven hundred under the dual dynamism of an effective clergy staff and Vaughn's shrewd management team. The largest church in the area, Calvary drew from a forty mile radius of Sedona and boasted a one point nine million dollar budget. The congregation worshiped in a newly enlarged sanctuary with a computerized sound system, and a mini-health club complete with swimming pool had been built on church grounds. Whatever it took to snare the bodies with bucks, was Vaughn's private motto. Then, the senior pastor, Dr. Guthrie, drowned in a freak accident while wading with his son in spring-swollen Oak Creek, and the congregation was left in a quandary. They had associate ministers for music, for youth, for the elderly, for education, for general pastoral care. Each had superior talent in their field of expertise, but not one had the rich voice, the marvelous delivery of Dr. Guthrie.

Vaughn advised the district bishop of his intent and restored his old customer database on to his computer to cull the records for names of IOG ministers who might qualify for Calvary's needs. He did not want an aggressive person who might try to usurp his authority. The right candidate would be charismatic in the pulpit and charming as an ambassador for faith at public functions, but beyond that, he could not have any ambition. It was a formidable chore to find such a man. Having associated with plenty, Vaughn rated most ministers as controllers; they enjoyed the power that they wielded over other lives.

CHANDLER, GLENN M. appeared on the monitor screen.

Vaughn had an excellent memory and the image emerged of a slight fellow from a seminar in San Francisco. Chandler had not been interested in instituting any of Vaughn's ideas. He had even admitted that he had gone along to the seminar just to keep the trustees happy. After the seminar, Vaughn had gone down the coast for a brief vacation and had been in Carmel on Sunday. He had attended Chandler's church and caught one of his sermons. Vaughn smiled. Chandler had a voice and a theme that uplifted a congregation. His outstanding oration made a person forget about his short stature. The man would be perfect as an inspirational figurehead while he, Vaughn, retained command.

Vaughn selected the function key to print out Chandler's record on his laserjet. Would he still be in California as an associate pastor? But where he was presently did not matter. Districts kept files updated and a central administrative office in Kansas City, IOG national headquarters, maintained a databank. He would find Glenn and strike a deal.

CHAPTER EIGHT

A week following Kristen's wedding, Theone returned from Lake Femvivant just after dusk. Sam was engrossed in his programming and Erik, driving the Jeep that his stepfather had given him for graduation, had gone to the movies with a cousin, Patrick's son from his first marriage. Theone found Brigit before her altar set with pink candles and potted white lady's-slipper orchids, flowers often found growing wild in woods. Brigit nurtured hers beyond their spring season in the greenhouse that Sam had built for her on the property.

"It's time," Theone said.

Tears misted Brigit's eyes, but she turned and smiled at her daughter. "You had your sign?"

Theone considered the cold, hazy day. A mesh of thin clouds had veiled the sun, but a full moon had been directly opposite; its gossamer image suspended in the pale eastern sky. Gray and white puffs had choked the glory of sunset, leaving the horizon dull, but tonight the moon would not be so overshadowed. As of today, the masculine power of The Deity no longer ruled her path. Rather, the feminine power, originally the premier power of Truth, would gain supremacy as it had for most of her existence.

"There's a man in Texas that I'm going to see," Theone explained.

"Can your truck make the trip?" Brigit's voice was calm.

"Yes, it needs minor repairs which can wait."

Brigit nodded. "You'll need money for travel. Sam will give you anything, Theone. His hands are such an incredible gift and he cannot ever express..."

"Maybe a credit card for emergencies and enough cash for basics?"

"Your usual modest request. Will you pick up Mike on your way?" The young man called every Saturday morning for Theone, and Brigit believed him destined to serve her daughter's ministry.

Theone smiled in acknowledgment. "Not yet, but I'll speak to him so that he doesn't worry. Mike will have his part soon enough."

"His part," Brigit repeated and stared at Theone. "And do I have...a further part?"

Theone opened her arms and like a child, Brigit nestled against her. She is the parent now, Brigit thought, Theone is the Mother. The Mother Incarnate of us all.

"You had a big part, Brigit," Theone whispered, "but you're entitled to a break; you are deserving of a time just for you and Sam."

"Erik will be okay?"

"Always."

"But not Kristen."

Theone felt Brigit's pain and wished that she could fib, but outright duplicity was never an option for her. "Kristen's soul veers off course."

"Is that the plan? To juxtapose sisters in a plain lesson of right and wrong?"

"She has free will! She can change!"

"But you know that she won't."

Theone released Brigit. "Her soul will not advance on this journey."

"And there will be a confrontation."

"Not between us. I'll be leaving in the morning."

Brigit looked at Theone whose eyes were a warm, healing blue. "My love goes with you," she said.

"Just as mine stays with you," Theone answered.

Near midnight, Theone stood in the frost-capped courtyard of the house amid Brigit's withered garden. Animal sounds, wild and domestic, soared in a symphonic tribute, and in the overcast sky, the moon glittered like a silver hole burned into thick gray batting.

༄

Jasper Stroud's whitewashed two-story, Spanish adobe abutted the flagstone *Paseo del Rio* which overlooked lush landscaping and the San Antonio River in the city. Careers in journalistic writing or religious reporting were not generally the kind that provided for such lavish quarters. In Jasper's case, he had inherited the property from his late mentor and companion, a professor at a local Christian university.

Xavier had been the last of a family that had lived on this property for generations before the Alamo had rallied American interest in Texas. Other than regularly upgrading his computer system and being forced by neighborhood crime to install a sophisticated security system, Jasper kept the antique furnishings and territorial decor.

The house had been featured numerous times in an assortment of publications from historical periodicals to architectural magazines. Jasper acknowledged the sin of pride and thereby permitted himself to enjoy the recognition accorded for owning a landmark. Adjacent property had been zoned commercial, but he resisted offers to sell.

His successful writing career was another source of pride, but one which he was vigilant to maintain at a high moral standard. Being a truth seeker in spiritual matters could easily lead to a judgmental role; as a homosexual with Native American ancestry he was especially sensitive. Jasper's upbringing in a Bible church in a small East Texas town and graduation from an affiliated college had instilled guilt which had taken him years to vanquish. The experience had also left him with a stutter that he had learned to control unless he was agitated.

Xavier had been one of his professors in graduate school and had helped Jasper to accept that he could be gay and Christian. Xavier encouraged him to approach their faith with a compassionate heart, to seek miracles and enlighten others. This influence inspired Jasper's articles. Articles which eventually Jasper compiled into a well-received book; as a result, he was offered a nationally syndicated religious column. He shied away from the lecture circuit, though. His stutter thwarted him and he was not keen on leaving Xavier for long periods.

Xavier left him, but not by choice. In his late thirties, Jasper lost his fifty-five year old beloved companion to an excruciating death from bone cancer. Prayers had not manifested a miracle and the failure affected Jasper's attitude. He did not lose his faith because Xavier had been so strong about his to the end, but he developed a skeptical edge. Jasper became a zealous, yet objective sleuth who reached for the bizarre and felt by so explaining such events that he provided Christians with a valuable, thought-provoking service.

Then he had stumbled on to the phenomena of Theone Jones and for the first time in two decades, Jasper questioned his beliefs. He gave up his column and ignored the leads from his sources. For almost three years he pondered and wrote about Theone, but never concluded the project or showed any of it to his anxious publisher. Finally, in November, 1991, the uncertainty, the sense of waiting, ended.

"I'm in by the vestibule," Jasper called to his housekeeper, Rosita. "I can get it." He seldom answered the bell because old fans, crackpots and curiosity seekers stopped continually.

In a shadow of the massive, carved door, Jasper peered at the locked, scrolled-iron gate by the street-side, prepared to advise the visitor that the owner was not in residence.

"I have a story for you to write," Theone said.

"It's written except for the finish," Jasper replied as he hurried across the entry towards the gate. It was *her* face, but Xavier's vibrant, chocolate eyes gazed affectionately at him! This was the final confirmation that Theone was truly who he had come to believe that she was...

"Already written? Oh, not quite," she said and gave the lanky man her charismatic smile. Theone had always been aware of Jasper Stroud, but had not paid attention. Now, she studied him. He had a high forehead, a soft chin marked by a deep horizontal scar and snowy wings at his temples; coarse black hair brushed the collar of his white short sleeve shirt. A neat mustache capped the lip of his small, pursed mouth, and wire rim glasses magnified his bright ebony eyes. This sensitive, intelligent man would be a conduit for Truth.

∽

November, 1991, was significant for Glenn Chandler, too. Vaughn Ulrich's search for him took several months because Glenn had not updated his PAF since returning to college.

The first phone call came on the 14th and several days later, Vaughn arrived in person. (Knowledge of Glenn's doctorate had Vaughn euphoric. The IOG profile was one of an educated, affluent conservative and degrees impressed them. Additionally, members were evangelical, anti-crime, big on community awareness, pro-life and pro-family. Chandler espoused it all and had a pregnant wife.)

During Christmas break, the Chandlers traveled to Arizona for a formal interview with the trustees. The visit confirmed for both parties that the match was excellent and the bishop concurred; the contract signed had an effective date of February 1, 1992. Glenn could finish his semester teaching obligation and submit the final draft for his thesis.

Kristen loved everything about being married to a minister and was delighted over Glenn's job offer. Sedona with its red rock grandeur was not a bit cold as she was accustomed to in winter. The congregation had gushed over her, the expected baby and her intent to sing in the choir. The other pastors' wives had welcomed her into their group like it was a special sorority, and under Tawi Ulrich's maternal care, the differences with her mother faded in importance. It was also a relief to be settling into a new location where no one knew their wedding date; she could wear maternity clothes without worrying about how big she was becoming and having people count the months.

CHAPTER NINE

Pilar

Officially, Pilar Gutiérrez Nuñez was Roman Catholic, but it was more from tradition than an espousal of faith. Hispanic culture and Church were closely woven in life's celebrations. Baptisms, confirmations, marriages, funerals - all were solemnized in ritual, then socialized with a party. If not a family member involved, then it was a friend who likely shared a common ancestor. Add birthdays, anniversaries, saints' days and holidays - an event was constantly being planned or attended.

Because of family, Pilar could not remember a time when she was alone. As a child there were sisters, one older, one younger to share the small room, the meager clothes, the few toys. There were brothers, too, to be waited on and catered to, in addition to their father and his younger bachelor brother. Barely past seventeen, Pilar was a bride and a mother herself.

Three more babies rapidly followed. By twenty-five, Pilar decided that four sons was plenty proof of a man's virility. On the sly, she saw an Anglo doctor to obtain birth control pills and counted on her guardian angel to express her regrets to God. She was not being flippant, just pragmatic. Besides, her commitment to church had lapsed since her mother's early death. Too many babies had contributed to the weary woman's demise, Pilar determined. It would not be her fate. She was positive that the angels had something important in store for her.

Pilar had been fascinated with angels since first understanding who the magnificent figure was in the stained glass depiction of the *Immaculata Concepcion* that filled the wall behind the altar in the sanctuary at their church. *Es Gabriél*, her mother had whispered in awe, Gabriél who had heralded to the Blessed Mary that She had been chosen to be the Mother of God. In catechism, Pilar learned that winged messengers watched over you and along with saints, could be prayed to for intervention with God who had more important things to do than listen to the pleas of mere mortals. Pilar took this very earnestly and believed that nothing really bad could happen to her if she kept on good terms with the angels. When she was several months pregnant with her fourth son, a vivid dream of a divine cherub with silver eyes further reinforced her conviction that celestial beings took special notice of her.

During adolescence, a relative had given Pilar a counted cross stitch pattern book filled with angel motifs. The preciseness of counting stitches appealed to her sense of order and from then on, Pilar always had an 'angel in progress' stretched taut in her embroidery hoop. Everyone who knew Pilar Gutiérrez could produce an angel kitchen magnet or a miniature picture of an angel or a Christmas ornament angel or a tee shirt with an angel decorated pocket.

Jorge Nuñez, her husband, was a distant cousin who had returned to San Antonio following a four year stint in the Air Force. Jorge was smitten with the intelligent, statuesque Pilar.

The Gutiérrezes encouraged Jorge because his kin owned a salsa factory; he was judged quite a catch to a family whose principal wage earner was a mason. But Pilar had an excellent grade average, and she held secret hopes to enroll at the local junior college for a business education.

Later, Pilar considered that she had been lucky to finish high school. Jorge had pressured her into sex and she got pregnant. A month after graduation, she was living in her husband's family compound four blocks from her paternal home in San Antonio.

Jorge supervised quality control at the salsa factory and the men often joked that seeking quality controlled Jorge in his personal life, too. He liked beautiful women and had a macho attitude about it with his wife. Pilar had a fine home, he said, and unlike many, she had no need to work because he provided very well. What he did was his business.

Pilar's entreaties to the angels were useless and she suffered much mental pain in the first years, but she had plenty of company among her female relations. Philandering men were rampant in her family and Jorge's. Jorge was just more flagrant than the rest. She did not abandon her trust in the angels, but she did amend it to a less naive sentiment. Bad things did occur; there was no way to avoid it. But she believed the angels always softened the blow; they helped her to cope. And deep in her heart, Pilar still felt that angels had something extraordinary planned for her life.

Finally her last son reached first grade, and she defied Jorge by signing up for a bookkeeping class. Pilar earned an 'A' and promptly took the advanced class. When she earned another 'A', she received unanticipated support from her brother-in-law, the factory president. He offered her a job assisting the Nuñez brother who was the factory comptroller.

Jorge ranted that his wife did not belong at the factory; he berated his brothers for interfering in his marriage arrangement, but Pilar's tenacity won. She threatened divorce, and Jorge acquiesced. In Jorge's world, divorce meant a man's failure to keep his wife in line; it was not permissible under any circumstance. Pilar had to continue with her household duties and provide care for their sons who emulated Jorge, but she had won a degree of independence; it was worth the steep price.

At age thirty, Pilar reflected that she had managed quite well to improve her lot. A conscientious, honest woman, balancing numbers had a great appeal and she found the perfect job in bookkeeping. She had her own personal funds and by standing up to Jorge, she gained respect from both sexes in their community. In spite of Jorge's dictates, she hired a cleaning service and paid relatives to watch the boys when she could not. Men at the factory flirted with her, but Pilar had no interest in another Jorge who would present a bottle of cheap perfume and demand a quick lay. The angels had not disappointed her, yet they had not brimmed her cup either.

Ten years passed. Jorge was not a handsome man, but he had charm and money. His attention to other women persisted. Not surprisingly, it had been ages since he charmed Pilar and been able to evoke her wonderful, infectious laugh.

But she made her own sufficient life. Early on, her boss recognized how capable she was, trained her accordingly, then transferred responsibility to her. Gradually, Pilar assumed a large portion of his work in addition to her own. He kept the credit and the big salary. Pilar was too happy to have her independence to object.

Because of Pilar, the Nuñez marriage had a cordial surface bound tenuously by their sons, although she hoped that in middle age her husband's infidelities would end. She prayed to the angels, hoping for Jorge to be enlightened so that they might attempt to build some semblance of a real relationship. But their marriage fared no worse than anyone else's in their acquaintance. Pilar spent hours in various activities with female kin and their grumbles about the men were the same as hers. She wondered if she was the only one who yearned for more, but never voiced her desires. It was not encouraged. The prevalent attitude was that if you were unhappy, it was of your own doing.

In November, 1991, Pilar's youngest son turned twenty-one. The evening of the birthday celebration at the Nuñez house, Jorge left early to visit his latest paramour, an eighteen year old illegal alien from Nuevo Laredo who had been hired in the packing department at the factory. During a second session of strenuous lovemaking at a shoddy motel, Jorge suffered a mild cardiac infarction. The young woman was so frightened of the authorities that she fled rather than risk telling anyone until she returned to her living quarters several hours later. Without the benefit of immediate health care, a naked Jorge, stinking of cheap perfume, died alone.

CHAPTER TEN

By Jasper's gate, Theone watched the busy sidewalk above the river. At an upstairs window, Jasper observed Theone, his love for her overwhelming his emotions. She had been with him four days and they had done little else other than talk intensively. Correct that. Theone had spoken while he had absorbed and accepted. The spiritual changes that had begun twenty years ago with her birth were about to converge in a spectacular way, and The Deity had elected to honor him with the privilege of transcribing *"The TRUTH of PEACE"*.

He pushed the start button on his tape recorder and listened again to her impelling voice.

Despite the simplicity of Truth, free will governs every soul and it's a potent force in directing the journey...I'm not the first messenger, just the latest one to remind humans of The Deity's Presence and The Deity's Hopes for their souls...

Some of you have been here before or places like this environment...yes, there are different environments. Humans have a tendency to be smug and believe themselves solo forms of life. The qualities you think of as 'human' are consistent, though. From the first, pure souls had choices... pride/humility, hate/compassion, greed/generosity and so forth...

Hell? There are incorrigible souls who spend intervals in dark environments, but no space has to be permanent. Souls exist at imp and demon level, but angels exist, too.

...Angels are souls on journeys in an environment close to this one and sometimes their presence overlaps. Let me explain. Certain souls get stuck. No matter what choices are offered to them, they make no progress. Our Deity recognizes that these souls require more visible signs than others. Angels have the privilege of revealing personal Glimpses of Peace to help these souls out of their spiritual sandtraps...

Jasper chuckled. Oh, how public knowledge of *her presence* would cause a stir! And it was a given. Her words would fail to have an unanimous influence; there would be those who would never believe, who could never recognize the distortions present in organized religion, but hordes of people would. Intrinsically, they would *feel* how right she was. Like a celestial traffic cop, Theone possessed the authentic directions for the soul to advance; she bore the correct map for those who elected to make spiritual gains in this journey.

He listened to more of the tape.

Sin? This means an offense against God, but Our Deity does not determine our soul's sentence! We do by our choices. And the worst ones the soul can make are those of hypocrisy and a judgment of others. For example, abortion is not right or wrong. It is a choice that an individual makes. How it affects her spiritual path is not another's concern. What is wrong is censure. Anyone who deliberately casts their will on another, endangers their own spiritual progress.

Jasper forwarded the tape.

...Sex is the celebration of fecundity. The act is meant to be pleasurable so that we will propagate; physical reproduction is an advance, but without responsibility, it is a limited one. A new soul must be given full opportunity to understand the choices for progress and a responsible nurturer provides it.

This is why the family unit is so important. We must be family units, and a family unit is any loving, nurturing environment...whatever combination of couple or blend of group is parenting the young.

He depressed the pause button. Despite his own self-confidence and Theone's vehement assurances, the shackles of his repressive childhood reared. Involuntarily, he steeled himself and listened again.

...Contrary to certain religious practices, celibacy has no impact on the soul's progress just as homosexuality does not. The soul who endures the physical pains of labor progresses because another soul is brought forth to travel again. From the standpoint of sexuality, the soul that makes the greatest single advancement is the woman's who loses her life to give a new chance to another soul.

Theone had been baffled by his distress. Why was he dwelling on something so unimportant? His sexual propensity may not be a gain for his soul, but it was not a loss, either, just as was the case for heterosexuals who chose to remain childless. It was simply one choice. Every soul made a myriad of choices, and the balance tipped in his favor; he had made exceptionally progressive ones. The Deity was not judgmental, and Jasper must separate human opinions from Truth. The soul's total journey was quite complex; the point was to strive for maximum attuning of which you were capable on this particular journey. He was doing so and in a magnificent way.

Jasper sighed. Theone would offend staunch conservatives and ardent liberals, but taken as a whole, her message was palatable to the common spiritual appetite because basically it adhered to the Ten Commandments and the direct teachings of Jesus. She readily acknowledged the Messengers who had been her predecessors. What rendered her unique and had convinced Jasper of her divinity was her magnetic presence.

The Deity had designed her as a perfect emissary for Truth. Modest Theone had no pride or any desire for recognition and she minimized her abilities. Yet, she comprehended that her essence would attract worship and seemed at ease with it. She was also nonchalant with what Jasper had deduced was a total dominion of life.

But no prophet ever had an easy time, he considered, especially a woman challenging the patriarchal structure of organized religion. Powerful religious bodies would lose in a big way when their supporters embraced Theone's Message. Financial empires fed by the dollars of the faithful would dwindle. He foresaw that initially, this unpretentious young woman with her straight directive would be deemed harmless, but the impact of who she embodied would ultimately threaten the structure of every major religion, and she would encounter mighty adversaries.

...You wonder why certain individuals seem to have so much. Beauty, wealth, fame, talent...life's scale appears inequitably out of balance. This is not Our Deity bestowing bounty, but is related to the soul's prior choices. Often a soul with an outward manifestation of success has retarded growth because the more trappings accumulated and hoarded in this life, the less a soul progresses. Yet I am not suggesting vows of poverty or recommending a mass embracing of strictly spiritual matters. Part of a successful journey is achieving harmony with your environment and with other souls. Some exchange, some accumulation of resources is necessary. Destitution makes too many demands of the body, leaving nothing for the soul. Poverty can stunt a soul's journey because human opportunities are limited. Sharing resources, then, can help to free another soul's roadblock. It also advances your own soul because love has been extended...

...Prayers offered for a sick body and a seemingly miraculous recovery is a Glimpse of Peace. Such a happening can serve to advance all the souls touched by it...Yes, I meant seemingly. Our Deity always listens, but does not intercede in this manner. Rather, humans can generate healing energy through concentrated focus...advanced medicine plays a part...and some bodies are just capable of recovery...

...Prayer is not irrelevant unless you pray for foolish things. Invoking God's Name to win a sporting event is frivolous! Thanking God for winning the lottery is petty! You are at a lengthy stop light if this is a sign of your faith! But prayer for direction, for enlightenment, for the understanding to cope during stress is answered.

...Good intentions and best possible efforts accelerate the soul's travel. Sincerity does, too. Honesty prompts a faster rate because truth, good or bad, pleases Our Deity...

Jasper had to incorporate Theone's information into his manuscript and get it to his publisher. And prepare her. In spite of her evident divine parentage, she appeared so innocent of life's reality. He had not delved beyond the surface of her poised remarks and kind admonishments about the nature of souls. Would she be braced spontaneously by The Deity to handle the harsh, picky questions about the universe? The explicit whys for inequitable behavior? The reasons for rotten things? He had not finished his queries of her and intended to be very thorough because she would be interrogated. As tests, as proof to those who scoffed at the possibility that God would send a woman. At the notion that God was half female; in Truth, the better half. Jasper punched the start button on the tape recorder.

...*Whereas Our Deity is God, Our Deity is also Goddess. The Goddess has superior essence because She embodies those souls most advanced towards Peace. Furthermore, she rules first as Giver of Life, but She is naught without Him.*

Let me clarify. Our Deity is of Dual Nature and like Self, created Life with the sexual division of organisms, male as fertilizer and female as bearer. As Life evolved, certain gender traits developed in the organisms. In humans, the male entity acquired greater physical strength and an aggressive nature. It was an issue of survival in a primeval environment just as the female entity who bore the next generation acquired a nurturing quality and a finer psyche. Our Deity further imbued humans with complex souls. They were not balanced equally, the male being the cruder, the more corporeal, but they were given the same measure of free will. The combination in the male has effected the genius of Mozart and the brilliance of da Vinci. But five thousand years of warfare is also a result as is the preponderance of male-superior religions.

In general, souls of females are much further advanced on their journeys than souls of males. Men's severe treatment of women throughout history has widened this spiritual chasm. In this environment, of course, there are males whose souls progress and females with souls that regress.

Regardless of our sex, we all have equal access to Our Deity. How we choose to respond is our solitary responsibility...

Mix the preeminent female essence concept with Theone's fomenting dialogue on Christianity, which so far took up an hour tape by itself, and guaranteed, she would be marked as a wacky cult figure by main religious groups until enough individuals had experienced her to comprehend her genuineness. Christians, particularly (until three years ago himself included), were so complacent, Jasper thought. They would not recognize a Second Coming if the heavens split and the image of a fatherly God in white robes personally announced that Theone was The One. Some self-righteous cynic would proclaim that a magician had fostered a mass illusion.

Jasper gazed at Theone who stood like a sentinel at the gate. She watched for someone, he realized. A specific someone. He felt a pang of jealousy, then let his soul rejoice. Theone could not be possessed or contained. She belonged to the world, and just by being a part of her future, his own spiritual journey would be strengthened.

Behind the pallbearers, Pilar walked flanked by her sons, one ashamed at his father's gross manner of death and three proud of the way the old man had died. Even the priest at the venerable Spanish mission on the river, the family parish for generations, had smiled more than once as he recalled Jorge's life during the eulogy. Jorge's funeral had attracted a huge group of mourners who clogged the *Paseo del Rio* for half a mile of its almost three miles that wound through downtown San Antonio.

Jorge's fatal indiscretion humiliated Pilar and she resented the men's admiring whispers about her late husband, but she felt no remorse at being rid of her marriage. And there would not be another, Pilar had already determined. She had been mindful of the sly glances and appraising looks, including from several of her brothers-in-law! But surely now the angels would direct her to the purposeful life that she was meant to have.

From his window, Jasper spied the funeral procession on the bend several yards from the house, but apparently Theone had been anticipating it. She was already out of the gate when Jasper checked her position. Fascinated, he watched her cross the flagstone path in front of the coffin and through a gap, saw her smile at...the widow who...shrugged off the support of her male kin and angled away from the mourners. Theone swept her gaze over the inquisitive crowd who had slowed at Pilar's action.

Jasper chuckled as he had done often these past few days. The crowd collectively blinked and moved forward to catch up with the casket. Not only did Theone possess the ability to read the soul and in her eyes, evoke the memory of a significant individual in a person's life, but she elicited strong empathy in others. In his interviews with the people she had touched, consistently he had recorded vague recollections of fact, yet extraordinary, durable transformations of spirit. This was the first time he had actually witnessed her power over humans, but he had observed her with animals when she'd been a mail carrier. Now, he was able to study her authority at close range.

His gardened terrace by the river walk had turned into a zoo with dogs appearing regularly outside the iron grill fence. From skittery hummingbirds to inquisitive lizards, creatures could not resist her, but they also manifested utter respect for her and after receiving her notice, would promptly be on their way. Traditional enemies such as cats and birds temporarily suspended their rivalry because, it seemed, paying tribute to their Mistress took precedence. His own two snooty Abyssians maintained a courteous distance, but would not let her out of their sight. He would not test a wild theory that his cats would attack him if he threatened their Goddess.

That first day, Rosita, his housekeeper, had peered at Theone and startled at whatever she saw, had crossed herself before disappearing. Then, for several hours she had appeared intermittently in the study where he had taken Theone. Rosita had excuses. She brought refreshments, mail, the newspaper. The moment Theone smiled at her, though, Rosita would vanish again. Finally, Rosita had timidly approached Theone and prostrated herself on the chilly ceramic tile floor. "Blessed Angel," she had whispered in Spanish, "my life is yours."

Rosita had kept mum about Theone because her multitude of relatives were not swarming the adobe. Theone's empathetic elicitation. She was not ready for the masses.

Yet here was a convert that Theone had deemed necessary, Jasper considered, as she led the widow to the gate. The woman displayed the same expression of wonder and surrender as Rosita. Upon entering, she started to kneel, but Theone gripped her hands, urging her to stand up.

Jasper was torn. Did he offer hospitality? His home was Theone's now and anyone else's she chose to bring here. Or would Theone tell him when she wished for him to be involved?

Theone suddenly looked at him and he understood to wait.

"You are the Cherub," Pilar kept exclaiming as she struggled to rise. The hem of her black silk dress fell below her calves and made her awkward. "You are the Cherub in the dream. The angels have answered my prayers!"

"Our Deity has always heard your prayers, Pilar, and has always noted your soul's progress despite the many temptations you have had to deviate from what was right and what was good. Life's tests can strengthen us or crumple us. Your soul reflects your success."

Pilar got her balance and stared at the young woman whose silver eyes and lashes gleamed like newly minted quarters. Like a Goddess would. She was no mere angel...

Theone loosened her hold.

"Do you need someone to take care of your money?" Pilar inquired. "I wish to be useful to you."

"It's why you are here, but money will not be complicated. We won't keep more than we need."

Pilar looked at her surroundings. She had been by this landmark house countless times and on occasion had lingered to glimpse inside the fence. Had the Cherub been living here all these years?

"Jasper Stroud owns this property," Theone said, "and will shortly make your acquaintance. Then you must return to your family..."

"I have nothing to return to!" Pilar beseeched Theone. "My whole life I have been waiting for you!"

Theone smiled at the attractive woman. "You must say 'goodbye' and settle things."

"There is nothing," Pilar replied, "nothing that can take me away from you."

"No, nothing in your soul ever will, but I'm staying here for some months. Come inside and we'll talk."

⸺

Glenn Chandler Junior's first birthday fell on the fourth Sunday in April and coincided with the induction ceremony for the two-thousandth new member of the church. Sedona's weather was balmy and the church grounds, under the care of Dickie Shinkawa, bloomed in resplendence. At Tawi Ulrich's direction (Glenn Junior's godmother), the women's organization had planned a party for after worship services. Members of Calvary IOG Church were thrilled with their new senior pastor whose eloquence surpassed his predecessor's, and they followed the lead of Tawi; everyone adored the pastor's pretty wife who had so happily immersed herself in church activities.

In turn, the Chandlers were ecstatic with the call. Fawned over and the center of attention, Glenn had the position of his dreams. He preached weekly, taught occasionally and had been asked recently by the Northern Arizona District's Bishop in Phoenix to chair the Evangelism Committee. He did not have to deal with people's problems or administrative issues. Vaughn ran the church which he did excellently. Glenn's salary was so generous that he did not have to scramble for other work to supplement his income. Kristen was free to spend as she pleased. Vaughn had arranged as a gift a down payment on a virtual mansion; fine furnishings and other items had been offered free or for purchase at a marked discount. Both Chandlers now drove new Nissans, courtesy of the dealer, a member of Calvary. Part of Glenn's job was to play golf on Tuesdays and Thursdays with Vaughn, influential church members, other denomination heads and local bigwigs. Vaughn remarked that their participation was ecumenical.

As Glenn had anticipated, Kristen proved herself to be the perfect wife, and he was very proud of his rambunctious son, G.J. There would be more children, too. His and Kristen's original passion had deepened; lovemaking was an important part of their relationship.

Vaughn and Tawi Ulrich lived just up the road from the Chandlers, and despite the wide age spread, they shared similar minds about everything. The four considered themselves best friends.

In all respects, Glenn and Kristen each felt that they had arrived at their rightful destiny, but did not shortchange the One Who had made it possible. As often as they could, they took a moment to sit on their balcony, which afforded a breathtaking view of a red rock canyon, and evoking the name of the Savior, thanked the Heavenly Father for their rewards.

∽

Six months after Theone's arrival in San Antonio, editor Ian Leahy, a diehard Manhattanite, swallowed with difficulty and gingerly placed Jasper's manuscript on the floor by his water bed. Was Theone Jones for real? Real or not, the controversy over her would be enormous. He could receive acclaim for publicizing the story of the century or more likely, he would be branded a heretic and be the recipient of some zealot's fire bomb.

Ian took off his reading glasses and rubbed his eyes. Jasper had always been levelheaded and cautious about his information to insure its accuracy. Could someone as seasoned as Stroud be taken in? It could not be an issue of sexual attraction to the young woman because Stroud was gay. Jasper could not be seeking endorsement of his lifestyle because Theone neither condemned nor condoned it. Yet Jasper's admiration for her bordered on infatuation...no, reverence.

The only traits Theone damned were pride and dishonesty. Was God as impartial to human foibles as she claimed? Was the individual his own true master for salvation...for attaining Peace? Her comments about the world's beauty, Glimpses of Peace, affirmed the notion that a heavenly abode existed; this would appeal to people. Given the symmetry of nature, it made sense that The Deity was of a dual essence and a godly testimonial would thrill feminists. Theone had a lot of sensible answers for important things that interested people. But the lengthy criticism of Christianity...

Ian decided that he had to meet this Theone Jones before he took such a big risk. Jasper had not even sent a photograph of the woman. He'd call at a decent hour in the morning and as soon as possible, have Jasper bring her to New York.

"She doesn't fly? Why not?" Ian's tone was incredulous, and he resisted making a crack to Jasper about angels and wings.

"Theone has to breathe natural air and she has to be in touch with the Earth. It's limiting, I know, but she is not...ordinary." Jasper would not be getting her on a train or a ship, either. The extent of motorized travel would have to be by private vehicle so that she could stop often and in her words, *embrace the intangible of Our Deity.*

Ian groaned. For the book to sell big, Theone would have to make personal appearances to verify to readers that she was for real. It usually involved lightning trips to as many cities in as many days. Now, he would have to find time in his busy schedule to leave town and make a trip to San Antonio just to see if it was at all worthwhile for him to bother recommending for publication *"The TRUTH of PEACE"*.

⁓

Brown-speckled blue eyes full of empathy - Aunt Kathleen, Ian thought with astonishment as he gazed at Theone. The saintly woman who had taken in her wayward sister's abandoned boy and raised him with her own two. Aunt Kathleen who had worked full time at a florist shop and managed to care for an invalid husband, too. She had believed in him and encouraged him to apply for the scholarship which had been his ticket of escape from humdrum Elm Falls, Iowa. Seventy plus Aunt Kathleen, the selfless volunteer, who one day a week still read to patients at a nursing home and on another, cared for children at an abused women's shelter. Without knowing it, Aunt Kathleen was a disciple of Theone's...

On Jasper's terrace, Ian dropped his brief case and held out his hands to Theone who stood with her back to the landscaped slope that met the river. Above her, feathery clouds of coral pink and purple sheltered a rosy horizon where a hidden sun set.

She glows, Ian realized, she is pure. Theone is truly of God...of The Deity. Why had he doubted?

"You are making a significant choice, Ian," Theone said as she clasped his hands. "It is one that you will have to defend and one that will cause you hurt. Be assured that it counts highly in your soul's favor, and Our Deity is listening to your meditations on this matter."

Ian's knees sagged, but Theone effortlessly held him upright.

"Look at me," she whispered.

He peered into her eyes which had changed from Aunt Kathleen's. For a second, they were clear like windows and he saw through them a place of splendor oddly familiar; then, her irises blended to hazel.

"That was Peace," she explained. "There are Glimpses of It everywhere in this environment."

"Yes," Ian said, "yes, yes." Jamaica Bay at sunset with Jenny, he remembered. South of bustling, jammed New York City and abutting the harsh atmosphere of JFK Airport, a thriving wildlife refuge existed. Jenny Yates, an ecological writer under their imprint had insisted that he see the marvel of the water birds who settled at Jamaica Bay for summer breeding. Grassy knolls rose from the water, and numerous fowl had been etched against a horizon blazed vermilion from the sinking sun. At the time, Ian had felt what he could only ascribe as a metaphysical uplifting. Later, he had been embarrassed at his lapse of sentimentality and therefore had not pursued a relationship with the woman who had been interested in him. He wondered if he could salvage Jenny's feelings...

Theone released Ian and stepped away.

"Welcome to spiritual renewal," Jasper declared and hugged a dazed Ian.

"She is definitely a transcendent experience," Ian finally replied and shook his head to clear it. Settle business here, he decided, and not only would he contact Jenny, but he was going to see his aunt to tell her about Theone. "Let's talk promotional strategy for the book," he said. "Tomorrow when I return, I'm authorizing priority publication."

Theone had turned to view the remnants of the sunset. "Pilar can contact Mag Ingram and Mike Zimmer now," she said. "It's time for them to settle things and join us, Jasper."

Pilar's expression showed relief and she noticed Jasper's as similar. Theone wished to keep them close, and to both, it was all they desired for their lives.

~

No pictures would be possible, Theone had said curiously to Ian, and it had to be printed in paperback so that it was most affordable, she had instructed about her book. And Jasper had been no support, Ian thought, disgruntled. Jasper was the author of record, yet reduced royalties had not swayed him to contest Theone's stance. As far as he was concerned, *"The TRUTH of PEACE"* could be printed on cheap newspaper and bound with staples. People would read the story.

Exactly. The book was going to be a bestseller and people would pay for a bound copy. Jasper did not have to deal with a board of directors who would gripe at the loss of revenue from skipping hard cover sales. Or so Ian figured.

The senior publisher at his company was impressed with the story and admitted in private to Ian that he was a little in awe of Theone Jones. And what did she look like, anyway? Wasn't she photogenic? How about flattering sketches of her? Could Ian arrange for him and his family to meet this Theone?

Ian berated himself for his skepticism. He should have recognized Theone's influence on the whole process.

She did not visit people, however. To see Theone and hear The Message personally, you had to go to her, an issue in itself, because of the few, obscure locations. She had presented Ian with a schedule before he left San Antonio, and he had faxed the dates to his superior.

Now, in a month, which would be early October, Theone would make her first public appearance on the Allagash Wilderness Waterway in

Northern Maine. Theone had indicated that she would hike to the area, but paddling in by canoe would probably be the easier means. Easier? Ian chuckled. Currently, she and her four chosen companions were already on their way to the region from San Antonio.

The appearance in Maine coincided with the blitz publication of *"The TRUTH of PEACE"*. The media would receive their official copies ten days prior, but Ian had not been surprised to hear that the senior publisher at his company and anyone who could get the time off had arranged to be at that remote spot in Maine along with every major communications source. Despite the rustic travel, they could all detect a sensational event and did not want to miss it. But Ian bet few of them had an inkling of how Theone might affect them personally. *That* would be the real sensation. The one that would transform their souls.

When Mag Ingram received Pilar's phone call to summon her to San Antonio, escrow had just closed on a cash contract at full asking price for the delicatessen. Thanking the Deity for the opportune moment, she packed her personal possessions and with Theone's approval, accepted title to her aunt's Airstream travel trailer. (Years before, Mag's metamorphosis from her contact with Theone had converted Eloise to The Message. A Goddess had come? Eloise had exclaimed. *The* Goddess! At last the world would right its balance! Whatever she could do to help spread the word...)

Eloise had purchased new in 1979 a 31' Airstream, but degenerative arthritis had discouraged her in recent years from driving long distances. The streamlined silver trailer had a rear bath, air conditioning, double awnings and comfortably slept four. Cupboard space was limited in the upper part of the trailer due to the curve-shape, so Mag intended to buy a roomy vehicle to haul the trailer. Pilar, though, already owned a late model royal blue Suburban. On their way to the first stop in Maine to promote *"The TRUTH of PEACE"*, they would pick up the trailer in Dana.

An ecstatic Eloise gazed at Theone and saw the same kind-hearted eyes of her first lover who had died of kidney disease at a youthful age. She agreed with Mag that Theone was exactly whom Mag had claimed her to be.

Jasper had been doubtful of the tight arrangements in the trailer - there were five of them, not four - yet traveling in proximity, they discovered that their personalities and talents meshed quite compatibly. Precise, energetic Mike was chief driver and in charge of supplies. With Jasper, he dealt with site arrangements. Quiet, sweet-natured Mag tended their domestic needs and served as main cook. Responsible, sharp Pilar handled financial transactions and kept a ledger on her laptop computer. Amiable, protective Jasper had a laptop, too, in which he logged their activities.

He had been argumentative when Theone indicated that they would stay at park campgrounds. She would be besieged by the world and there would not be adequate security! Theone had smiled. The public appearances would not preclude her contact with individuals. She could not stop touching souls and sharing The Message. The Deity would safeguard their presence.

An empathetic elicitation again, Jasper had concluded; wherever they stopped, no matter who she blessed with her attention, the Suburban-Airstream and its occupants maintained anonymity. The inability for anyone to track her added to her mystery.

And the trailer was not as cramped as Jasper had worried. At first they were disconcerted when Theone set off with a goose down sleeping bag and an A-frame pup tent to camp at some unknown spot. The open windows during the day, though, convinced them that she was better off outside if they were going to be warm at night.

A part of every day, Theone spoke to her companions about the Deity and Peace, girding them for the questions that others would pose. When the weather allowed display of the sunset, they paused to meditate. They tuned to the phases of the moon and pondered on its symbol for their souls.

They marveled at Theone's phenomenal singing, but she gently insisted that music was merely a Glimpse of Peace to be shared, and many hours they sang together. Also, Jasper and Pilar would read aloud, everything from newspapers to poetry.

The love they had for Theone overflowed to each other and the strangers soon bonded into fast friends.

⌒

Behind Theone, the midafternoon sun cast a metallic glaze on the deciduous trees scattered among the pines on the hills. Purple cloaked the ashes, and orangy-red veiled the maples; lime-green aspens and golden birches shone brilliantly against the mass of dark evergreens. A fellow from St. Francis, a small village on the Canadian border, had brought in a news team from Bangor. He remarked that the cool weather had come on slow this year and a lot of sunny days had been a boon to the dying leaves, allowing them to develop their full color range.

Midst crimson-leafed blueberry bushes, Theone stood on the shore of the river tinged pewter from the sun. Noisy whiskey jacks postured around her like wardens.

Ian had been amazed at the number of whiskey jacks that had escorted Theone, his fiancee, Jenny, and Mike Zimmer on their hike. Jenny, an instant convert to Theone's Message, had commented that the friendly gray Canadian jays seemed particularly attentive to Theone; she kept exclaiming, too, at the numerous rabbits, squirrels and deer that were about so openly. And porcupines were nocturnal creatures! Theone had said nothing, but she was also aware of the coyote family, an elusive fisher cat and several devoted moose tracking their journey.

Jasper, who along with Mag and Pilar had been brought in by canoe from Dickey, approached Theone. She calmly surveyed the people before her flashing cameras, but interestingly, they were not barking questions at her or trying to get too close to her, either. Well, Jasper thought, the whiskey jacks might be intimidating. Or it could be that these people were trying to figure out Theone's hair. Rather, trying to understand the source of luminosity giving it the halo effect.

"They are wasting their film. Didn't Ian advise them?" Theone said.

Jasper shrugged. "This is The Press. They don't listen and even if they did, they'd have to try. The whole world is going to want to know what you look like! What about the camcorders?"

"My image can be broadcast live, but it won't leave an impression on video nor will my voice record."

"Can't you lift...the ban? It's important for you to be credible and part of that is being visible."

Theone sighed tolerantly. "The Message is important, not me. Jasper, you understand this. And there will be no applause. I'm not here to entertain, but to enlighten."

Mike joined them. "Are you speaking from this spot? No one will be able to hear you over the jays."

Theone glanced at Mag and Pilar who were with Jenny on the edge of the activity. They looked anxious, and she smiled at them. Their faces relaxed. Then she pivoted her head to view the whiskey jacks. The birds ceased their trilling. Jasper and Mike stepped aside, and the crowd automatically hushed.

"Your soul is on a journey," Theone stated in her irresistible voice, "and I have come to remind you how to get it on the right road because Our Deity wants you to succeed. Our Deity wants you to reach Peace which is at the end of your ultimate journey, and to inspire you to seek it, Earth has been endowed with Glimpses of Peace." She swept her arms to the blazing hills. "Success hinges on your actions as an individual, not on your piety to a creed. Whether you focus on the Moon or the Cross or read the Talmud or the Koran, adherence to existing religions will have little impact on your progress if you ignore the Universal Rules of Our Deity. Wealth hinders your journey unless it is shared generously with those who have less. Integrity with others insures progress. Judgment impedes it. Selfless love guarantees advancement because Our Deity prizes it highly."

Theone held out her left hand where the emerald ring glittered like a torch, and a whiskey jack flew to the finger. As if bowing to her, the bird lowered its head.

She smiled. "Free will is your gift and dilemma, so you must be vigilant in your choices, and understand that no intermediary is needed to interpret for you; you alone are responsible for your soul. Listen to The Message and open your spirit to it!"

Theone lifted her hand and the whiskey jack soared off. "Oh, the rules are simple," she uttered, "but not easy. So keep close the vision of this Glimpse of Peace, knowing that it is only a small part of the Supreme Peace that all souls can anticipate."

Jasper had been observing the crowd and making notes while Mike had been taping close ups of their faces with his VCR. Both repressed smiles. They had recorded the same perceptions. Hopeful expressions were now exultant. Curious expressions were now hopeful. Cynical expressions were now either angry or afraid. Every one had been affected. Thirty seconds of silence ensued until several perched whiskey jacks bickered and took off in flight.

A bristling reporter from a widely broadcast Christian station shouted at Theone. "What are you claiming here? That Christ's Salvation is a lie?"

Theone's answer was gently delivered. "Sincere repentance counts immensely, but Grace alone does not finish your journey."

"Merciful Father in Heaven protect us from this daughter of the Devil!" The reporter cried.

"Cork it, Schreiber," a voice exclaimed. "There's plenty who believe differently, like 50% of the world's population. You don't have an exclusive on salvation!"

Christians in the crowd murmured, but did not rebut.

A woman executive from a large bookstore chain asked, "You refer to The Deity to promote gender equality, but in Truth, don't you purport that in the dual nature, a Goddess has greater power than God?"

"The essence of Our Deity is a balance of feminine and masculine. Yet in the past two thousand years, human males have fallaciously overpowered, encouraging the masculine essence to dominate reason and spirituality. Now, the feminine essence is asserting authority because man's choices have been...less than successful."

Women in the crowd laughed.

"...But who is greater is unimportant," Theone clarified. "The achievement of your journey is not in having every answer to the universe, but in gaining ground for your particular soul. You have been reminded of how to do so." She stepped backwards until shadows from the pines obscured her presence.

Numerous questions had been left unanswered among those assembled, but Theone was finished, and a general acceptance prevailed. Conversation rose and without dissent in their midst, both those with negative or positive feelings began packing gear for the watery return to civilization.

Mike grinned at Jasper. "Do you see that? No hecklers, no fist fights, no complaints about the arduous trip here for ten minutes, no wrathful stampede...she is one incredible, divine soul, huh?"

Jasper stared at the vague form of Theone outside the sunlight, then back at the individuals readying to leave. "Yes, but as these people reflect on this experience, their devotion or their scorn will solidify. Discord will result. May Our Deity protect her."

Since winter approached, Theone had plotted a southern itinerary first. After the riverside address in Maine, the group traveled to the coast and downward, their destination being the Outer Banks off North Carolina, a chain of barrier islands that extended seventy-five miles eastward to the Virginia border.

Theone chose to speak at the northern end of Hatteras Island by Pamlico Sound where a stiff, cold wind whipped about the golden sea oats growing on the dunes. She walked barefoot just above the water mark on the ocean side of the island. Willets and turnstones, shore birds, had abandoned their investigation of the shell fragments in the beach's fine sand and paced with her. Seagulls swooped around her.

Widespread interest had grown, and Theone's formal appearance garnered national attention. This time, though, the news media had sent sketch artists, not photographers, to capture her image, and TV networks had satellite uplinks to insure live transmission. Along with spectators, the communication teams had located northeast of Theone, well away from the invading tide. The crashing of a mighty surf muffled their activity.

Apart from the escalating crowd, Mag and Pilar, dressed in parkas and lined boots, discussed their concern for Theone's health. Mike joined the two women, chuckling at the frustrated artists trying to draw Theone with accuracy.

"Mike, take her this blanket that I brought," Mag said.

He looked at Theone in her calf-length jean skirt and a dazzling silver windbreaker accented with bright gold that he was positive no human had stitched. She did not appear fazed by the harsh wind, but he did not expect her to be. She was never hot or cold. Theone belonged as one with nature, and he had understood this for years. They would have to learn this about her. Mike shook his head. "Accept that she has an internal thermostat. It's part of who she is."

Jasper joined the trio. "It's gotten too rough for the ferries to cross, and I've just learned that the police have now closed off the bridge to the island because of the volume of people trying to get here. Have you noticed the state troopers?" He frowned. "With all the change at churches that has been reported in the news, I expect there are more than a few religious folks, including a range of clerics, who would like to...well, I hope the authorities haven't gotten any inklings of specific trouble today. Surely, they would advise us..."

"Feel the peacefulness here!" Pilar interrupted. "Theone won't allow dissension in her presence. It would detract from The Message."

"You're right," Mag said with certainty. "She is determined...not to be a leader, not to be...worshipped. No matter what their feelings before they arrive or after they leave, the people who are here are...peaceful."

"You are to remember The Message, not the Messenger," Mike reiterated. "Theone has made that statement again and again."

Theone stopped her movement center point to the range of cameras trained on her, and human noise ceased. She cast a glance at her bird escort, and they halted.

"Why are humans drawn to the ocean?" She asked. "Why is it through the ages humans have been fascinated by the tides? Why is acquisition of the land near oceans so highly prized?"

A minicam photographer looked puzzled, adjusted his earphones, then shrugged. "I can't believe it with those waves in such a frenzy, but she's clear as a bell," he said to his associate, a cable TV newscaster sent from Raleigh.

Theone turned towards the ocean, stretched her arms and walked into the foamy swell pummeling the shore.

"Gracious, she'll be knocked down," Mag murmured, "and drenched."

"No," Mike assured.

A powerful water jet cascaded over Theone, but she did not lose her balance or appear wet. She faced her audience and declared, "Oceans captivate humans because oceans are powerful Glimpses of Peace! The ocean soothes the soul and is meant to be a glorious reminder of the destiny waiting. View the ocean now as an encouragement, an incentive for you to make the right choices for your soul to advance."

She stepped away from the water just as a peaking wave loomed behind her. The wave seemed to lift and carry her to dry beach where it set her down gracefully. Later Jasper mulled whether or not it had been one of her empathetic exercises; regardless, every face watching her mirrored awe.

"Our Deity has a Plan for the Earth and the Moon, the Sun and the stars," she said. "Liken it to a treasure map for the soul with the hints of treasure being the Glimpses of Peace such as the one you are witnessing today." Theone looked at the overcast sky. Through the gloom, the winter sun shone brilliantly, banishing a wide stretch of clouds and flaming her hair. "Our Deity has also provided simple Directions to aid the soul in reaching Peace, but humans need reminders. It is why Our Deity has found it necessary to send messengers." She smiled, and sighs rippled through the crowd. "So I am here to remind you. For your soul to advance, you must be honest; you must be humble; and you must care about all life that is here."

She strode off into the grassy dunes towards Pamlico Sound, her retinue of birds forming a shield around her.

From the crowd, a voice piped faintly, "We are in the presence of God's Daughter."

Theone pivoted and called, "Each of you has a soul and is thus a Child of Our Deity. Who I am is unimportant. Take to heart what I say and live as Our Deity desires for you."

Despite the wind and waves drowning out sound, her words were heard clearly and fully echoed several times before fading.

Out of habit, Pilar crossed herself and knelt. Weeping, Mag stared in reverence at Theone while Mike grinned in delight at her retreating figure. Jasper rocked to and fro as he fought to dissolve the lump in his throat.

∽

Theone and her group continued to travel in a southerly then westerly path. On an island in the Okefenokee Swamp of Southeastern Georgia, Theone delivered The Message against bald-cypress draped in silvery Spanish moss which twinkled when the vapory sun beamed through. The arrival of lethargic alligators amid the water lilies inhibited the humans who had gathered in canoes and small motorized boats, but the reptiles did not deter the other species drawn to Theone. Mike video-taped deer, squirrels, rabbits, opossums, raccoons and otters stirred to gather by her presence. In the shadows lurked a bobcat and a sluggish black bear. A multitudinous variety of birds - winter visitors and permanent residents - chirped and cawed while ducks honked for Theone's notice.

At the rugged Wichita Mountains NWR in southwestern Oklahoma, a giant golden moon, low on the horizon, lit Theone's presence as she spoke in the middle of a bluestem-grass meadow. The meadow abutted the boulder strewn, red granite mountain range, dome-smooth from erosion. Throngs of bats, mixed with a variety of raptors, shadowed the sky, spooking people, but not the animals attracted to Theone. Drawn from their preserve to the public area, sleepy buffalo and longhorn cattle ambled around her. Elk appeared, and elusive bighorn sheep silhouetted the lower cliffs behind her. Snakes skimmed her ankles while cottontails, prairie dogs and other field rodents nestled serenely nearby. Coyotes and foxes crept close enough to be seen. Hoots resounded from great horned owls.

Thus far, bland questions had been raised by observers, which Theone had answered with gentleness, and no disputes had ensued. At any rate, no disputes had occurred during her appearances. 'Theone's Hand of Peace' was Jasper's explanation because elsewhere, controversy seethed. Presuming The Message here in Oklahoma concluded, Jasper had already closed his notebook, and he was surprised when a cleric strongly criticized her position on Christianity.

"You deny Christ's Message of Salvation, young woman, and thereby refute Grace! You talk nonsense about the soul and are damning your own to Hell!"

"To begin with, Jesus never offered Grace!" Theone said firmly. "Just as humankind has pursued corporeal and technological matters to improve physical existence, remnants of Truth pertinent to the soul have been revealed along the way. The Dead Sea Scrolls at Qumran are such an example. Why would Our Deity limit salvation? Why do organized religions, specifically Christianity, feel as if it has the only answer? Christians have always suffered from tremendous pride. The death and rebirth of a god was a central belief of the Goddess religions, as old as Inanna, the Sumerian Queen of Heaven, and Isis of ancient Egypt! The important thing from Jesus is what he taught to humankind and how they are to lead their lives to reach Peace!"

"You deny that Jesus, the Son of God, died for our sins!" A mainline Protestant denomination bishop shouted.

"I say that the path to Peace is not just a simplistic issue of salvation. To achieve Peace the Hindu concept of spiritual progress is more in keeping with Our Deity's Message which was offered by Jesus, but edited by Paul and the recorders of early church history!

"But I am not judging those whose sincerely believe in the Christ myth. What I'm saying is *don't judge those who don't*. If focus on a death and a resurrection helps your soul to advance, then it is right for you. But don't continue to think that the Christian religion is the only way."

Before the bishop could quarrel further, bats swarmed Theone and in their midst, she stepped away from the crowd towards the mountains.

Later Jasper and Mike compared notes. No wolves were known to be in the region and they might have been coyotes except for the color and the distinctive howls. The two men agreed. A small pack of red wolves, considered to be extinct, *had* joined her as she walked into the darkness.

On Anacapa Island, part of the Channels Islands National Park near Ventura, California, the assemblage of sea mammals amazed the human crowd who had boated the eleven miles from the mainland to witness Theone speak. Splashing and crying in guttural pitch, multifarious species of whales, dolphins, sea lions and seals contended with noisy pelicans and other sea birds for Theone's notice. Yet the moment she spoke, the quiet was instantaneous, and above her, a pallid, inverted half-moon suddenly impressed the sun-bright western sky.

At the end of The Message, a pair of sea lions swam towards her and she waded into the water, thick with golden kelp. En mass the sea mammals either entered the ocean or those already in, moved to join Theone, inundating the spectators and creating a deafening noise.

The usual furor never distracted her from studying eyes, though. Theone always sought to communicate personally with an aching, susceptible soul and in the mob of humanity and creatures, Bobby Lon stood out prominently. She leveled her smile to beckon him.

CHAPTER ELEVEN

Bobby

Yolenta Kolaski, Bobby's mother, was a first generation American whose anti-Nazi parents had the foresight and the resources to leave Poland before Hitler's troops marched into their country in 1939. Her father, a bilingual physics professor, offered his talents to the British government and was later transferred to the Allied Command when the United States entered the war. In return for his service, the Kolaski family qualified for the first visas issued following the cease fire in Europe, and because of the location of sponsoring relatives, they settled in Chicago. Yolenta, their fourth child, was born shortly after their arrival.

Dr. Kolaski's patriotic sentiments and brilliance gained him a tenured position at the city's most prestigious academic university. Her mother, an orchestral pianist before starting a family, found her own function at the college - accompanying student musicians during their recitals. Yolenta was raised in a stimulating, intellectual atmosphere which steered her to liberal causes and led to an involvement in women's rights, the sixties' peace movement and to a minor extent, the freewheeling drug culture. She was also the youngest Kolaski child and coddled. Her generation's rebellion fit with her disposition. Yet lengthy, tangled brown hair and dirty denim on an unwashed body detracted from, but could not fully obscure Yolenta's Slavic beauty. She did nothing to enhance her prominent cheekbones and limpid green eyes, but with her curvaceous figure, she stood out among student protesters at the university. Young men could espouse revolution and champion equality, but beauty still influenced their sexual attitudes. Yolenta was coveted as a companion. For her part, her preference in men was based on a shock equation, which was the reason she initially slept with Tym Lon, a fellow student who had matching high cheekbones and similar political sentiments.

Tym Lon was a fourth generation Chinese, native Chicagoan whose conservative Buddhist parents were herbalists/acupuncturists with a thriving practice. The oldest son, he had been trained in the ancient healing arts since childhood and his family expected him to enter the business, but Tym wished to be free of the stereotype. He could sing on key and dance well; in high school, he had always won character roles in the drama department's productions. When he met Yolenta at a campus rally, he was enrolled in theater classes at the university with the idea of pursuing an acting profession.

Yolenta and Tym were involved in the tumultuous Democratic convention the summer of 1968, but they were not core activists subject to the police brutality or the sweep of arrests. They did, however, spend the night together in Grant's Park with other dissidents, smoking pot and making love. Yolenta, sporadic about birth control, conceived.

Their families were appalled at the cultural complications if they married, but the issue was moot; neither had any inclination to do something so bourgeois. They packed their knapsacks and hitched a ride to New York City. Tym reasoned that he could always find work in the Chinese community while he pursued acting parts, but it was not necessary because his luck was phenomenal. His first audition he was hired, silencing his critical parents until they found out what he was doing. The contemporary musical, featuring frontal nudity, called for a racially balanced cast. Tym was hired as much for his ethnic makeup as for his talent.

The production was a smash on Broadway and by the time Bobby (for Kennedy) Aquarius Kolaski Lon was six months old, Tym was a minor star. Yolenta was also pregnant with Bobby's sister, Cecila Starshine Kolaski Lon, soon modified by baby Bobby to Celee. With children born so close together, Yolenta's focus became her children and the pursuit of homemaking. She baked bread, sewed in natural fibers, pureed her own baby food, and cultivated a tiny herb garden on their Greenwich Village apartment balcony. Tym's radical young actor crowd, who disdained the establishment, and Yolenta's back-to-basics women's support group overlapped congenially; therefore, the Kolaski-Lon relationship benefited each partner economically and emotionally.

Tym stayed with the musical for two years until a Hollywood studio casting agent caught the show during a visit. He had come up dry for a special Oriental thug needed to be cast in a soon to be filmed epic. Tym could act and he was photogenic - the marquee featured his picture. Add twenty pounds to his slim girth and shave his head. The agent knew he had a winner.

With no career stakes in the East, Yolenta was willing to move. The Kolaski-Lon household left their crowded Manhattan flat and moved into a Glendale rental near the California studio.

Tym's movie was a hit and he received positive reviews for his repellent portrayal of the thug. Unfortunately, the weight he added for the role increased rather than decreased, but Tym's ego did not require a lot of artistic massage. Steady work appealed more, and he developed into a reliable character actor who consistently had some sort of a role lined up when the last one wrapped. The Kolaski-Lons bought a house in Sherman Oaks, a community just north of Beverly Hills.

With the children in school and Tym often on location, Yolenta needed an outlet for her energies. Because her interest in natural methods had extended to medical remedies, over the years Tym had shared with her his knowledge about herbs, and Geraldine, her advertising executive friend, suggested that they go into business on a local basis. Ti-Mu Herbs (so named for the Chinese earth mother goddess) were merchandised for women. Yolenta's herbal supplements and tonics were merely mild sedatives and stimulants, but cleverly packaged to target cramps, menstrual blues, conception difficulties, childbirth ease and menopause coping. She used the herbs herself, particularly the kind she could not sell without legal trouble - birth control and fetus expelling. As a result she served as her own best advertising and often appeared at health food stores carrying the line.

Women responded enthusiastically and Yolenta soon outgrew her leased greenhouse workshop. She and Geraldine arranged their own financing and bought a warehouse with plans to market Ti-Mu Herbs nationwide.

What had once been Yolenta's concentration on her children, then, transferred to her successful business. Bobby and Celee were already in private schools; now, a disinterested housekeeper laxly supervised their leisure hours. Like other affluent children with absent parents, they were given too much spending money and had too much free time to squander.

Only fifteen months separated the siblings who had inherited features so similar that they were often asked if they were twins. Each had more than a hint of Yolenta's translucent green in their sloped, tan eyes; they shared her generous mouth, Tym's straight black hair and their parents' medium height. Prominent cheekbones were inevitable. Peasant-breed either way, Yolenta said; in truth, their looks were a provocative Eurasian mix, making the Kolaski-Lon offspring strikingly attractive individuals.

Bobby and Celee once compared their earliest parental memory. Both agreed - it was of a proudly unwed couple who always smoked a joint with their wine cocktails.

Drugs were easily available. They regularly witnessed parties at their house with guests snorting coke off the kitchen work island, and their peers came from the same atmosphere in their homes. LSD, Quaaludes, diet pills, assorted designer drugs were as much a part of growing up as doing minimal homework. Parties with sexual kicks started in 6th grade and to offset boredom, grew kinkier by high school. (Yolenta induced fourteen year old Celee's first abortion, father unknown. Rather than show any moral concern, free-thinking Yolenta just made sure her daughter got a prescription for birth control pills.)

The lack of restraints gnawed at their vulnerable temperaments, and often they felt bewildered by the abrupt turn they had taken from a mother-centered, organized life to one unstructured and permissive. Bobby's shield was to behave in a foolhardy manner which progressed from being the champion who could shoplift the most from the same store without getting caught to being the last driver to turn off while playing chicken with his Corvette convertible.

Tender Celee suffered frequent melancholy and feared getting fat like Tym. She had little discipline about her diet, though, and developed bulimia from purging to combat calories.

Because they could confide in the other, they managed to buffer the world, and this kept them fairly stable until Celee received one too many blows from life's hammer. She was truly experiencing happiness when her lesbian lover jilted her. Celee eschewed handy drugs in favor of a messy suicide with razor blades on the white carpet in her bedroom.

After the shock faded, twenty-one year old Bobby considered her fatal stunt with sad admiration. In death, Celee had finally made a statement which she been unable to communicate to their parents during her life. LOOK AT ME. SEE WHAT I AM? FUCKED UP AND IT'S TOO LATE TO DO ANYTHING ABOUT IT. LIVE WITH IT.

Yolenta and Tym cried in baffled tones about children given every privilege. They grieved indignantly about children granted unwavering financial support to explore anything they wished. It sounded to Bobby like they viewed Celee as ungrateful and her demise was a personal affront to their excellent parenting! Disgusted, but not stupid, he demanded a substantially increased allowance or he would do the same as Celee. Yolenta and Tym, anxious to assuage their guilt and unwilling to call Bobby's bluff, afforded their son the opportunity to move into an upscale Venice apartment. They also replaced his beat-up convertible with his choice of a factory-new conversion van because he had an undefined notion that he would need it if he traveled.

In Venice, he welcomed a parade of roommates and lovers for temporary company, but found no confidante like Celee had been. He lived this way for three wasted years, cavorting on the fringes of beach society, sponging off his parents and indulging himself in whatever fancied him, until he heard that a former sex partner had died of AIDS. Frightened that he had been infected, he went for the test. The results were mixed. He was HIV-positive, making him a carrier, but when or if the disease would develop would depend on time. Regardless, he was contagious; no present cure existed. To protect others, he must use a condom without fail in every future sexual encounter.

The night he received his bad news, Bobby was getting drunk at his favorite hangout. Word that Theone Jones would be speaking on Anacapa, one of the Channel Islands, diverted his bitter, self-pitying mood. She had a New Age thing about souls, he recalled vaguely. Did she do cures? It would be worth an overnight trip to Ventura to find out.

Eye contact with Theone Jones riveted Bobby. He was compelled to reach her and despite the mob, a path opened just for him. He was able to wade right to her. The pandemonium and congestion receded...

She has the same eyes as Celee! or he was looking in an illusionary mirror. No, he was positive. This pair was feminine. It was Celee, all right, and...his sweet little sister was...okay. Not super great, but...improving? Whatever, it was a relief! Until this moment, Bobby had squelched an uneasiness about where Celee might have gone. Tym had once mentioned that Buddhism was a spiritual spire to nothingness; obviously he wasn't into it. He believed with Yolenta in a sort of self-power. They mail-ordered motivational tapes and tuned into them during freeway excursions. Religious training just had not existed in the Kolaski-Lon household and until his AIDS test, death had been a remote concept.

Bobby realized that he was gawking. "Thank you," he stammered. "I miss Celee, but it's okay for her, and I guess I can feel..."

"Celee made a choice that ended her mental suffering, but did little to advance her soul," Theone said kindly. "Her next start will be at similar point and hopefully it will be in an environment that will nurture her spirit rather than tear it down. Some are capable of taking positive steps in spite of negative circumstances, but Celee could not."

"Yeah, well..." Bobby had fooled with hypnotism at parties, but had scoffed at it. Now, he felt like this must be how it really works. Theone Jones could probably make him do anything! He felt powerless to refuse.

"Well, you still have choices, Bobby. Are you ready to try the positive?"

He looked at the sky and swore he saw Celee's face in the pallid moon. She was smiling joyously at him. He grinned at Theone. "I am ready. I am! Can I join up with you? I don't know how to do anything much useful, but everybody can use a gofer. Do you have a gofer?"

Theone knew that Bobby did not possess any skills; he was out of shape and in no condition to keep up with her active, fit group. Yet most souls had lives that would be enriched by their newly found faith; the transformation affected their attitudes about self, both spiritually and physically, and their relationships. But Bobby had nothing to reclaim and no one with whom to share. Also, the recent knowledge of his illness caused him despair. If his raw, tender soul was to be funneled on to the right track, he would need special support...it risked their harmony, but The Deity had prompted this connection. Perhaps getting along with Bobby was a lesson for the group.

She made a decision. Room did not exist for him in the Airstream, but she envisioned his new van. "You are welcome to join us," Theone said, "if you drive your own vehicle for your shelter. Everything else is ours to share."

Bobby's eager expression faded. "You can tell I'm getting AIDS," he said resentfully, "and you're afraid of getting it."

Theone regarded him with patience. This was why Bobby needed bolstering. "Our trailer is full. My friends spend too much time on the road to be uncomfortable during relaxation."

"Oh." Actually, Bobby realized it was better to be separate. He liked his own space and would need some privacy for the occasional joint or pill he enjoyed popping. "I have to get my shit...stuff together, then. I can meet you in a couple days. Where will you be?"

"If you join us, you do it now, Bobby. Other than calling Yolenta and Tym, you have nothing in the past to return for."

"But...my stuff!"

"Choices," Theone said in a calm, but uncompromising tone.

As he stared at her Bobby fidgeted with the gold hoop in his pierced left ear. Celee's eyes were gone and in their place were ones not so arresting for their fickle hazel hue as they were for the message emanating from them. *This woman could make a difference in his life,* he comprehended, *but only if he took responsibility. There would be no more handouts or copouts. And it wasn't an issue that he could think about or negotiate. His...his soul was at stake.*

"I'm parked somewhere on the inland," he said. "How can I find you?"

Pleased, Theone gave him her fullest smile. "Go to your van and wait. We'll find you."

Bobby's heart flipped. She was extraordinary, as well as in a sexual sense, and he speculated as to what his chances might be to make this new direction turn to one of a more personal nature.

༄

From the Pacific coast, Theone's group with their new companion tagging behind ventured east. In Kings Canyon National Park on the western slopes of the Sierra Mountains, the giant redwoods seemed insignificant in Theone's presence. Northwest of Salem, Oregon at Baskett Slough NWR in the Willamette Valley, she had to speak to the human crowd at a distance of fifty feet because the trail became so congested with attentive ring-necked pheasant, California quails and ruffled grouse, game birds common to the sanctuary.

More impressive than the public phenomenon, though, was the effect on individual souls that Theone connected with during her travels. From bankers to carpenters, from Christians to agnostics, both sexes and all nationalities, Theone's candid words and ephemeral touch transformed lives. Unlike the others, Jasper could frequently see and hear the exchanges. He noted each one.

Simultaneously, faiths of every denomination suffered from the consequences of The Message. In a mere six months of Theone's public tour, membership in organized religion sharply declined and the contributions counted on to fund the system slumped, too. Inspired by Theone, people sought direct means to help others; dollars which had not only provided for denomination causes, but had supported the ecclesiastical bodies, were now diverted. Soup kitchens, food banks, day care centers, ghetto medical clinics - donors funneled their dollars and volunteer hours into any area where they could be a viable, tangible part of the process.

This movement towards personal involvement also affected conglomerate, national charities. People demanded to know exactly where their funds would have the most impact with the least retained for administrative costs. Money earmarked for causes outside the country included specific donor instructions to specific relief organizations. But rather than downsize their administrative budgets, major charities, like religious denominations, used their shrinking dollars to maintain governing body expenses, allowing the reason for their existence - programs and research - to dwindle.

The bureaucratic quagmire, then, prevalent in many non-profit associations began to erode. Jobs and perks at every level were threatened; pet projects were jeopardized. However, while hot, internal debates raged as to a means to counteract Theone's influence, neutral public statements were issued. She was becoming too popular to attack overtly; her message was too benign. Thus, no unified effort among the assorted groups was made to combat the peril to their existence. No one wanted to be cast in the villain role as the first to speak against Theone until Glenn Chandler learned of her endeavors.

⁓

"How's your scalp this morning?" Kristen asked Glenn as she placed scrambled eggs and toast in front of him.

"Improving," he said. "it's the final treatment, so I can bear it." He rubbed his crown gingerly where he'd had his latest hair implant. The IOG denomination provided superb medical insurance along with generous pension benefits for its ministers, but hair implant surgery was elective and not covered. Vaughn had negotiated with a physician, a member of Calvary. In return for waiving his fee, the physician was being given full credit on his donor statement for a mission contribution. Glenn justified that his image was important for Calvary's image and legitimate to maintain church prosperity.

"I get my hair frosted this afternoon and it's done by picking strands through a plastic cap," Kristen said. "I sort of know how it is." She patted his cheek and turned her attention to G.J. in his high chair. He had oatmeal in his blond hair and he'd pried off the lid on his mug. The apple juice had spilled and dripped on the terra cotta tile. Glenn teed off in an hour, after which he had a lunch date at the country club and at three o'clock, he was being measured at his tailor's to order custom pima cotton shirts. Vaughn swore by them for fit and comfort. She'd bathe G.J. following Glenn's departure since her child helper was not due today until noon. Currently, Lupe, their housekeeper, was doing laundry. She would take care of the mess in the kitchen.

"Do you recall the date of my next eye appointment?" Glenn said. "I'm fairly certain I need new contact lenses or I've reached the point where I need reading glasses because this print is blurred." He held the newspaper further from his face and gasped. "Your sister has been written up on the front page!"

Kristen moved behind Glenn's chair and peered at the article. The headline jumped at her, THE TRUTH BE KNOWN - THEONE PHENOMENON. There's no picture, she thought, her stomach queasy. There have never been any pictures. Theone was from the Devil and her dark mission had gone public!

"She is spouting some rubbish which denies that Christ died for our sins, and the media is giving her credibility with their coverage!" Glenn said in a shocked tone. "It says here 'statistics support that women form the backbone of Christian congregations, and certain denomination leaders, who decline to be named, have admitted that the impact of Theone Jones has been felt critically at churches in those areas where she has appeared. Christian feminists, who in recent years have been calling for equal power in sacred matters such as ordination, are abandoning church and joining the Theone Movement. Other active Christian women, including a number of nuns, are openly challenging the patriarchal structure of the Trinity and demanding that the Goddess be accorded her proper place in worship. A growing group of female Jews are heralding her as the Messiah.

'In the broader population, lesbian spokespersons and their gay counterparts applaud Ms. Jones for her non-judgmental doctrine. They urge their factions to heed her message.'" He rattled the paper. "She can have all those perverts, but get this, Kristen. There are people coming forward in the Midwest and the Mid-Atlantic region who claim Theone brought The Message to them personally about five years ago! I quote, 'Our lives were transformed by the Truth she shared with us and in turn, we have shared It with others who have further shared It. Off the top of my head I can name forty folks right here in our small town who profess to follow the Messenger of Love.' Messenger of Love? God Almighty, this is preposterous and Believers must challenge her!"

Kristen straightened her posture and stared at the wall by the built-in microwave where a hand-carved mesquite Cross hung. The pastorship at Calvary was an excellent position for Glenn, but he deserved a bigger audience; he was good enough for his own show on TV. The Ulrichs had commented about it, yet life was pleasant and prosperous where they were. Why seek more...except for recognition. Public attention...

"You must rebut her in the pulpit," Kristen cried. "You must not only distance us from her blasphemy, but go on the offensive and denounce her!"

Glenn dropped the newspaper and looked at Kristen. Her eyes glowed and he particularly loved her zealous expression. Desire hit him and he glanced regretfully at the clock. She was right and because of their relationship to Theone, who better than himself to lead the opposition? Who better than him to gain prominence as the defender of the True Faith...national recognition...global..."

"I'm calling Mother!" Kristen said. "I can't believe she hasn't been aware of Theone's activities. I hope she comes to her senses now about this...this daughter of Satan that she spawned. Her soul is in terrible danger. She needs to get herself in close touch with God or she'll be dragged to Hell with Theone!"

"I'm getting hold of this book of hers today," Glenn said as he stood up, "and I am mapping out a whole series of sermons to discredit her. I'm also calling Kansas City to find out why the denomination hasn't seen fit to inform us about what's going on!"

"Oh, Glenn, you are the one to do it and I will tell you all the evil things about her, specific things that really happened..." Kristen embraced him.

Glenn smiled and gave his wife a passionate kiss. G.J. clapped his hands.

CHAPTER TWELVE

Arela

Arela Pedersen was set again to leave Denver for a while. Her travels were as much for titillation as they were a desire to settle an indistinct restlessness. One day a daring adventure might just satisfy the ache, and it would leave her. Meanwhile, she had white water rafted the Amazon River; she'd done a photo safari in Kenya; she'd been bobsledding in Norway; she'd been hang-gliding off a chalky Dover cliff and dunked in the English Channel. Each time she would return from thrill-seeking to her teaching job at an inner city school, which was plenty risk for her associates. A teacher had been raped in the parking lot by a student, and several muggings had occurred. Arela did not let it worry her.

She taught first graders and they weren't as hardened as their older siblings. Six year olds still had a sweetness, a remnant of innocence, and if she could make a difference in a life with so many obstacles ahead...Arela loved working with young disadvantaged children and augmented her meager supply budget with her own funds. She gave the children money, too, for lunch, for books and sometimes, for spending which she knew was not a wise thing to do. Yet if there were days when futility seemed to rule, then there were also days when a child would show the grit to rise above circumstances and hope imbued her. Possibly, she could make a difference in an indifferent world.

Arela's looks did not match her personality; her slight build disguised the toughness. 'Fragile blonde with melting blue eyes' had been one suitor's description of her. She'd attracted plenty of those in twenty-seven years, but Arela had only a casual interest in men. Her father, Brett, had been a handsome, gregarious substance abuser who never grew up. Her mother, Natalie, a former beauty queen, had grown up when Arela was eleven and subsequently divorced Brett. Arela was not crazy about her staid stepfather, an engineer, or her preppy half-brother, but her mother's ordered household offered stability whereas her father's lifestyle guaranteed chaos. Since her parents had agreed to share custody of her, the extremes were confusing, but like most children from broken homes Arela learned to adapt to the moment. She was a B average student, first-string varsity tennis player and never took any boy seriously because she already had one permanent boy to cope with, Brett.

Arela's paternal grandfather, an owner of a tool-and-die company, had invented a machine part which eliminated a human phase in the manufacture of photocopiers. At age fifty, he sold the company, then died suddenly, leaving his only child, twenty-five year old Brett, a million dollars with stipulations.

Brett had briefly tried college and had held a superfluous position at his father's company. Fancying himself an artist, he dabbled at wood carving and bonsai horticulture, but chiefly, he liked to play in between his self-described power naps - golfing, partying with thin, exotic-looking women, traveling to trendy, sunny spots like Cabo San Lucas on the Baja tip or Newport Beach in California - and he did so in a functioning fog of premium marijuana, inhaled from a pocket-size shooter, fortified with an occasional cocaine snort. His drug habits left him a high roller at the beginning of the month, then at various levels of low until receipt of the next dividend check. Fortunately, Brett's father had exercised foresight for Arela's sake because upon majority, half of the million-plus inheritance diverted to her.

Arela used some of the money to pay for her elementary education degree at a state university, finishing in three years by going straight through without break. She'd hardly put a dent in her inheritance.

After purchasing a condominium in Denver and furnishing it in white Danish Modern like Brett's, the dent decreased the amount a little more, but Arela still had money in excess of her needs. She placed a $25,000 nest egg in one mutual fund and the balance of the principal in another for Brett who could only draw on it if she co-signed. He had frittered half of it when he was killed several years later. Brett plowed his 280Z into the back of a Rolls Royce Corniche driven by an elderly man who had changed lanes without noticing the low vehicle tearing up on the left. Brett, who considered the mandatory seat belt law an affront to personal freedom, was ejected through the Z's sun roof into oncoming traffic.

Brett's sum religious conviction had been a simplistic one based on the karma concept. A person's actions gained them either good or bad karma. You strove for good, but you did not scold yourself, either, if some bad accumulated. Arela shuffled his philosophy with Natalie's fixation on her spiritualist's advice revealed through exorbitant tarot readings. Yet neither parents' surface-skimming beliefs could be attributed for galvanizing Arela's passion for the youth she taught. She had actively sought the inner city school position just because she 'felt' it was where she belonged.

At Brett's death, Arela had re-assessed what to do with her inheritance. Since she enjoyed cross country skiing and snowmobiling, she had shopped the real estate market bordering the southwestern edge of Rocky Mountain State Park and had bought a partially furnished three bedroom house on Lake Latimer. She had passed papers just at the beginning of summer vacation. The next full moon was on a clear night, and she rowed out with the box containing Brett's ashes to scatter them in the glistening water. Brett had been exasperating, particularly in the last months when his brain had begun to fuzz from the damage inflicted by the narcotics. Natalie knew very well what Brett was like and had frequently admonished her daughter to cut the ties, but Arela had spent her life being the responsible one, the nurturer in the relationship; she could not just turn it off. Now, a sizable void existed where Brett had been, and despite his behavior, she had loved him. With this final act, though, Arela could sit on her redwood deck any time and view the exact spot where his ashes lay. It seemed an odd comfort, but one that eased her loss.

In the next year, teaching and vacations at her new home absorbed Arela, yet the restlessness in her simmered. When Pam, a fellow adventurer, suggested that at the beginning of summer break they fly into Gustavus, Alaska, and catch a bus to Bartlett Cove where they could then kayak into the back country of Glacier Bay, Arela quickly agreed.

An advocate of Theone's (a former Protestant minister), married Ian Leahy and Jenny Yates on a Long Island beach in late April, but the newlyweds postponed their honeymoon to coincide with Theone's early June stop in Alaska. They chose to voyage into Glacier Bay from Juneau on a ship specially chartered by a cruise line for Theone's appearance.

Dressed in raingear and under her wool clothing, thermalwear, Jenny stood on the ship next to Ian gawking at the immense tidal glaciers jutting through the haze shrouding Glacier Bay National Monument. Twelve of the glaciers had snouts at water's edge which 'calved' bergs into the ocean. She had recognized a large number of whales - orca, minke, humpback - migrating into the Bay and now she witnessed hordes of cormorants and gulls jostling for position on loose icebergs. Jenny bet that Theone was the drawing card. She was scheduled to speak on Muir Inlet which afforded access by trail and water.

"Hello!" Jasper shouted from the shore.

Ian waved from the ship which had been granted a permit to moor close enough to provide a good view of Ms. Jones. The park service office had smirked at the request. A good view? Precipitation was the standard forecast. Today, however, the sun had been glimpsed intermittently, and the haze had thinned. At the head of the bay, lofty Mt. Fairweather was visible, a rarity.

Jenny scanned the rocky, ice-dotted area, dismissing the mixed throng of media and general spectators on the shore. Silver windbreakers with gold collars and gold striping the sleeves dominated the scene, making it difficult to distinguish the authentic one...There. Theone was with the new fellow, Bobby, her hair flashing just as brilliantly in wan sunlight as when the rays were strong. In spite of her determination not to be a focal point, Theone's shiny nylon jacket had caught on with devotees resolute in having a badge of their faith, and numerous clothing manufacturers had rushed to produce facsimiles. People needed symbols, Jenny mused. They needed that sense of identity with the one they worshiped. She knew Theone was saddened by the need. Pilar nicely refused all attempts by companies to gain an endorsement and further recommended that if they must commercialize Theone, then they should donate the related profits to the less fortunate. Jenny wanted to believe some actually did, but those with souls that advanced on their journey usually would not be ones that sought to achieve wealth by exploiting public demand.

A depressed Ian spotted Theone. He had not told Jenny yet about losing his job because he had not wanted to spoil their honeymoon. He'd gotten a message to Jasper, though, since it affected publication of *"The TRUTH of PEACE"*. Rather, the cessation of printing and no options by another publisher to buy out the contract, irrespective of the book's rank on the bestseller's list for non-fiction since the beginning. Distributors had been pressured to cancel orders and retail outlets had been requested to return unsold editions. But plenty of books circulated. People wanting to read it would find a copy.

The job issue would not be solved so handily. The publisher and the entire staff supportive of Theone Jones had been forced out by what Ian could only describe as a malevolent Christian majority of stockholders who, atypically, had chosen dogma over dividends. For Jenny's sake and this trip, he was trying not to dwell on his subsequent blackballing in the industry.

Perhaps Theone would have some solutions for him, Ian thought. Late today, he and Jenny would disembark at Barlett Cove where they had reservations at the Lodge. Theone's group had driven to Alaska through British Columbia, ferried to Gustavus and were settled at the campground in Barlett Cove. Tonight, they would gather for the evening in the Airstream.

A sudden commotion shattered the solitude of two women maneuvering kayaks around a bend of Muir Inlet. Being summer, darkness did not exceed a maximum of two hours, but for most of their vacation, scarlet fireweed sprouting on the banks had added the only cheer to drab, foggy days. Today, the sun had broken through regularly, and they could see the hemlock and spruce forest in the distance.

"What's going on?" Arela queried Pam who in the front had a better view of the shore across the inlet.

"Gosh, people, boats, marine mammals - I can't believe it! There are whales all over the place!" Pam exclaimed. "It must be something spectacular. I think every seal in the park has congregated along with scads of birds, and I can see moose, brown AND black bears...something incredible has made them leave their forest haven. Let's get closer so that I can photograph it."

Pam, a manufacturer's rep for a sports shoe corporation, was given to superlatives, but Arela compliantly dipped her paddle just as a familiar groan echoed in the inlet. The twenty glaciers in the region constantly shifted and broke, sending tons of ice crashing into the bay and a mile off, a sérac (a complexly woven, icy pinnacle formed on the upper surface of a glacier), had rent free to plummet loudly. Humans and animals silenced in awe of nature's "white thunder".

As if heralding the event, a bald eagle soared over the inlet and landed on a chunk of bluish ice very near to a barefoot Theone who stood balanced on two large rocks lapped by water. The onlookers remained motionless as the eagle flapped its wings, then meekly bowed to her.

Theone smiled at the bird's tribute. "One of Our Deity's beloved creatures," she said, "and as Our Deity intends, the magnificence of the bald eagle inspires the spirit of many souls." Her smile faded. "Yet there are also those who would kill this bird without any remorse in their souls just to have a trophy. Tell me. Which soul is elevated? Which soul is degraded? Which action advances the soul on its journey towards Peace? Where on the spiritual road is your soul?"

A mist had set in again, obscuring the sun, and the air temperature had dropped below forty degrees, but Theone gracefully stepped off the rocks into the frigid water. Although incongruous to the site, salmon appeared in the shallow depth and gyrated about her as she walked towards a colony of seals settled on a rocky point. The seals fixated on her with rigid concentration.

A hiker contemplating the eagle remarked, "Tha' ol' bird's gonna hav'a fine dinner."

A journalist who had followed Theone faithfully since Maine, chuckled at the man's naiveté. "Not on those salmon," he answered confidently. "In Theone's presence, respect for her supersedes instinct."

The hiker shrugged cynically, then realized that Theone was looking directly at him. Momentarily he puzzled, then rapture filled his face. The journalist nodded knowingly as he made notes. He'd seen the expression on plenty of faces, including his own, and recognized when she had touched another soul. Yet, he'd also witnessed those who became disturbed at what they saw upon looking at her or ashamed or recalcitrant. It was hard to imagine for him because he believed, but not every soul responded affirmatively to The Message. Was it free will exercised in subconscious resistance, he considered, or a soul so off track that the detour had grown too complicated for the soul to find its way back without major effort? At death, what environment did that qualify you for? He realized that he had a dynamic premise for a book! The journalist remembered where he was and chided himself for not absorbing every moment he could in Theone's glorious presence.

He checked on her location. The water had reached her knees, soaking half her beige twill skirt. She stopped moving just as two women in kayaks reached the promontory where the seal colony resided.

Intent on the still seals, Pam said in a baffled tone, "No barking? Have you ever been around a bunch of seals who didn't bark and bark? What the heck is going on?"

Arela saw Theone and frowned. Why was this lightly dressed woman standing in the water? Why hadn't even one person in this immense crowd had the sense to get her out before she suffered injury from exposure? People were so apathetic to others...what could she do to help her...

The mist abated and the sun flared. Arela tilted her head and gazed at Theone whose image had sharpened as the surroundings receded. Even at this considerable distance, she could see Brett's gorgeous blue eyes! No, blue eyes that were a mirror of her own, lucid and focused, not dope addled and bloodshot like Brett's had been. This was no ordinary woman, Arela thought with surprising calm. Her hair glowed as if a higher being had endowed it with its own power source.

"From earliest memory, you were conditioned to equate responsibility with love," Theone said. "Love should have no such strings, Arela. Accept now that you will always be loved, regardless."

The vague yearning which had driven her for years vanished and tranquillity enveloped Arela. Had she just encountered...the Divine?

Theone's smile made Arela grin.

"I am joining you," Arela declared.

"Yes, you are meant to," Theone said. "Come ashore and hike back to our camp with me. We have a lot to discuss."

The feeling of communion with Theone left Arela and she became aware again of her surroundings.

"I'll be damned!" Pam exclaimed. "That's Theone Jones! Have you read the book? I heard at the place where we rented the kayaks that she was going to be in the park. How interesting she looks."

Her looks were interesting? Arela retorted mentally. Her *presence mesmerized*! Her *quintessence altered lives*! She stared at the back of her friend's head. Pam had not experienced the same effect. But perhaps she was not meant to, unlike herself, whose spirit, whose *soul* felt akin to the sublime freedom expressed by the bald eagle presently ascending into the sky. No, she hadn't read the book. She wouldn't have to. She would be privileged to learn The Message directly from Theone. Tears brimmed her eyes.

"Paddle to the shore," Arela instructed as she sniffed. Surely someone would assist Pam in kayaking back to their camp, and she would join her friend again tomorrow to pack up since, fortunately, their vacation was scheduled to end. She had to get back to Denver as soon as possible to rearrange her affairs because from this moment forward, her destiny was tied to Theone's.

Jasper, Pilar and Mag had returned to Barlett Cove by motor craft, and by the time Mike, Bobby, Theone and Arela hiked into their campsite, Mag had a chicken roasting. Shortly thereafter, Pilar arrived with Ian, Jenny and additional groceries.

It was a reunion of dear friends and despite being a new acquaintance, Arela was welcomed like she was one, too, except by Mike. As they had hiked the rough, wet terrain, Arela had been too enthralled with Theone and in absorbing The Message to pay much attention to him, but he had noticed her. Women had never interested him because, unswervingly, Theone had always been the only one who mattered in his life. This Arela, though. There was just something about her which had diverted his singular devotion to Theone.

But what he felt would not make any difference, so why was he letting it bother him? Arela would be attracted to handsome Bobby with his soft, shaggy hair and rakish earrings; plus, their frequent walks with Theone had gotten Bobby's physique in good shape in a very short time. Girls clustered around Bobby when they stopped even though he paid only a cursory attention to them. Bobby loved Theone like he did. Well, not exactly. He sensed that Bobby's love had a sexual undercurrent, presumably because Bobby had a lot of experience with sex whereas he had none and it showed. Sometimes he wondered if Theone loved Bobby more because he was so attractive, so well-acquainted with life matters, but then he would rebuke himself. Theone did not have favorites. She ministered to them with a perfect balance.

"Mike?" Theone said.

"Mm?" Slouched on his bunk away from the others talking in the rear section of the trailer, he'd been pondering for an hour what he considered a crisis in his commitment to Theone.

"Walk with me for a bit?" She requested.

He sat up and swung his legs to the floor. "Let me get on my down vest."

"It's snowing. Put on your poncho, too."

Outside, Theone offered her hand to Mike and he looked at her in surprise. Bodily touch was rare on her part and always brief. Because it was inessential, Mike reasoned. She could touch profoundly merely with her eyes and her smile.

"You're fleet footed, but it's quite rocky and our Moon is hidden," she explained. "I'd rather you didn't fall."

You wouldn't ever, he thought, even if a canyon ruptured as you stepped. He took her bare hand, wishing his own wasn't cased in a heavy leather glove. Physical contact with Theone had never repelled him like others had aside now from Arela. The idea of touching her, amazingly, excited him.

"Ian has lost his job because of his association with me," Theone said, "and Arela has offered to finance his own imprint. It would be a small enterprise and specific to certain writings such as Jasper's about Peace or Jenny's ecology articles, but that is the extent of publishing Ian cares to handle. They plan to start their family soon and Ian intends to be an active parent. Arela did not request it, but the Leahys have decided to relocate to Denver. Things work out."

"I'm glad for them," Mike replied mechanically.

"Arela is very special," Theone said.

Mike stumbled, but Theone kept him from pitching into the muck. Could she read his heart by touching his hand? Or like a cat, could she see his eyes in the dark and fathom the truth? He'd never had a reason before to concern himself with the possibility.

"She's supposed to be special, Mike. Why are you brooding about her?"

He stiffened. "What?"

Theone laughed gently and grabbed his other hand. "Oh, Mike, with your wonderful, wonderful soul. You're just responding to a kindred spirit! Arela is a match for you."

"I'm younger than she is by a lot," Mike mumbled. "It doesn't bother me, but wouldn't it bother her? I didn't finish college, but she has done hours for her masters'. She's so lovely, really stunning, and I'm so...homely...Bobby would be a better pick."

"You're being too surface-minded," Theone teased. "Arela's appearance is pleasing, but it's not why you're attracted to her. You're turned on by her beautiful soul and she has it in her heart to love you back for the same reason."

"I never expected to love anyone else but you, Theone! I'm happy just to be with you and help you..."

"Your love for me won't diminish if you love a woman because it will be a different kind of love. In reality, you will experience a deeper, greater love for a companion with whom you can share friendship as well as sex. You are entitled just as I am."

Mike gulped hard. "What about Bobby?"

"He isn't competition for Arela's heart."
"How about for yours?"
"I'm not in any competition. We're going back now," Theone said.
"Don't think on what you feel for Arela, just trust your heart."
He laughed nervously.

As Mike entered the trailer behind Theone, he hesitantly sought Arela. She was looking at him with...genuine affection! He relaxed. Why did he doubt Theone? Thank you, My Deity, he thought.

"I'll drive Ian and Jenny back to the Lodge," Mike announced. "Why don't you join me, uh, join us, Arela?"

"Okay. Perhaps tomorrow I could talk you into escorting me to my camp inside the park so that I can help Pam pack our gear."

"I'll not only escort you, I'll even help! I've got the whole day."

Mag and Pilar exchanged glances. Mike...flirting?

Theone caught their eyes and winked at them.

Bobby repressed a jubilant smile. He had evaluated Theone's companions and where he would rank with them. Jasper was gay and no snag other than to Bobby's bisexual appetite, but a dalliance with Jasper would complicate his goal. He wanted Theone more. Pilar had a thing for angels which seemed to elevate her above carnal considerations. Mag was an asexual mouse. Bobby concluded that neither woman had any latent lesbian tendencies. He had deemed Mike the singular barrier to achieving Theone's special affection and therefore, had done nothing other than to think about cultivating it. Arela's appearance and Mike's lovesick expression had given Bobby hope that they would connect, thus fortifying his position with Theone. Now, he could show some boldness. Stake his claim so to speak. With caution, of course. Theone had shown him no particular outward favor, but Bobby detected a passionate nature just waiting to be unleashed. He aimed to be the one to do it.

CHAPTER THIRTEEN

Sam found Brigit in the courtyard, but she was not gardening as he had expected. She sat in a fan-style wicker chair just staring...at the cirrus clouds? He wheeled next to her and noticed his cellular phone in her lap.

"I remember at lunch hearing a remark about weeds in the snap beans and 'must do'," he said. "It sounded like a rather grave situation that needed immediate tending, but I'm always in favor of discounting the imperative and lazing away the day. Am I rubbing off on you, Babe?"

Brigit's hands trembled as she covered her face.

"Brig, Honey, what's wrong?" Sam swung his wheel chair into a position where he could clasp his wife.

She fell against him. "Kristen called to gloat. Apparently, a growing number of righteous Christians have been listening to that dreadful preacher she married and he has been asked to give the keynote address at the IOG National Conference in August. Glenn met Theone once very briefly. What makes him an authority on who she is? Who gives him the right to judge her? Certainly not a real god! And where does he get off saying her message isn't valid when it's the same as his without the grace bullshit? How can my own daughter be so damn smug about a faith which is so limiting to the female spirit? Grandchild or not, if she forces me to make a choice between her and Theone, she'll lose!"

Sam let Brigit rave on without adding any comments. He knew Theone was truly of The Deity. But it was a plain fact in history; prophets attracted formidable enemies. Whether or not the truth was being addressed did not matter; leaders of established religions resented the challenge to their authority. In the name of their god, they could justify any action to retain their power.

Power. A hunger for it was a worse crime for the soul than a hunger for wealth, Sam thought bleakly. Avarice was a shallow, tangible greed, but the greed to control, to dominate others with your opinion, your ideas, had deep, toxic roots in the psyche. Yet, ancient Egyptians' belief to the contrary, neither wealth nor power survived the physical conclusion of the grave. Every body ended in dust, but the soul had a reckoning...there was accountability...

Mindful of Brigit's grief at the attacks on Theone, Sam curbed a grim chuckle. Somewhere in Peace, along with those souls who, despite the odds, had sincerely embraced Truth, prophets had the last laugh.

The fine lace collar on her raspberry-pink silk crepe de chine maternity dress would be a nice contrast in photos and in camera-pans, Kristen thought as she sat down with Tawi and Vaughn in the front row of the convention center's main hall packed with IOG members. The baby was not showing enough yet to warrant loose fitting clothes, but the dress was so pretty on her. Ever since Tawi had taken her to be color draped, Kristen had carried her SUMMER swatches and had been very strict about her wardrobe choices. Today's speech was sure to catapult Glenn to prominence beyond their denomination, and both their appearances would become very important.

Her husband was seated on the stage and she admired him in his alb, a white liturgical robe spun of flax similar to the style commonly worn by monks. The robe tied with a rope called a cincture, under which were placed the ends of his colorful new stole, a long scarf custom-woven by Navajos with the IOG symbol of ordination. The cleric garments had been gifts from their appreciative congregation. Glenn had wanted to wear his traditional black robe which he felt would be representative of unity and authority in the denomination, but Vaughn had asserted that Glenn should be a stand-out in every respect. Kristen realized that as usual, Vaughn was right.

Glenn noticed her attention and winked.

Kristen smiled. The decision to give up contact lenses had been smart. His new bifocals projected an image of benevolence and stability. Vaughn had assured her that the sophisticated video cameras in use would minimize any glare off Glenn's glasses.

The pulpit had been elevated at Vaughn's discreet suggestion, and Glenn felt the Power of God filling him as he waited next to the exuberant moderator currently introducing him.

This was BIG TIME, Glenn thought, touching briefly the remote microphone clipped into a fold of his robe. A microphone that he did not need during usual preaching, but this hall held eight thousand, quadruple the capacity of Sedona's sanctuary.

He could see people squeezed into the rows; just before he had left his seat to approach the pulpit, Vaughn had passed him a note saying that the staff was scrambling for folding chairs to accommodate the overflow standing in the lobby. Ushers had even patched auditorium microphones to outside speakers in the hall's central courtyard where additional people milled. In separate meeting rooms and behind the pulpit, wide video screens had also been erected to further enhance communication.

Glenn hoped the smile that kept curling the corners of his mouth would not betray the serious demeanor he was trying to project today. The power he exerted over these people almost made him giddy; they were a giant

amorphous mass to be manipulated and formed by him into whatever he desired.
    Applause.
    Whistles.
    Amens.
    Praises to God.
    A number of folks on their feet and he had not uttered a word!
    Savor the moment, Glenn, and suppress the smile of satisfaction. The best part is that it's just beginning.
    The moderator stepped down and the crowd's response continued. Glenn modestly waited for ten seconds, then raised the requisite glass of bottled water from the lectern and took a sip.
    Quiet settled over the room in anticipation.
    Glenn assimilated well the career lessons from Edgar Nicholson; from Vaughn Ulrich he had polished his external image. The hours spent cultivating high school debating skills, though, had been minor compared to the time he had dedicated in refining his present technique, and this afternoon he intended to use every speaking tactic at his command. But verbal manipulation of the masses had been an artifice worth working hard at to perfect; his efforts were paying off by way of a straight road to greatness and power.
    He had admitted to himself early on that he was not a profound thinker. Rather, he became an expert at stringing together like beads others' ideas and twirling them into a bright chain of captivating expressions that mesmerized a listener. Like a master fisherman tantalizing an elusive catch with fine bait, Glenn fed a congregation bits and pieces of information, philosophy and dogma before he finally reeled them into his net. His timing and phrasing combined with a sonorous voice that could launch a whisper across a jammed sanctuary; a whisper that conveyed he personally shared an intimate secret with each individual in the room. People caught their breath and listened, believing that he was speaking directly to their hearts and minds. This was a key strength; he raised verbal volume to emphasize a point, but he never ranted or raved. He soothed, he caressed, he admonished, he demanded gently. Always in control, yet in a caring way. The Reverend Doctor Glenn Chandler led his flock - and they followed.
    Glenn sipped again from the glass, replaced it on the lectern, and fixed his gaze on a grandmotherly-type halfway back, mid-center.
    "I am here today to offer you an apology for myself and the belief we embrace which is our only hope and salvation." Glenn felt a tinge of condescension as a questioning murmur rippled through the assembly. How inadequate was people's knowledge of words!

"My apology is not an expression of error or regret for some transgression. No!" His voice reverberated through the great hall and echoed back from the outside speakers. "My apology derives from the Greek word 'apologia', originally translated as 'justification' or 'defense.'"

Slowly he raised his open Bible in his left hand, the pages facing the audience. "I stand in the shadow of the great Christian apologists - Justin Martyr, Tatian, Theophilus - and tell you that the truth can be known only to humanity through the revelations of this Good Book, revelations which culminated in the birth of our Lord. My apology is for a faith which made our forefathers strong, girding them to conquer adversity and establish communities in a new land; my apology is for a faith in eternal values that has stood the test of time. My apology is for a faith that has come down through the ages and remains as bedrock for the institution we worship in today. Yet belief in this faith, this precious faith, is presently being forced to tread dangerous ground. *Belief that is threatened on all sides*, yet...yet it continues to stand strong. Our faith is one that will never be defeated, no matter what scurrilous attack is made!"

Glenn paused for the scattered 'amens' which he expected to ensue. After the last one, he placed his Bible back on the pulpit and spoke in a paternal tone.

"The Word warns us of false prophets who come in sheep's clothing, but inwardly are ravenous wolves. Oh, yes, there are those in the world who would tear and shred our faith as ruthlessly as a wolf would rip out the throat of a helpless lamb. They have the facility to combine truth with deception. With signs and wonders, these deceivers will dazzle the world so that even the followers of our Blessed Lord will be fooled and led astray." He raised his hands in supplication, then regarded the audience.

"You sit before me and I know the question in your minds. 'Glenn,' you ask, 'is there no way for True Believers to discern who these charlatans are? How do we protect ourselves and our loved ones from those who would destroy our eternal souls?' My brothers and my sisters, I tell you that God will not allow True Believers to be deceived. He will never abandon us if we trust in Him."

Glenn picked up his Bible and flipped the pages as if finding a verse. "Matthew tells us that we will know these evil ones by their fruits. He queries, 'Are grapes gathered from thorns, or figs from thistles?' He continues with the admonition that every sound tree bears good fruit, but the bad tree bears evil fruit."

He rested his Bible, grasped both sides of the pulpit and leaned forward, enunciating each word. "Matthew also states unequivocally that 'every tree that does not bear good fruit is cut down and thrown into the fire.'"

His gaze swept the audience.

"Time and again, we are told to separate the good from the bad, the wheat from the chaff. We, the True Believers, will be gathered like wheat into the granaries of heaven, but the chaff will be burned with unquenchable fire."

Glenn noted the body language. Some sat bolt upright straining for every word, others leaned forth as if doing so would get them in closer tune with his message. Those standing in the rear were mute and motionless. *The crowd was his!*

His words rose in volume, "Saint Thomas Aquinas stated that 'Evil is the absence of good.' Some uphold that evil is simply a counterpoint to good. Others would have us believe that evil in the world...is a necessary evil." Glenn waited for the light wave of laughter to ripple through the audience. "But is there any reason, any...possible...reason for evil to co-exist alongside the good? At the risk of sounding trite I can only utter a firm, simple, No! Increase that to a thousand times NO! The Bible warns that these evil angels will be cast into Gehenna, the Lake of Fire. The sole reward they shall receive for their profane labors will be eternal damnation."

His voice softened. "Our Master warned us, 'Do not think that I have come to bring peace on Earth; I have not come to bring peace, but a sword.' Why would the Prince of Peace use these words of conflict? Because, he cautioned, a man's foes will be those of his own household. Yes, if we allow it, the very sanctity of hearth and home will be violated by those we have loved and trusted.

"As I stand before you today a deep pain in my heart wrenches me to the very depths of my soul." Glenn bowed slightly and dabbed a finger at his left eye as if to catch a tear. "This very violation Our Savior warned against has touched me and my loved ones," he whispered.

Other than sniffling and restrained nose blowing, silence.

Glenn permitted it to last for his standard ten seconds.

"Yes," he said in a trembling tone, "Theone Jones, a false teacher, has ties to my family through my beloved wife, Kristen. Kristen tried to lead her sister back to the fold, but she resisted my wife's loving appeals. Theone Jones rejected the care lavished on her, and eventually retreated from the abode of the faithful. Long before we met, Kristen had no choice but to denounce the theology of her sister, Theone Jones, a separation that might have crushed her had it not been for her powerful faith." Glenn gazed compassionately at Kristen, then slammed his fist on the pulpit. "*No Grace? No Resurrection?*" He roared. "*...Re-in-car-na-tion?? God-dess Wor-ship? For-tune-tell-ing? Mag-ic spells equated with Prayer?* I ALSO repudiate the prevarications of Theone Jones who has strayed far from the path preordained for us by our Master! Theone Jones, the heretic, seeks to lead astray God's Select!"

Affirmations of faith resounded and applause interrupted Glenn. He smiled gratefully to convey appreciation to the audience for their show of support in this terrible circumstance afflicting his family.

As if regenerated, he said in a clear, strong voice, "Great writers often have keen insights into the human condition. Mark Twain commented that 'one of the striking differences between a cat and a lie is that a cat has only nine lives.' A cat is limited by its nine lives, but a lie endures, feeding on deception and duplicity. A lie grows in strength, breeding new generations of deceit and falsehood. Finally, it metamorphoses into a beast like the multi-headed Hydra in mythology. Destroy one lie and two grow back in its place.

"Now, I am going to make a request of the media. No, a plea to those who hold the power to cultivate the misrepresentations and wayward ministry of Theone Jones by placing this false teacher before the public eye. I beg you to look beneath the surface and ask some hard, serious questions. As purveyors of the news, you are responsible for the public trust and as such indebted to search for the true person who lies behind the public persona of Theone Jones. The indiscriminate coverage and instant fame that has been accorded her by those who pander to the baser instincts of society must be tempered by responsible reporting and a search, however difficult, for the truth."

Glenn took a deep breath and exhaled slowly. "Lies of monumental proportions such as Theone Jones speaks threaten the very fabric of our social and religious institutions. They must be stopped at their source before they are allowed to infect our moral fiber with their insidious poison.

"Oh, but you say, Theone Jones is unassuming. She appears so harmless in her bare feet and jeans. Surely, she is just a fad like the rest of this New Age business." He shook his finger at them. "Don't think that lies will be presented to you by a malevolent being horrible beyond description. No, no, My Dear Friends, Satan has many names - Lucifer, Beelzebub, Dragon, serpent and Prince of Darkness - but the most important one for us to remember is that he has also been called the Angel of Light. Yes, Paul tells us in II Corinthians that Satan disguises himself as an Angel of Light. Satan, who with his minions, manipulates humanity by telling lies that delude people into believing they are truth. In the Old Testament, Isaiah tells us of the Day Star, the son of Dawn fallen from heaven. It was the Day Star who dared to ascend to heaven, above the stars of God to shine the brightest. He who would make himself like the Most High."

Glenn stopped to scrutinize faces, looking left to right. "Remember the con man isn't the one who beats you into submission and then takes your possessions. The ultimate con man or in the case of Theone Jones, con woman, is the one who makes you believe that she only has your best interests at heart, yet in the end you find your soul is forfeit to Satan for eternity.

"Understand that we war not against flesh and blood, but against principalities and powers and the spiritual hosts of wickedness. Theone Jones in her delusion is part of this panorama that seeks to engulf True Believers in a deviant and wayward lifestyle diametrically opposed to what the Word teaches. She is a storm that assails our faith.

"When the disciples were caught in a storm while fishing on the Sea of Galilee, Jesus came to them walking on the troubled waters. Peter asked Jesus to command him to come. But once on the water, the storm took Peter's focus away from Jesus, and he began to sink into the depths. *Peter let the winds and rain and raging waters divert his attention from the Only One Who could offer him safe refuge.* Only by refocusing on Jesus was Peter saved from the turbulent sea."

Glenn nodded with commiseration. "So it is with the True Believer. The storms of life rage around the faithful. Our attention is sidetracked by daily cares - the job, the children, troubles at home, plus a myriad of smaller distractions until our very being cries for release, for peace, for a quiet resting place. Alcohol, drugs, sexual promiscuity, New Age cults - we live in quick fix times and too many of us settle for these easy ways out.

"New Age cults are deceitful because they seem to offer a simple, yet caring answer to our problems. Come to us, they say. We will take care of you. We will give you a rock for peace, understanding with a charm and a sense of belonging in some witch's circle. Sadly, their answers for today's problems come at a horrible price. Channeling, spirit guides, spiritualism, the occult, psychic phenomena..." Glenn chuckled disapprovingly. "The Age of Aquarius is not dead, it has only been recycled by the false prophets and renamed the New Age. It's true, the adage, that there is nothing new under the sun. I reiterate what Matthew wrote two millennia ago, 'For false Christs and false prophets will arise and show great signs and wonders, so as to lead astray, if possible, even the elect.'"

He raised his closed Bible over his head. "I exhort in the name of this Book against the Theone Jones of the world who seek to take our focus off the only One who can deliver and save us from the wickedness and profanities teeming around us! Never, NEVER lose sight of the fact that the center of our deliverance is the Lord! NEVER take your eyes or mind off the Word, for this is THE ONLY path to salvation."

Glenn smiled at the congregation. "I say to you, put on the armor of God to withstand the Evil One. Take the shield of faith and the sword of the Spirit and you shall persevere. Then we shall sing with the Psalmist, 'The

Lord is my strength and my shield; in him my heart trusts...' Let us 'fight the good fight of the faithful' so that we can say with the Saints, 'I have fought the good fight, I have finished the race.'"

Raising both hands above his head as if to enclose the congregation in benediction, Glenn's voice rose in volume and resonated with rich appeal. "We have been promised that 'In My Father's house are many rooms'; the Faithful shall have a place prepared for them. Be assured that one day, after our life here is finished, we, as True Believers, shall rest and rejoice forever with Jesus Christ Our Lord."

Dropping his arms, Glenn lowered his head and bade, "Let us pray."

On the perimeter of the auditorium, two men, in addition to the official church recorders, checked their equipment. Each had videotaped Glenn from different areas of the hall so that a full perspective could be analyzed. As they reviewed their work, a third man waited to approach Vaughn Ulrich, understood to be Chandler's proxy. This man represented a group that shared the concerns expressed so eloquently by Dr. Chandler, and they had a proposition for the IOG pastor.

↩

From Alaska, Theone and her companions drove east across Canada, then south from Banff into Montana to trace the path of the Great Divide, the continental watershed where water falling to the east flowed to the Atlantic Ocean, and water falling west went to the Pacific Ocean. They sojourned for a while in the meadows of the alpine region to savor summer's vibrant flash of wildflowers. In barren, stony areas, Mike used a telephoto lens to video-tape the mountain goats and bighorn sheep charmed by Theone, who trod the crags and ledges as nimbly as they did.

Bobby's hopes to get Theone alone for a lengthy period were frustrated. His stamina was limited in the high altitude; he could not keep up with her on her jaunts. No one else could, either, but he yearned to prove to her his worthiness. (Because he suffered no symptoms, he had rationalized that being constantly in Theone's healing presence, eating Mag's healthy meals, and the abundance of clean air had cured his illness. This was not an issue critical to a relationship.) At night, even with a flashlight for security, he felt too afraid of the vast darkness to venture far in trying to locate her tent, and he distrusted the Moon as a reliable means to light his path. Alone in his van, then, he mulled how he could awaken her sexually if they were always surrounded by the others. Could Theone not feel his vibes? Jasper and Pilar had noticed and given him more than one quizzical look. She would not reject him because he possessed no special talents like the others, would she? He genuinely tried to make himself useful and they all, particularly Theone, expressed appreciation. If they would just stop somewhere long enough to expand their personal space. Bobby was sure he could persuade Theone to accept him as a lover.

Below the timberline, the group meandered through national forests of spruce and fir - Flathead, Lolo, Deerlodge, Beaverhead, Targhee, Teton, Shoshone - and Mike chronicled hours of footage of the wildlife Theone attracted the moment she stepped away from their vehicle. Moose, elk, antelope, both whitetail and mule deer, became a routine occurrence as did the appearance of hawks, ravens, eagles and other birds like jays, warblers and grouse. Periodically, they saw red fox, marmot and mice. Less common were the lynx and mountain lions; they also sighted a few gray wolves along with a cougar and several bobcats. Rarely frightened for Theone, even Mike gave pause and failed to push the record button when she had walked alone to a stream edge to acknowledge a beaver family and the first grizzly showed. Six feet away from her, it reared and roared, the sound petrifying the others, but within seconds, the bear plunged to its knees in obeisance. Regardless of how often they encountered grizzlies, Mag always trembled afterwards.

On purpose, they circumvented the major recreational areas, including Yellowstone. Tourism was at its summer peak, and now the park service also had to cope with the extra number of people roaming the preserves, seeking Theone. Searchers figured she traveled in the vicinity because she was scheduled to speak mid-August at Seedskadee NWR located on the Green River in southwestern Wyoming.

Golden eagles and Red-tailed hawks overshadowed the sky during her appearance in a sagebrush-covered field at Seedskadee, astounding a restrained, but crushing crowd. Anxious officials closed entries, but people tramped into the sanctuary any way they could find, which unfortunately included fragile areas. Jasper speculated that Theone elicited a lot of mental cooperation that afternoon to avoid confrontations between upset refuge management and the spectators.

After her speech, Theone requested that they go directly east into the Great Divide Basin. In the Basin, no trees grew and it was a place few people visited. Theone chose to linger. Mike rationed their water supply and he serviced their generator daily to insure power. Her five companions expressed concern among themselves, and the endless wind and resulting dust especially bothered Pilar, but the bleak, forbidding territory appealed to Theone whose mood had been pensive since speaking at Seedskadee.

Besides coyotes and antelope, roaming mustangs inhabited the Basin. The wild horses seemed to cheer her and curiously, she took to riding bareback on one lucky pinto. As Mike watched her race across the dry, scrubby land in the midst of a devoted herd, he wished her image would record. Bobby wished he knew how to ride a horse. He'd begun to think that his lack of skill at anything important was the reason she eluded his advances.

Finally Theone indicated her readiness to proceed again, and as they crossed the Colorado state line, she spoke to Jasper who sat next to her in the backseat of the Suburban. Mike was at the wheel. Mag and Pilar had chosen to ride in the Airstream while Bobby followed behind them in his van.

"It's time to reassess my approach," she said, "I believe damage is being done to the eco-system by all these people trying to hear me."

"You could eliminate the delicate locations," Jasper suggested. "Parks are designed for visitors whereas refuges aren't as popular so they're not as environmentally sturdy."

"But refuges are such strong evidence of Peace! They are places that humans have had to recognize *consciously* and preserve for the lesser creatures who inhabit Earth."

Her heavy-heartedness was unusual, and Jasper's tone was conciliatory. "Yes, those who believe The Message know and respect that, but the souls who have yet to experience you don't understand. They are typically human. They are often 'self first' motivated."

Theone leaned forward and rested her arms on the front seat. "Mike, do you think you can drive straight through to Arela's?"

Being with Arela again was upper most on his mind, but quite a distance separated them. "We're in the midst of winding down the Rockies and getting to Denver will be a stretch."

"She'll be at her home on Lake Latimer. When we stop for gas, you can call to tell her to expect us."

Mike grinned at Theone in the rear view mirror. "That's half the miles! We can be there this evening."

Theone smiled at him and then at Jasper. "There are going to be changes," she said.

The men waited for her to elaborate, but she settled in her seat and concentrated her attention on the rugged beauty outside her open window.

Jasper got an inkling that part of the change included a man and started to worry that it might involve Bobby. Jasper was sexually attracted to him, which Bobby, consciously or not, reciprocated. It indicated to Jasper that the younger man had gay tendencies and Theone in her innocence might be mistaking Bobby's sensuality as hetero. He did not question Theone on her decisions, but the one to introduce Bobby into their group might yet result in dissension. Jasper could not shake his dire feeling about it.

∽

Just before daylight, Arela joined Theone who had slept down by the lake, but now sat on the house's deck in a redwood chair, watching the dreary sky.

"When I looked at properties, I considered the view," Arela said as she sat on a bench by her mentor. "Did I want the sunrise or the sunset? The east view won because I realized how renewed the rising sun has always made me feel. No matter how bad the past, optimism and hope arrived with each dawn and by being reminded of it, I could face anything."

"Your soul is a joy to Our Deity," Theone said, "and it is why you are the one to take my place in public."

"I can't even begin to deliver the Message in any manner close to yours! I understand why you wish to stop speaking, because faith is getting too focused on you, but you are...The Messenger. How can you retire?"

Theone took Arela's left hand in her right one. "Your previous journeys have culminated in your wonderful gift for teaching. Combined with your tremendously advanced soul, you will be more successful than I could ever be. You can go to other continents and share what I cannot." She smiled at Arela. "Mike is the dearest friend anyone can ask for and as partners you will convey the full essence of Our Deity."

Arela blushed. "I never believed I would find someone like Mike. It's so fast, but so...natural. I really do love him."

Theone laughed gently. "Mag will go with you, too. Don't let her quiet, compliant nature fool you. Her soul is as elevated as yours, and she will be a source of strength. They will be resistant, but Jasper and Pilar will return to San Antonio to handle the secular end of things. We get so much money thrust at us on the road and tons more at Jasper's address which Rosita's daughter, Isabelita, has gotten expert at forwarding to us. She has been a treasure assisting Pilar, who deals with a lot of the financial matters by modem and mobile phone, but it has still been difficult with our transient lifestyle."

"Except for this house, which I feel I should keep for a haven, and a certain sum to maintain it, I wish to give Pilar my assets, too, the bulk of which will be for underprivileged youth. Surely, she'll have an idea for it?"

"Oh, yes," Theone replied. "It's her gift and her soul's assurance of progress. Through an angel Pilar has her own unique connection with Our Deity, and she has an unerring sense of which envelope contains a sincere request and what causes are genuine in their need for support."

"And Bobby? His romantic feelings are transparent. Are you and Bobby meant..."

Theone smiled sadly. She could offer Truth and set an example with her own behavior, but she had not been bestowed with her powers to sway human conditions unless The Deity chose for her to do so. In Bobby's case, The Deity had repeatedly made clear her passive role. "He will soon follow another path, Arela."

"Then where do you fit in? You can't just stop! You can't retreat into a solitary existence!"

"I won't be alone again, but I will limit myself to where I feel I am most effective, spontaneous meetings and touching individual souls."

Arela tried another gambit. "I truly believe I am meant to spread The Message, but I just found you. I wish to be near you for a while, to love you and learn from you..."

Theone nodded. "It's part of the plan. Our friends are weary from almost a year on the road and conveying knowledge to you is important. We'll settle here for a period." She glanced at the dull horizon where nimbus clouds concealed the sunrise. Lightning striped the gloom, setting off a rumble, and she raised her face skyward.

"I acknowledge My Deity and give thanks for Your Presence," she intoned, "as always I am of Your Will, not my own. I am grateful for the companions You have chosen for me and pray that their choices in this life's journey will steadfastly advance their souls towards Peace."

Arela felt The Deity's Tranquil Presence, a 'presence' that she recognized as the same that had touched her the first time she met Theone. Aspire to this mental serenity and live each day with actions to advance your soul, she thought, because on your last successful journey the Ultimate Peace awaited. Arela hoped to be ready this time around, but first she had a mission to tell others about Peace and to encourage them to seek the right path.

A steady rain started falling, but neither of them noticed. Lightning flashed and more thunder blasted the atmosphere, but they continued to meditate, their hands still clasped.

Inside the closed sliding doors facing the deck, Bobby jealously observed them, aching to hear their intimate conversation. What was Theone doing? Arela was supposed to be with Mike! Had she set the couple up just to cut in on the guy's time as a lesson in authority? This display with Arela confused him. His experience in these matters gave him the distinct impression that Theone was straight.

Bobby shelved his seduction plan. A nocturnal visit to Theone's tent erected by the lake might not be a good idea until he had a better handle on the situation.

Vaughn Ulrich did not like San Francisco, anymore. He objected to homosexuals and the once charming city now had a blatant crop of such inhabitants. The last time he and Tawi had visited the waterfront, used condoms littered the walkway among the strolling gays, and they had witnessed two women kissing at a scenic overlook by the Golden Gate Bridge. But it was here or New York City, which had been the first choice. The event had to happen in cellar-linked Victorian row houses or brownstones on an anonymous street in a cosmopolitan arena where the common destination of powerful men would not trigger curiosity. Activities had to occur in a location that would not draw attention to itself, yet would be easily accessible. New York City, however, was in the midst of one of their infernal strikes and besides the inconvenience, media focus was greater than average. Vaughn appreciated that those who convened were opposed to publicity and this meeting was being held in absolute secrecy. It was not his interest to be at the forefront, either; his passion was power, and he enjoyed knowing that he was the key person invited to this assembly. He controlled the desired commodity, Glenn Chandler; thus, he held the winning hand to run things.

Four rectangular walnut dining tables extended thirty-two feet from the formal dining room through open French doors into the front parlor of the house being used for the main meeting. Chandeliers and glass shade floor lamps in Art Nouveau styles provided light because the mauve damask curtains in both rooms were kept drawn.

Situated mid-center, Vaughn glanced around the span of tables, wondering who would moderate this coalition of influential, but public unknowns. Christian, Jewish, Islamic - in front of each man was an identity card as to creed or ecclesiastical affiliation, but no personal name or title. Interpreters and the domestic staff were also men. Vaughn supported this gender imbalance - no women to muddy issues.

Across from him, a distinguished chap with peppered white hair and in a custom tailored navy suit stood up. A mainline Christian fundamentalist, Vaughn noted approvingly.

"In the equitable drawing of lots," the speaker said, "my denomination received the distasteful chore of steering this gathering. It by no means reflects our desire for leadership or our consent to lead on any action determined by this group. We, like you, believed that an urgent need had developed to discuss current situations and wished to establish a unity of purpose for the future."

Heads nodded amid murmurs of assent.

"We've had plenty of time in the last year to stew in our own juices and I am not going to beat around the bush. We may differ on our approach, but each of our religions has in commonality that God/Yahweh/Allah is monolithic and supreme. He rules us and we yield to Him as Our Master. Therefore, we are not here to debate theology, but to establish cohesion and find a viable plan of action." He sipped from a crystal goblet and waved his hand. "In addition to delegates of every major...concern, joining us is a representative of the IOG pastor who has made headlines in recent months courageously refuting Theone Jones and quite admirably, upholding Christianity. At this time, I would like to draw your attention to the large screen televisions at either ends of our table. A videotape of Dr. Glenn Chandler has been prepared for your viewing."

The lights dimmed.

Vaughn grinned in the darkness. From liberal to conservative, whatever spectrum of faith, each man present had a worried, but hopeful expression. Oh, there had been grumbles from assorted pulpits, but not one other religious leader had summoned the guts to articulate what Glenn preached and the important part, with such a surge in following. Glenn was a shoe-in as the head of this premiere body which would support the policies Vaughn deemed crucial for victory over the Satanic influence of Theone Jones.

As Vaughn had sensed would happen, the true champions of faith, the fundamentalist Christians, had no qualms about what had to be done and dominated the meeting's direction. Liberal and moderate Christian protests against the group's decisions were feeble and easily quelled; they wanted desperately for Theone Jones to be stopped, but neither did they wish to appear intolerant or condemning. Her ministry had drained most their mainline denominations, effectively polarizing traditional, conservative believers and those open to change - those in their membership who challenged the rationale for the continued restrictions against women and homosexuals.

Muslims, a minority, abstained from voting on motions which had no influence on their doctrines. Action taken by the group would be in the name of Christianity, yet the issue would be resolved to Islamic satisfaction.

The Jewish contingency, too, refrained from voicing any opinion other than to go on record as stressing for reason, but the decisions pleased them. They had suffered the rap for two thousand years; now this Theone Jones was going to be assaulted with the clout of Christian religious militancy.

CHAPTER FOURTEEN

Gabriel a.k.a. Spider
   As a youth Spider often wondered what had attracted his parents. Not something that had kept them together - they'd divorced before he was five. Both were workaholics but in different fields. Adriano Giovetti, his fiery Italian father, owned a successful wholesale tomato brokerage in Chelsea, north of Boston. Kezia 'Kizzie' Rosen Giovetti, his sharp-witted Jewish mother, was a Miami condominium developer's highest grossing sales associate.
   Early on, Spider eliminated personality type as the basis for their attraction. Tall, wiry Adriano had married a second, lasting time to a placid redhead with freckled white skin and few brains. Loud, abrasive Kizzie had dark hair, dark eyes and tanned, oily skin. She dated men for the size of their bankroll; men who were usually insincere creeps. Spider smarted off to her on one occasion that there was a connection between a big, flashy wad of bucks and a small dick. Kizzie had clubbed him with a metal vacuum cleaner pipe.
   Both Adriano's wife and Kizzie had in common heavy bodies with big tits. Would you marry a woman because of her tits? Had Adriano and Kizzie's ardent temperaments resulted in spectacular sex that they had mistaken for love? How had they met to begin with? Nobody offered any explanations and Spider did not ask any questions. He did not even find out the reason for his nickname until he was in puberty and on the annual visit to his father. Adriano inquired if the girls liked his long, lean body, saying that Spider had crawled before he could sit up and then had bounced on all fours before he got his balance, reminding his father of a gangling spider. Adriano bet Spider would have plenty of chances of doing the 'all fours' on the girls because he was going to be a dark, handsome devil. Just like his old man. Spider laughed. The truth was he looked better. His eyes were a trifle close set; his nose had a bit of the Rosen hook, and his upper lip was thin, but the flaws gave interest to otherwise classic features. He'd gotten the best from his parents' diverse gene pool.
   Gabriel 'Spider' Giovetti was also a bona fide genius, but an indifferent student and a terror. Adriano showed sporadic interest in him. Kizzie did not have the time or patience to cope with him. Spider desperately sought attention and acted outrageously to get it. His cussing in Italian was legendary at his grade schools. Unfortunately, his teachers had neither the time nor the resources to deal with him, either.
   At first, professionals diagnosed him as hyperactive with Attention Deficiency Disorder, then later as manic-depressive. One Ph.D. advised Kizzie that either Spider would grow up to be President or a master felon.

Another expert said Spider had the virtues of a psychotic. He was polite and considerate, but conceivably he could kill someone without remorse. Yet Spider was not cruel or belligerent unless provoked, and then he made sure that he was never in a position to be hurt. For the same reason, he disliked contact sports and refused to participate in gym. By 9th grade, he had been expelled from every school in the district where his mother lived.

Despairing, Kizzie requested that the state of Florida intervene. Spider was placed in an experimental school for misfits diagnosed as having potential criminal profiles. He was given drugs to level his moods and therapy to straighten his head. He excelled at computer games, but only because in the school's underground, a sophisticated gambling structure flourished. He stashed a sizable chunk of money.

At eighteen, Spider graduated from the state institution and enlisted in the Navy. He had read an article about SEALS and decided that he belonged in the elite commando group. He passed the rigorous physical exams, but being a SEAL required too much mental regimentation, and he failed the final psychological tests.

For the most part, Spider behaved while in the service; the special school had succeeded in tempering his behavior. In three years, then, he never landed in the brig, but he stayed in ship maintenance at seaman's rank, and on discharge had little to show for his military stint other than a black widow spider tattooed on his left forearm and a penchant for toning his muscles.

At the time of his discharge, Spider was stationed with the First Fleet at Norfolk, Virginia. Neither selling tomatoes nor condominiums appealed to him so he did not bother to visit Boston or Miami. He had trained for the SEAL program on Coronado Island off San Diego and had grown up in a balmy climate. Spider bought a chrome-laden, black Electra Glide Classic Harley-Davidson motorcycle and rode out to Southern California.

Menial jobs abounded on the Coast, and he worked as a grease jockey at a gas station or as a laborer on a new home site or as a janitor until he grew restless and moved on to the next shabby motel cottage. He got along with people, but did not care about cultivating friendships. Drugs turned him off. He'd had enough of legally administered chemicals in his teens, but for a period he hung around biker bars, drinking too much whiskey and smoking pretty heavily. He was also inspired to let his luxuriant hair grow out to a length easily kept in a pony tail.

His vanity was his body. He joined a fitness chain and worked out daily at the local club where he found girls in plentiful supply, too. As predicted by Adriano, women were highly attracted to Spider and he took advantage of them. Not that he was cruel, but he wasn't kind, either. Self-indulgent and vaguely unhappy, he figured that life was okay as long as he got laid regularly and could afford steak for dinner. He did not welcome any deep thoughts...until recently.

Recently, he had been channel surfing and pausing on the Christian evangelism stations. He ascribed it to latent curiosity because despite his lack of interest in formal education, his intellect quested for stimulation. (Spider deduced that he tended to watch PBS programs for the same reason.)

Religion had been an issue in his father's household, and Spider's three half-siblings were raised Roman Catholic. His step-mother gave it her best shot with Spider, but his visits were too seldom and his exposure too erratic to have much impact. He memorized the rituals and paid attention during Mass to avoid a hassle with his father, but the question of Spider taking formal instruction never arose. Kizzie's family, proprietors of two gift shops in Miami, acknowledged their heritage, but they were too materialistic to take seriously a religion that required a person not to work from sundown to sundown over a Saturday, the best day for retail sales. The question of Spider taking formal instruction in Judaism never arose, either.

Initially, the smarmy attitude and pretentious appearance of the TV evangelists fascinated Spider. How could even the most naive viewer be persuaded that these hokey characters in pompadours were worthy recipients of financial support? Then, he actually started listening to the gushy, fervent testimonials, judging the majority of the speakers as failed show biz types who had found an audience. Yet he also conceded that there might be some truth in this Jesus stuff to have prevailed for two thousand years, but the constant angle for money bugged him. Did a belief in the Cross come with a monetary price tag? According to the sermons, Grace was free for the asking, but these preachers twisted the message to their own advantage - support their ministry so that others would hear The Word and be saved, too. Spider translated the pleas as less a concern for a listener's soul than these preachers' need for air-time to feed their egos and to keep them clothed in six hundred dollar suits. He toyed with the idea of reading the Bible (every place he lived had a Gideon's version), to find out if he had missed some vital part of the real story, but it would take mental effort. He approached life on cruise control and it was hard to break the habit.

At twenty-six, Spider Giovetti was a misfit with enormous spiritual potential, but zero motivation to develop it until he witnessed Theone Jones.

⁓

"TV? Later, we can watch it later," Spider cajoled as he stroked the girl's knee. He had not dropped by her apartment to gawk at some inane sitcom! She had come on to him outside the weight room yesterday with all kinds of promises in her big violet eyes and had readily given him her address like she expected immediate action.

Nervous, Darci twisted out of his reach. He was overpowering just like she'd heard about the super sexy Spider with his buff body and fine features. She'd been dying to connect with the hunk and yesterday, she had been doing her thigh routine on a stair-stepper at the club when word went around that he was lifting weights with his shirt off. The instant she had seen him, she'd been smitten. From the blue-black stubble on his chiseled jaw to the silky black mat on his hard chest soaked with perspiration, sulky Spider represented Darci's ideal of the totally fabulous man. The totally fabulous man, though, should have some cool. Sex was great, but she didn't just do it without preliminaries, and she really wanted to watch this program. Everybody she knew was going to watch it.

"I didn't think you'd just, you know, appear," she said. "Like usually, it's good to call first."

"So I was supposed to look up the number in the directory?" Spider slouched lower on the couch and pulled out a cigarette package stuck in a rolled sleeve of his tee shirt. They were over eighteen; he *always* used a condom, whether requested to or not. No conception. No disease. NO complications. Just a nice fuck. This babe had clearly wanted one, so why the games now?

"Well, you asked where I lived, not my phone number," Darci retorted. "We work out at the same club. Like, I thought we'd see each other." She clicked the channel changer. "Uh, there's a live broadcast tonight of that Theone Jones. Everybody is gonna watch it because she isn't scheduled anywhere else so like she might be taking a long vacation. She just talks minutes, not like a sermon or anything, and we can do something after it..."

The screen flashed the station affiliation, and a prominent national newscaster announced that he was reporting from Grand Lake, Colorado, in the heart of the Rockies, where Theone Jones would be speaking momentarily. Behind him a huge crowd milled before the lake's edge. A phenomenal number of birds had flocked, and the late day sun cast a shadow-show on the purple-black mountains soaring beyond the water. The newscaster touched his ear-microphone and remarked that state troopers had just closed off vehicle access into town, but people on foot still pressed forward to the area.

"Isn't that a fabulous place," Darci said. "I mean we have the ocean and it's so great, but like, doesn't that make you want to go there?"

Pissed off, Spider got up from the couch. "You have any beer?"

Darci nodded. It was her roommate's, but no biggie. She'd pay her back. After the speech Darci figured they could order a pizza, maybe, or go out. "Help yourself," she said, "and there's an ashtray on the counter."

His expression bored, Spider popped the can, lit a cigarette and settled back on the couch. He'd heard of Theone Jones on the news and dismissed her as just another evangelist. But for sex as a reward, he could endure an hour of the woman's blab.

"Each of you possesses a soul which is on a spiritual journey and whether your soul advances is up to you. To help you, Our Deity throughout time has given you guidelines to make progress. How humans with their free will have interpreted the guidelines is why Our Deity has found it necessary to send Messengers again and again..."

Spider stared at the TV and grabbed the remote from Darci to turn up the volume.

She smiled at him, but he was riveted on Theone, his cigarette forgotten.

"...this is a Glimpse of Peace." Theone held up her arms and turned from her audience to gesture at the spectacular backdrop now aglow from a brilliant sunset. She was silent, allowing the crowd to absorb the beauty, then she smiled. "Each of you has a soul on a journey. How fast you reach Peace depends on you."

Theone stepped past the camcorders hogging the front row and into the people. Continuing to smile, she made eye contact with specific individuals, occasionally pausing to touch their hands as she walked alone through the hushed crowd separating in her path. The camera trailed her to a Ford Bronco parked on the street where several followers apparently waited to drive her away.

Transformed by the woman's simple words and her magnetism, Spider muttered, "Where's the applause? They should be applauding. She's... she's..."

"I have this friend who is really, really into Theone Jones. Ashley says Theone doesn't like applause because she is not speaking to entertain us, but to enlighten us. Theone Jones is a Messenger. Like, maybe Ashley is on to something?"

Spider stood up. "Theone Jones is speaking the truth," he said quietly. "For the first time in my life, I've actually witnessed the truth." He smiled at Darci. "Go find a guy who'll respect you and love you."

Startled at the change in his attitude, Darci replied, "Like I guess you're not a candidate."

"Our souls have gotten all they can from each other. Now, I need to get on with my journey."

As Darci picked up the half full beer can and dumped it in the sink, she thought with disappointment that Spider was the sexiest guy she'd met in ages. He'd been in such a hurry to split that he'd even left a full pack of cigarettes on the coffee table! Like it was really too bad their souls couldn't do some of the journey together.

Spider went directly to his latest dive and packed his worn Navy duffle bag. By nine thirty, he had passed San Bernardino and angled north on Interstate 15. 15 would connect him with 50 in Utah which turned into 70. 70 eventually tied to Route 40 that forked into 34. Grand Lake, Colorado, was on 34 in the middle of two national forests. It occurred to him that she may have moved on, but the possibility did not matter. Theone Jones had nothing in common with airwave evangelists; she had to be someone genuine to have touched him so profoundly. He'd find her. His soul was at stake.

In Grand Lake Spider rented a motel room to clean up with an intent, then, to check out the tourist town for information. A casual query to the motel clerk, a believer who referred to Theone respectfully as The Messenger of Love, narrowed his search. She was still staying somewhere on nearby Lake Latimer, but Spider would stand a better chance of seeing her if she made another public address because with cooperation from the neighbors, the location was being kept secret. Oddly to Spider, the clerk added, but nobody would bother her, anyway.

Spider was glad supporters were keeping her safe. Certain sickos got off on attacking celebrities. Yet he felt confident that he could find out where she was and get past the security.

In Arela's kitchen, Theone, Mag and Pilar stood by the counter drinking coffee. To the counter's other side, Arela knelt on the floor of the living room, packing a log with newspaper to start a fire. Jasper sat on one of the couches sorting road maps.

The kitchen door opened and Mike appeared. "You order a pizza?" He inquired. "There's a guy on a motorcycle at the entrance to the community who claims someone here ordered a pizza."

"If we had, we'd have told you," Pilar teased, "because we know how picky you are about toppings!"

Mike shrugged good naturedly. "I figured you would, but you know how it is with Chinese food. Arela's Szcheswan feast at dinnertime was great, but an hour later..." He winked at Arela, and she stuck her tongue out at him. Their attraction had bonded into romance, much to the delight of Pilar and Mag.

"What's on the pizza?" Theone suddenly asked.

"I can find out," Mike said and disappeared. He returned in a few minutes. "The guy says 'half green pepper, onions and half pepperoni, extra cheese.' Imagine the amount of fat and the nitrates! I'll just go back to cleaning the Airstream, thank you very much, but I'll send in Bobby. He goes for that junk stuff."

Theone's smile did not reach her eyes. "Have the man deliver it around on the deck," she said, "and make certain that Bobby comes inside immediately." Her expression remained enigmatic.

Mag and Pilar exchanged mystified looks, but they made no comment. Theone always had reasons for her behavior even if it seemed peculiar.

Spider swallowed nervously as he climbed the redwood steps to the deck. Now that he was here, his bravado had faltered. They knew...she knew...it was a ploy. A flimsy ploy. And why the hell did she not have better security? What if he had a bomb or a weapon to assassinate her? Other than a cursory inspection of the pizza, nobody had frisked him. His leather jacket had deep pockets! The guy who had escorted him here had acted unconcerned and had veered off, leaving Spider to announce himself.

The sliding door opened, and a balding man of the same height as Spider greeted him pleasantly. "We aren't aware that we ordered this, but we'll take it. Chinese food for dinner at five o'clock, you see."

At the fireplace, Arela looked up and mugged. Jasper chuckled mischievously.

Spider's eyes darted around the living room, dismissing the Eurasian guy inspecting him with a faint hostility. Where was she? He fixed on the Formica counter which split this area from the kitchen. A rather frowzy blonde, an attractive, heavy-boned Hispanic...Theone Jones had her back to him. He walked into the kitchen.

Pilar was closest to him and bent to the floor for her voluminous purse. "Well, the pizza man. How much do we owe you?"

Spider had his eyes on Theone's tumble of hair. He could not see her face! "Uh, the pizza is a gift," he mumbled and handed the box to Pilar.

Theone turned to regard him. "Thank you," she said and smiled.

Overwhelmed, Spider fell on his knees and bowed his head.

Theone gently lifted his chin. "Our journeys are at different levels, but we are equals, you and I. Supplication is only for Our Deity."

He opened his eyes to stare into hers. Spider was too agitated to see the affection and humor in them. "I am Gabriel Giovetti," he said stiffly. "I will do anything you need done to free you to spread The Message. And I want to give you all the money I've...not spent. It's a lot."

His soul poised on the brink of a great leap! But she had expected such. Theone turned his face to see his right profile, then asked, "Are you called Gabriel?"

"Spider," he said as if ashamed. "I have a nickname, Spider, but I am... renewed. I wish to be called...Gabriel now."

"Oh, but I like spiders. Their remarkable webs are Glimpses of Peace. Have you ever studied a spider's web?"

"No."

"I'll show you."

He blinked, to filled with emotion to speak.

"Stand, Gabriel, known also as Spider," Theone instructed.

He got to his feet, embarrassed by his physical reaction to this...saint. She turned him on! The only woman for whom he felt respect and honor and he had the hots for her! How inappropriate...how disgusting he was...

Theone gripped his shoulders and kissed his cheek.

Her friends were astonished. Theone did not kiss, but Spider didn't know that. He embraced her.

Mag's mouth dropped. Theone took hands to gauge souls, but *nobody ever* touched her. This stranger had a lot of gall, but Theone had encouraged it!

Bobby was outraged. She had never kissed him! She had never shown him even an ounce of the affection that this total stranger was receiving!

Spider's image was unmistakable; Theone hugged him in return. Besides, as anticipated when the right man appeared, The Deity would smile with approval on both of them. She could feel Their Pleased Presence.

Abruptly, Spider released her and took several steps backwards. "I'm sorry," he mumbled.

"Pizza, folks," Jasper said cheerfully. "Pilar, open the box, eh?"

Bobby rushed past Jasper on his way to the kitchen, fumbled with the deck's sliding door, and shot outside. Jasper, Mag and Pilar's faces registered little surprise. Unlike theirs, Bobby's love for Theone had surpassed friendship, but she had shown no return interest. Jasper immediately began to worry about the ramifications of this new man.

Theone gazed pensively at Bobby's exit, then addressed Spider whose woebegone expression almost made her laugh. "I've never been on a motorcycle," she said. "Would you take me for a ride into Grand Lake? I'd like some frozen yogurt instead of pizza."

He nodded.

"Theone, motorcycles are dangerous," Pilar clucked. "It's night. The combination is..."

"...is just right," Theone finished.

"Wearing a helmet is optional in Colorado, but you do have one and agree it's the only safe way to ride?" Arela said to Spider.

"She can wear mine."

"You have two snowmobile helmets, Arela," Theone said. "May I borrow one so that we are both safe?"

Arela shrugged at Pilar and introduced herself to Spider. Apparently, they were adding a member to their group, and the others followed Arela's lead.

It was September 23rd and temperatures this late in the month never got higher than the 60's; the nights cooled significantly. Spider was concerned that Theone would be warm enough in just a windbreaker.

"Don't you have a heavier coat?" He inquired. "The wind chill gets you pretty cold."

Strapping on a red helmet, she smiled at him. "I'll be comfortable."

That smile of hers captured him and he wasn't feeling it in a spiritual sense...no! Not with Theone. He shouldn't feel that way.

Her remark about being comfortable wasn't plausible, yet he believed her. Spider realized he'd believe anything she said which also meant that it did not bother him to relinquish control over his destiny.

As she settled behind him on the passenger's perch, he considered that Theone was his destiny. Just like everybody else who followed her. He was not special. He was not...worthy to be anything more to her...but she had not placed her hands chastely on his waist. She had leaned into him, hugging closely, and if not for his heavy leather jacket separating them, her breasts would be boring into his back...her jean-clad thighs were plastered to him...flustered, Spider powered the Harley and took off, scattering stones on the unpaved drive in front of Arela's house.

Theone rested solidly against him and sighed. The Deity had endowed her with every divine attribute and finally, her intense sexuality could be liberated.

In the shadows of the neighbor's A-frame cottage, Bobby could barely keep his presence concealed. Arela's sweeping front house light had revealed everything! He itched to lash out at Theone, to find the words to hurt her like she was hurting him with her behavior. And where did this guy get off encroaching on his territory? For going after HIS woman? ...Because Theone was allowing it. Promoting it! This guy wasn't any better than him. If anything, he, Bobby, was superior. This guy hadn't paid any spiritual dues or endured the hardships of travel in rough wilderness. He was not a part of their group!

Bobby had begun to build hope again when last week Mike left the men's quarters in the basement and moved into Arela's bedroom. Theone spent an inordinate amount of time with Arela, but evidently, she had changed her mind about interfering in the couple's relationship. The group still lived intimately, but they enjoyed greater space and the amenities of a home had made them relax, including Theone who had not actively sought to touch souls for several months other than at her recent appearance in Grand Lake. Yet her attitude towards him had remained annoyingly the same - kind, friendly, warm, but without a hint of sexual awareness. Bobby could not believe that she was so obtuse to his interest! Theone was inexperienced and naive, he had decided, constraining himself to weigh options other than an appearance in her bed to force her notice. *Until now.* Theone had gotten on that Harley and snuggled next to that guy like she wanted him to rape her! She knew all the turn-on moves like a pro.

The bike's tail-lights had long disappeared before Bobby could rein his emotions and return to helping Mike. But he had made up his mind. Her game was over. Theone was getting a visitor tonight and she would not be given an option to say, 'no.'

⸻

"I guess you don't approve of smoking, so I'd better not, even outside," Spider said as he pointed at a warning sign hung in the empty ice cream shop.

"I'm not around anyone who smokes," Theone replied, "but you have a right to your choice."

He shook his head and smiled hesitantly at her. "I just quit. So, are you a vegetarian?"

"No, are you?"

"I like steak and I figured you wouldn't because of the soul's journey. Isn't there the issue of reincarnation? You can't eat a cow because it might be your grandmother?"

"Hindus believe that souls reincarnate in different life forms. In Truth, only humans have complex souls. The souls of lower life forms are the supporting cast for the human soul. Their presence is part of the road's hazards or aids, depending on the human soul's journey. You understand about the food chain and the laws in nature. Carnivores are part of it."

The shop owner recognized Theone. Fascinated at the man's wondrous expression, Spider decided his own must have been similar. Theone took the man's hands and...

No sound, but clarity of motion. Spider could see the owner's wife coming from a rear room, her mouth agape. He could see Theone speaking, but he had been inflicted with instant deafness. Chocolate yogurt in a cup was given to him. It was what he wanted, but he had not ordered it or paid for it. Somehow, he got the communication to move outside to a picnic table and sit down across from her. The next thing he heard was a reference to their conversation like it had not been suspended.

"Your body is important to you," Theone said, "so you take care of it."

Strange that he did not feel confused or see any reason to demand what had happened. Rather, Spider was flooded with a desire to be honest, to come clean...*to bare his soul.* Something he had never been or done with anybody, especially a female. But she was not a female in the sense that he typically viewed females. This was a spiritual being. "I've neglected my soul," he admitted. "My body has been too important."

"You aren't wrong to care about good health, but it doesn't advance your journey to be externally beautiful."

"It's been...so important because of...women. That's pretty shallow, isn't it?"

Theone spooned some of her chocolate yogurt and reiterated, "A preoccupation with your external aspect can result in the ignoring of your spirit."

"I've sure done that, but what about...the women? I've been with a lot." She was trying to be tactful. So what had possessed him to insist on that confession? Spider felt like he was outside of himself watching. How was he supposed to impress her if he talked about other women? Scores of other women! *Impress her?* In exactly what respect? What was wrong with him?

"Have they meant something to you?" She probed. "Did you love them and did your soul and theirs gain from the experience?" Theone knew the answers of his troubled spirit just like she did others, but in Spider's case, he had to make the confessions. He would not be touched and left to fend on his own journey. Spider had to purge what hurt him before he could trust and grow with her.

His stomach roiling, Spider pushed away his yogurt. "I've never loved any woman, not even my mother." An urge to cry had caused his voice to crack and he ducked his head into a shadow.

She was relentless. "There is no love in your heart for anyone?"

"No one, except now...for you," he whispered, "and that's spiritual."

Physical, too, Theone thought with tender amusement, the physical unhinged him as much as the sore state of his soul. She may be in a hurry for progress, but he was feeling enough pain without her rattling him further with sexual pressure. Yet she had waited so long! Spider was the only man she could tantalize. The only person who could know her literally and with the privilege, be told the entire truth. He alone was the human she could allow to treat her as a female.

Free will. Trying as it might be, unless permitted by The Deity to make an exception, Theone could not influence any soul, including Spider's very special one, to do something the soul was not ready for on its own. This was not going to be one of those exceptions.

"Gabriel, love isn't something that is static," she said in a neutral tone. "Once you let yourself love, it expands. By giving love to others, your soul begins to make the right choices and your journey advances."

He rubbed fiercely at his wet eyes. "I want to love, I just don't think I know how to start."

"But you already have. You love me."

Spider forgot his embarrassment and gazed at her. "It's different. You're not..." He was going to say human! She sure looked human and felt human. A dim memory of Greek mythology flitted into consciousness. The gods and goddesses often took human guise and had human lovers, sometimes against their will. He would not resist Theone if she wanted him, but then, he might be so awed, he would fail to...to follow through, which would be an ego-bending disaster...

"Love in most forms is a positive choice for the soul," Theone said.

"Do you date?" Spider could not believe what he had just uttered. A goddess did not date!

Theone smiled and reached across the table for his sturdy hands. "This is my first date."

Spider experienced a tranquil, but invigorating current. Through her touch she released a unique energy...uplifting, yet not necessarily spiritual ...desire burst from his groin into the extremes of his body. Was she coming on to him?

He glanced at her yogurt. Half-eaten like his. Was she maybe feeling this lust, too? But surely not the vulnerability like he was feeling. It struck him. Is this how he used to make women feel? When he discarded them, how badly had their feelings hurt? Why did he keep thinking that Theone wanted to connect with him in any way but spiritual? Because sex had always been *his* motivation to connect with women. He had a lot to atone for.

She released his hands and picked up her helmet. "I'm ready to go back, Gabriel."

"Yep," he mumbled and knocked over his bench standing up. His previous conduct in life did not qualify him to be one of the worthy who traveled with her, let alone be a consort. He was damned lucky - blessed - to have received even an hour of her personal notice.

The narrow road from Grand Lake to Lake Latimer curled through heavy evergreen forest which blocked most of the sky, but the moon was full, and suddenly it appeared overhead. Conscious of Theone's interest, Spider pulled on to the shoulder and stopped. She eased off the bike and linked her arm with his before he could rise, too.

"Look," she instructed, "look at Our Deity's symbol of perpetuity."

He gazed at the Moon which appeared swathed in gauze and nestled in folds of black velvet. Distant lightning etched the soft void with fine gold threads. He'd never paid any attention before, but the moon was inspiring, the sight did give him peace. And a definitiveness had formed to the love he felt for Theone. He not only loved her for impressing his soul, but he was falling *in* love with the woman or the female she represented.

Spider shifted, and Theone released his arm. Kicking the stand, he swung off the bike, removed his helmet and came around to her. She had also removed her helmet and he could see her quite well. Had the Deity trained the moon on her like a spotlight? She was beautiful and desirable and *to touch her...she wanted him to touch her...*he moved closer and was almost within reach...

High beams hit them and Spider stepped away from her. One of the county patrol vehicles, its blue bubble flashing, pulled off the road behind them.

"You folks having a problem?" The deputy sheriff called.

"No, we're just admiring the Moon," Theone replied, "it's quite a spectacle from here."

The deputy peered at them, then got out of the vehicle. "I've seen you. You're that Theone Jones. My wife and daughter heard you speak the other day and were they ever affected. Finally, they're listening to me! It makes a helluva lot more sense to earmark our donations for helping run the local animal shelter than it does to remodel the perfectly good modern kitchen in the parsonage."

This time Spider heard Theone speak, but it was as if he was in the audience at a movie theater, and she and the deputy were a part of the screen action.

"Supporting the shelter is a fitting choice. Your soul is trying to get *your* attention, Irv," she said, "listen to the whole Message that your family has embraced because then, you, too, will find the way to Peace."

"I don't think much about peace in my line of work. We don't get shoot 'em ups like they do in big cities, but there's always some yahoo driving drunk into a ravine or getting lost up in the woods."

"Thank you for your concern tonight," Theone said.

The deputy touched the brim of his hat. "Be shoving along. One of those drunks might just pick this spot to drive off and knock you both dead. I'd hate to have to explain that to my wife and daughter." He got into his vehicle and was gone.

"He missed something, didn't he?" Spider said hesitantly.

"Not every soul is open to hear The Message," she replied sadly. "I can only offer it and hope for impact because every individual must determine his or her own journey."

"I got full impact from seeing you on TV! And now, in your actual presence, I intend for every step I take to be towards Peace. I have a lot of catching up to do, but I'll try like hell...like heck..."

Theone moved nearer to him. "Most souls have ordinary journeys with regular progress. Others lapse and take a moderate dip. Few have striking leaps or reversals, but there are exceptions, and they are usually spectacular such as yours could be. It's all in choices, and you're making right choices."

Spider's breath shortened and his engineer boots felt fused to the ground. She was the most captivating female alive, and he was a bum, a loser. What did she see in him to bother?

"Tell me about your parents," she said.

"My...parents? Kizzie is a saleswoman and Adriano is a tomato vendor. I haven't seen them in years."

"That's their jobs. Who are they?"

"You mean, who am I. I'm half Jewish, half Italian, but they weren't married very long so I'm probably more Jewish in nature because I was with my mother mostly." Spider fiddled with the gear mechanism on the handlebar of the Harley as he spoke.

Theone placed her hand over his on the handlebar. "Your heritage is the key. Think about it while we ride."

He lived by impulse. Spider leaned to Theone and kissed the springy hair by her right temple.

She turned slightly and his lips brushed her brow as he straightened.

"You don't kiss very often," he said with sudden conviction.

"Oh, I don't kiss," she said playfully, "save for one man."

She had kissed him earlier! Tense with hope, Spider asked, "It's me, isn't it? I'm glad if it's me, Theone, but why is it me?"

She held on to him in order to get her leg over the motorcycle. "Let's go. They'll worry."

But Spider had seen her pleased smile. He grinned the entire trip.

⁓

Arela's basement was semi-finished. Some of the floor had been tiled; the walls were partially paneled; the ceiling was open beam. The bathroom was in a portion of the area which still had concrete flooring and walls, but it was fully functional, including a shower stall with a curtain. By the adjacent washer and dryer, Arela had strung a rope line for hanging laundry. In the living section, a corduroy sofa and a pine dining table with a couple of matching chairs were the only furniture other than the three cots Arela had purchased for her guests. These, Jasper, Mike and Bobby had spread out around the room to gain a measure of personal space.

Bobby had set his cot closest to the stairs leading to the main level. Mike had judged which spot was beneath Arela's bedroom and had settled there prior to their recent decision for him to join her. Jasper had picked the wall by the front of the house. Each man still had an unobstructed view of the other, yet averted their eyes, respecting the limited privacy, just as Jasper and Mike had grown accustomed to in the Airstream. Tonight, though, as he and Bobby settled, Jasper planned to keep his eye on his roommate, at least until his breathing indicated that he slept. Bobby's earlier behavior had made Jasper suspicious, and Bobby had not joined them, either, when they congregated on the deck to laud The Deity's Full Moon. Jasper did not trust the young man.

Bobby tensed at the thrum of the motorcycle's approach. What if this guy came in instead of dropping her off? What if she took him upstairs or to the tent...blood pounded in his head. Theone belonged to him! He had done everything she had told him to do and he had earned her affection...he had a RIGHT to her affection, not this stranger!

Outside, Theone got off the Harley the moment Spider stopped.
"Collect your things and join us. I'll give you your answers about family and other things," she said nonchalantly and climbed the redwood steps.
She probably means tomorrow, Spider thought, scrutinizing her. Not a chance. He was collecting his possessions right now and coming back.
Theone judged his re-appearance to occur at 10:41 p.m., the moon's fullest sphere.

Alert, Jasper listened to the motorcycle depart as Theone came inside. She would change her clothes, then go out to her tent. He knew Bobby was awake and shortly, Jasper would know also whether the fellow was about to try something foolish.

Bobby was so obsessed with his plan to confront Theone and so incensed at what he perceived as being jilted, that he saw no point in muffling his rise from the cot. If he woke Jasper, so what. He was not his guardian.
The cot creaked, and Bobby's feet landed heavily on the floor. He had stayed dressed and now fumbled in the darkness to put on his sneakers.
"Let her be," Jasper said. "Theone has never given you any indication that you are more to her than a cherished friend. You won't be so cherished if you force your attentions."
"You don't have any idea about this because you're gay," Bobby replied hotly.

"And I can't understand feelings? Theone has been trying to help you, Bobby. To help your soul stay on the right path with her constant example. She lives Truth! You would repay this precious gift, which the few of us here have been privy to receive day in, day out, with an absurd...pass?"

"I suppose you think I should crawl into bed with you, instead. Jealous, Jasper?" Bobby started up the steps.

Jasper swept off his covers, got to his feet and cut around the vague shape of the sofa. "Bobby, don't do it!"

Bobby laughed as he kept climbing.

Jasper rapidly gained the stairs, flipped the light switch and was able to grab Bobby's ankle.

Bobby staggered to his knee. "Goddamn it, you asshole!" he cried. "We both could have fallen down to that hard floor!"

Keeping his grip taut, Jasper said, "Come back to bed. You are not going to bother her."

Bobby had violent thoughts, but acting on them was different. Jasper had martial arts training and about four inches height on him. It would not be a contest he was likely to win. He slackened his body.

"Do you think you're the only one who has ever found their feelings unreciprocated?" Jasper inquired softly. "It happens. You hurt for a while, but then you recover. Next time might be the right person for you."

"So who hurt you?" Bobby asked sullenly.

"As you pointed out, I'm gay, but getting rebuffed is universal. In certain respects the hurt is compounded because its not the kind of thing that you can tell many people and expect sympathy."

Bobby twisted so that he could sit on the step, and Jasper sat down on the one below him.

"Do you find me attractive?" Bobby said.

"Yes."

"I've been with men."

Jasper refrained from saying that he could tell.

"I'll bet you thought I was straight. Are you shocked?"

"No, Bobby, today's youth are freer to express themselves, and my generation could learn something from your ability to be so unabashed. It should be okay to explore different avenues to fulfillment without feeling any guilt."

"That sounds like a Theone statement." Bobby's tone was mocking. "She's a switch hitter, too, isn't she?"

"Theone attaches no judgment to choices, sexual or otherwise, nor does The Deity. Living The Message is the only..."

"I know. The only requirement for the soul to advance. Don't you get sick of hearing it?"

Jasper sighed with exasperation. "Being around Theone doesn't make you happy, so perhaps it would be best if you moved on, Bobby. I only hope that you don't lose sight of Peace."

"Speaking of getting on, do you want to get it on with me before I go?"

Jasper swallowed excitedly. He had fancied Bobby for months, but would never have mentioned it first. The young man was not doing this out of love, but through a twisted need to soothe his ego, yet they were consenting adults, and Jasper would like the closeness...

Bobby stroked Jasper's head. "Your cot or mine?"

"Find your condoms and join me." Jasper moved downward on the stairs.

"Condoms? That's gross."

Jasper turned to look at him. "That's safe."

"Forget it," Bobby retorted. The old queen couldn't give him anything he hadn't gotten already, and he could care less if he happened to transmit a disease.

"Okay," Jasper said quietly.

"I'm gathering my stuff," Bobby grunted, "and splitting, if you'll fork over some of the cash you keep around so I can pay for the trip back to the real world. This nature-spirit scene is a real bore."

"Yes, well, you can have money, and to make sure that you really do go, I'm seeing you out to your van."

Bobby thought about telling Jasper to go fuck himself like he was probably going to do anyway, but it wasn't worth the effort. "Suit yourself," he muttered and started locating his possessions.

In the living room, Mag kept silent as Jasper escorted Bobby out the side door by the kitchen. Shortly, his van peeled away from the house.

The basement door had been cracked, and inadvertently, she had over heard the men's conversation. She had been anticipating the young man's departure and with relief, now returned to her reading.

Spider timed it. One and three-quarters hours. At ten twenty-four p.m., he was knocking again on the deck's sliding door. Mag responded.

"Theone told me to expect you," she said, "so I waited up."

Theone knew, he realized, as he followed Mag inside. Theone knew everything, which included his desire for her. Where was she? Sleeping? Near anywhere he would be? Other than a lamp by a couch, the quiet house appeared dark.

"The house has a bedroom on this level which Arela and Mike share; Jasper and Bobby...Jasper sleeps on a fold-a-way in the half-remodeled basement," Mag informed as she led Spider to stairs at the far end of the living room. "There are also two bedrooms above. Pilar and I share one. Theone indicated that you were to sleep in the other."

Spider stopped mid-step. "So where does Theone sleep?"

Mag smiled at his bluntness. She and Pilar had discussed at length Theone's extraordinary reaction to Spider and had concluded that this man was the special one of whom she had hinted recently. They had expressed a mutual relief that Bobby was obviously NOT the one.

"The room you're assigned is officially hers, but she has yet to sleep in it," Mag replied. "As customary, when we settled here, Theone found her own place. She erected her pup tent down by the lakeshore. Rain or shine, she always sleeps outside."

Spider motioned for Mag to continue up the stairs. "I'll put my gear in the room, then I'm joining her," he said with confidence, figuring on maximum fifteen minutes to extricate his sleeping bag, dig out his sweats and skin his jeans.

"I would guess that she won't be surprised," Mag answered.

From the deck, Spider could see by a spruce the outline of the small tent, and the moon illuminated his path to it. He hesitated when he reached the spot, though. If she was asleep, he did not want to wake her.

Cautiously, he bent to check. She was sitting up and the moon shone in on her smiling face. He couldn't tell. Was she naked? She was inside her own sleeping bag and her hair flowed over her shoulders.

"Are you accustomed to camping?" She asked.

"I've done it without the convenience of a tent or a tarp," he said with a grin, "but not without my waterproof nylon mummy bag packed with goose down! Can I join you?"

Theone laughed as she lay down. He scuffed his unlaced sneakers, unrolled his bag, crawled into it and cozied next her, planning to start serious kissing.

Something good-sized thumped the tent wall by their heads. A lighter thud jiggled a side section.

Passionate intentions fled. Spider shot up and whispered, "We're in the Rockies. There are bears."

"There is too much civilization around for it to be a bear," Theone said calmly, "but in any case, you needn't be alarmed. Animals will be curious, but none will ever harm you, even if it's in their nature to be aggressive normally."

Normally? Spider propped on his elbow and stared at her face which he could see distinctly because the moon washed them in light almost like a wan sun would. Her eyes were the loveliest he had ever beheld. Blue, green and gray blended with a smidgen of amber into a unique hazel. "Are animals tame around you?" He inquired.

"In a manner of speaking. Having more primitive senses than humans, animals are capable of singular focus and they do tangible things to get my attention."

"And humans don't?"

"Humans already have my full attention. To deliver The Message about Truth, *I* have to *gain* their attention."

"And you're succeeding at it!"

"Not enough...not as thoroughly as I'd like, and there have been...big disappointments..." like Bobby, she thought sadly, "but I understand human nature."

"Aren't you...don't you have human nature?"

Theone studied his earnest face. He had taken out the rubber band in his pony tail and his shiny black hair hung to his shoulders. Spider's dark features were extraordinary, but he was not handsome to perfection. And to stay clean shaven like he was tonight, he would have to use a razor twice a day. She reached to his cheek and stroked it. "I don't have free will, Gabriel. My will is Our Deity's."

"Does that mean...you're divine?"

"Labels are always important to humans. Yes, I am of Our Deity."

"So you are God, uh, Goddess."

"I am not Our Deity, only of the essence, a facet."

"Incarnate."

Theone sighed at his stubborn persistence. This was going to be the most demanding, complex relationship she was to experience and already he tested her composure! But Spider had the right to know everything; although she was not to volunteer information, whenever he inquired or whatever he inquired about, his questions had to be satisfied. It was just difficult to let go of the restraints that had been in place up until now.

"Yes, incarnate," she said.

"Like Jesus?"

"Do you know anything about The Dead Sea Scrolls found at Qumran?"

"I've seen TV programs about them. They contain the earliest known writings about Jesus and have shed light on his life historically. Scholars are still sorting it out."

"Scholars are still attempting to classify and interpret what writers of the Scrolls *originally* attempted to classify and interpret about a being not meant to gain such great importance! Political motives and the personal ambitions of the writers enhanced the distortion!" Theone's voice softened. "The being, Jesus, was only a Messenger."

"A being like...you."

"Yes, not what humans have put in the Bible. Mary was a surrogate the same as Brigit, my mother, but with a significant difference. *Joseph's* lineage was the determining factor. Jesus' pedigree established legitimacy in human terms and guaranteed notice. My mother's notable Celtic lineage is hers, although ancestry is not the big issue that it was in Jesus' day."

"The Holy Ghost impregnating the Virgin Mary is b.s.?"

"There are angels, one of whom visited Mary to herald Our Deity's intentions, but no such being as a Holy Ghost. 'Virgin' designated an unmarried woman, not a physical condition. Mary was already sexually active with her betrothed, Joseph, which was custom. Our Deity impregnated Mary as father AND mother. Jesus was not of human conception."

"Have there been others like you two?"

"No, only us with parallel human-type lives, but many have come who are divinely inspired. Our Deity has also appeared in various, temporary forms, giving rise to the many names by which Our Deity has been known. You learned from your Roman Catholic teachings that Mary, a Deity Ordained nurturer, has evolved to a godly level. This has happened to a lesser degree with human designated saints. There have been prophets, too, with whom Our Deity has communicated directly. In some manner, Our Deity *always* answers human petition for spiritual guidance, including with the appearance of a deific being."

Spider mulled that for a second. "Did Jesus really die on the cross?"

"Life as humans perceive it left his body, but his passing was not meant to forgive human errors. Those in religious power were determined to destroy The Message. The concept that each human soul, regardless of sex or race, had the same right to approach The Deity threatened their defined order."

"...And their self-important positions."

"In some ways they did succeed in their destruction because The Truth was misconstrued, but for genuine seekers, of which there have been a host to the present day, Truth is still intact and is practiced to their souls' great benefit.

"Jesus rose from 'death' because he never truly died. His offering of The Message about the soul's journey here on Earth and travel in different environments to attain Peace was twisted into the Christian religion of grace and heavenly salvation." Theone quivered with indignation. "As a dogma, Christianity has been such a mixed bag, inspiring goodness, true, but also the worst atrocities. Think of the Crusades! The Inquisition and The Burning Times when a vast number of innocent people, particularly women, perished because the Church was determined to consolidate its power!"

Spider settled on his back and put his arms under head. He was wide awake, his intellectual thirst almost a physical sensation. "Do you tell people this?"

"Just you since you are entitled to the whole truth. It isn't important now. Jesus' authentic Message is the same Message that I'm bringing."

"Ha! It would blow their minds!" Spider turned to face her. "But you're right. It isn't important. To me, either." He touched her hair and caressed around her ear. "So, Jesus. Was he the celibate emulated by monks or is that a myth, too?"

Theone smiled impishly and nibbled Spider's wrist. "Jesus was born into a Hebrew order which equated celibacy with piety, but sexuality is an element of Our Deity and every Messenger is thus endowed. Contrary to the habits of his sect and early church doctrine, Jesus loved special humans."

Spider inched so that their bodies were in full contact. Packed goose down separated them, but the idea was arousing as his erection verified.

"Who was she?" He murmured and continued to stroke her head.

One human, Spider assumed only one. Theone said, "She was a high priestess in a temple of Ishtar. Ishtar is another name for Isis."

"A wanton? A...pagan?"

Mildly vexed at his ignorance, she responded, "An independent, intelligent woman of fine matrilineage, a Goddess worshiper for whom lovemaking with different partners was honored as a sacred rite. Children born to a priestess were granted every right in society. For centuries, Goddess-God beliefs co-existed, although in some cases, specifically in Canaan, at great cost to those who deemed the Goddess holy. Elohim believers, subjugators of women to an extreme, were very intolerant and with the alleged endorsement of a wrathful god, they frequently slaughtered those who did not agree with their philosophy. The Old Testament is filled with accounts of such actions and with admonishments by prophets to women to behave chastely or be banished as harlots. Yet, in some regions, despite the fact that the knowledge has been eradicated, Goddess-God worship had co-mingled fruitfully which was real spiritual advancement."

"It makes sense."

"Our Deity conceived Jesus with the purpose to reconcile finally Goddess and God veneration into one abiding faith which is the truest path to Peace. So, at a time when Hebrew women were on a footing with chattel, Jesus encouraged them to leave their traditional roles. He taught that Our Deity was of an equal divinity, and enlightenment was for all souls. Spiritual progress depended on love, honesty and humility. No one was the property of another, and judgment was detrimental to the soul."

"Sounds like you, Theone."

"The Message has never changed! Anyhow, as a result, women who worshiped God and/or Goddess embraced The Message and became actively involved with his ministry. One woman in particular was meant for Jesus, whose intentional birth into the Hebrew faith was to solidify the merge. Unfortunately, the words selected for preservation by the early church and the theology thus evolved..."

"Has her name been lost, too?"

"The Bible refers to her as a repentant whore who renounced her wickedness to follow Jesus. 'Whore' was common derogatory verbiage used by Hebrew scribes to depict women who worshiped Isis or Artemis, one of the Hellenistic forms of the Goddess."

Spider gaped at one of the thin tent poles and pondered. It couldn't be Mary. Her status in the Catholic Church approached Goddess level like Theone had mentioned. She had gotten pregnant outside marriage, but no one had dared call her a whore in Scripture, had they?

"Mary Magdalene," Theone said. "Her origins were obscured in the New Testament, but not scribal opinion of her previous Goddess faith."

"The Easter story! Mary Magdalene was at the tomb and the angel asked her why she was weeping," Spider uttered. "No wonder she was weeping. Was she Jesus'...wife?"

"She was."

"And were there children?"

"No. Jesus' public time was brief, but Our Deity felt that The Message had been stated conclusively. No insurance was necessary, there was no need for further...clarification of the path humans needed to follow to advance their souls."

"But we humans altered it. In two words, *free will*." He smiled at her pleased expression. "I really listened to you that night I first saw you. So, what's the deal with Mohammed, then? He had to be a Messenger to have such impact. Since he came after Jesus, he should have gotten things back on track at least in Arabia, but Islam is a major male religion."

Theone marveled at Spider's quick grasp and easy acceptance of Truth. She thanked The Deity for choosing him so wisely.

"Muhammad was Our Deity's answer to Arab spiritual need," she said, "and his revelations which resulted in The Koran show plainly that he did try to convey The Message. He certainly respected women. Before his advent, most women in Arabia, like their Hebrew counterparts, were no better than slaves. The Koran forbids the killing of female children and reprimands those who show disappointment when a girl is born. The Koran gives women legal rights of inheritance and divorce, which Christian and Jewish women did not gain until the 1800's. Muhammad's revelations often address women explicitly, and 33:35 of The Koran stresses the moral and spiritual equality of the sexes." Theone recited, "'Lo! men who surrender unto Allah, and women who surrender, and men who believe and women who believe, and men who obey and women who obey, and men who speak the truth and women who speak the truth, and men who persevere and women who persevere, and men who are humble and women who are humble, and men who give alms and women who give alms, and men who fast and women who fast, and men who guard their modesty and women who guard, and men who remember Allah much and women who remember - Allah hath prepared for them forgiveness and a vast reward.'"

"Aha. Men got hold of it, interpreted to their own satisfaction and the result is..."

"Yes."

"And you are here to try once again."

"Yes."

"Will you at last succeed where your predecessors have failed?"

"One way or the other. Our Deity has tired of humans' errant choices."

The moon had risen to a point above the tent opening, and Theone's face was now in shadows. Spider settled against her, his head on her chest.

"What about me, Theone? Why me? I was a bum with no direction...I wasn't nice to girls. I wasn't nice to anybody! Why should I be the one privileged to love the embodiment of the perfect female? Where do I fit into this?"

"If the records existed, Kizzie's lineage could be traced back to Canaan. She is descended from priestesses of Asherah. Adriano's ancestry is Roman and ancient Egyptian."

"So, are we something like...soul mates?"

"It's a very romantic concept, but humans don't have soul mates. How would your soul ever progress if you kept ending up in the same relationships and pursuing the same patterns of behavior? A cosmic connection to other souls exists, but not in a *human* sense. Understanding it is unimportant. You were just born with the right combination of heredity. Plus, despite your previous behavior in this environment, you have an advanced soul, Gabriel. Your last name is another indicator."

"Giovetti?"

"*Giove* in Italian translates as Jupiter or Jove. There is truth in mythology." Theone yawned. "And like my mother, you were born to be one of Our Deity's nurturers."

Spider also yawned. "Okay, *that* message is clear. It's time to sack out. I'll bet you're up at dawn."

"Mm, hm."

"I will, too." He was so tired suddenly that he forgot to kiss her. A heavy creature brushed the tent, jarring it, but Spider was already asleep.

The next morning, Theone awoke and sat up to look at a smoky arbor of clouds skimming a creamy buff horizon. She crawled from her sleeping bag and went outside. In the gray southern sky, a soft yellow moon still shone along with a couple of diehard, twinkly star-points.

She stretched, and her midriff bared between her sweat shirt and sweat pants. "I feel most vital when the sun and moon are in the sky at the same time," she said to Spider who was putting on his sneakers inside the tent.

Staring at her exposed skin, his sight dropped to her feet. "Where are your shoes?"

"I seldom wear shoes."

"And your feet don't get cold?"

"No. Do you have to urinate? In those spruce there's a hollow with an incline above the water where I go. See by the cattails at the edge of Arela's property?" She walked away.

He scrambled after her.

Casually, she stripped her pants and squatted.

Spider shrugged, loosened the front of his pants and aimed at the water, but he observed her with curiosity.

Finished, Theone patted herself and stepped into the water to rinse her hands. She faced him as she dressed.

He hastily finished and hauled up his pants before an erection embarrassed him.

Theone took his hand and led him back to the tent area.

"Watch the horizon," she whispered and leaned against him. Several rabbits and squirrels joined them.

Spider put his arm around her and focused.

White, then bright gold dazzled them as the sun made its ascent.

"The sun and earth nurture human bodies," Theone explained. "They serve the physical self whereas the moon is for the psyche, the spiritual self. Acknowledging and respecting each is integral to the soul's journey."

Spider's mind was not on the lesson. She was so perfect and he had such glaring defects...

"My heritage aside, I've done nothing to deserve you," he said meekly, "and I was with my first girl when I was thirteen or fourteen. I can't count the number since."

Theone turned and placed her arms snugly around his torso by his ribs. "Physically, yes, I'm not experienced and you are, but emotionally, you're a virgin and I'm not. It's balanced. Why is your will so resistant to me?"

"I'm not resistant to you, but you should be resistant to me." But he had not hesitated to hug her back. And tightly.

She shook her head and laughed. "Oh, Gabriel, trust your heart!"

He stopped thinking and kissed her.

...Music? There was...celestial music! No, birds. Different birds, lots of birds singing...in harmony? Or was this a chorus of angels?

Theone tasted sweet, but tangy, too, and he could spend the rest of his life like this. Just kissing her. Exploring her lips, her tongue, her throat...lower...well, not JUST kissing her...married. They had to get married.

Spider broke contact. "Jesus married. Can you?"

Theone grinned. "In Our Deity's perception, I'm already married."

"Already?" His expression was anguished.

She was baffled. "To you, Gabriel. I'm married to you. Your profile is imbedded in the moonstone that hangs about my neck. Our Deity sent it to me as a child to hearten me. I would not always have to stand alone in this environment, but would have a consort. You've been meant for me from the beginning, but you have free will. You have to make the choice..."

He cut her off with a kiss. "How do I marry you back?"

"Make your commitment to me before Our Deity."

Spider faced the vibrant sun, fully visible now. He held out his palms and closed his eyes. Smiling, Theone closed hers to feel his modest words.

Then, he spun to her. With a crafty look, his hands shot up her shirt around her back and forward to cup the under swell of her breasts. Rapidly, he swept down into her pants, creeping to her pelvis and joining his thumbs in her pubic hair. "Just like I figured. You aren't wearing any underwear!"

Her eyes widened at the sensation. She brushed him away and ran her hands up his back, then into his pants to clasp his bare bottom. She came forward and her thumbs just touched his erect penis. With wonder, she said, "You aren't wearing any either, Gabriel!"

"I never do. It's a laundry issue."

"I don't to bed."

Passion kindled in their faces.

Spider grinned slyly. "I know two sleeping bags that will zip together."

Theone shook her head with regret. "Mag has already started breakfast. There isn't time now."

Spider was disappointed, but along with his newly discovered feelings of love, he understood about appropriate moments. "I was in such a rush last night, I didn't bring anything with me so its just as well."

"Anything?"

He gripped her head and kissed her. "Condoms, Theone. But maybe I don't need them because...you can't get pregnant?"

"I'm very fertile, Gabriel. Why would we want to prevent conception?"

"Holy sh...cow! I feel hot and dizzy. I'm probably going to burst from desire."

Theone laughed. "On this whole earth, I can be myself with only you. I can be a female. With you alone, I can be a wife and if so blessed, a mother."

Tears gathered in his eyes. "I won't leave you, ever. Not for more than hours and only when it's absolutely necessary."

"We will have to legalize our union. It's important for us to conform to society's rules."

"Today!" Spider shouted.

"My uncle in Wisconsin is a judge. He'll marry us at Lake Femvivant in a few months."

"Theone, can you predict the future?"

"I can foresee certain outcomes," she said cautiously. What was he about to ask? She couldn't lie to him!

"Will you stay with me until we are very old?"

"I will stay with you as long as you need me," she promised truthfully.

"Then, we'll be very, very old!"

Spider was too happy to see her fleeting expression of sadness.

From the deck, Pilar yelled to them. "Breakfast!"

"You go on," Spider said. "I have to wait...a minute."

Theone took his hands. "You are sated and content," she said.

He looked at her with surprise. The urgent, throbbing desire had just... dissipated. "You won't do that every time, will you?"

"Why would I want to do that? I just wanted you to be comfortable. For the time being only!"

Spider chuckled and grabbed her hand. "Just checking, My Love. Just checking."

Thoughtful, Theone climbed to the house in silence while Spider exuberantly greeted the chickadees and bluebirds fluttering in the crisp air around them. Different from other humans, she got only a general warning about Spider's behavior. She could not accurately predict what he would say or what he would do...*blithe laughter...a melodious feminine voice joined with a rich masculine voice...*

Theone comprehended. She was to guide Spider, but she was also supposed to inhabit and adapt to his life as much like a woman as she could. It included envisioning, but not of everything.

And The Deity was enjoying this. Theone glanced at the sky and winked at their jest.

⁓

Theone licked her fingers and smiled at Mag. "I do like crunchy bacon! Thank you for being a super cook."

"Thanks from me, too," Spider said. Every bite had been delicious. The coffee was the best he had ever tasted, and he did not miss a cigarette for finish, either. He felt totally alive and it was only going to get better. All because of Theone. Because of The Message. Because of the love she had brought to him.

The others at the table hid their amusement at his rapturous expression. They could well remember their own initial reaction to Theone and Spider as her consort was more than entitled to his awe.

Mag nodded at the couple and stood up to clear the table.

Arela rose, too. "I'll do the dishes," she offered, "since Bobby is gone and you have no helper."

"No, I can handle it myself," Mag said congenially, but firmly. "The deed may say it's your kitchen, but from now on when I'm in it, it's mine."

Mike came by the counter from the hall. "Which means, Ari, that you and I can go for a short hike."

"Pilar," Jasper said, "we have some business. Shall we adjourn to the deck?"

Pilar finished her coffee and pushed back her chair. If this business related to Bobby, she hoped that it meant his departure was permanent. Earlier, Jasper had been vague about details.

"I'm taking a shower," Theone announced and looked at Spider.

"Uh, I'll take one after you," he mumbled.

"Oh, take one together," Mike suggested in a joking tone.

"The idea has appeal," Theone replied gravely, but her eyes twinkled.

Spider grinned sheepishly as the others laughed.

Upstairs, Theone shut the door to her bedroom. "I want to see you," she said, "do you mind undressing in front of me?"

Spider gulped audibly at her straightforwardness. Modesty had never been a problem for him until this moment, but he got his clothes off, striving not to be self-conscious of his stiff penis.

Like a Renaissance statue, Theone appraised as she inspected him. He was lean, yet beautifully muscled, in perfect proportion, not obscenely over developed. It had taken many hours to achieve such fitness, but to survive with her he had to maintain a robust body. His stamina had to be exceptional. Stroking the tattoo on his solid forearm, she asked, "Your strength is important. Will you miss working out?"

"You hike. You climb. I've got a pair of lug sole lace boots and I'll be right there with you, buffing the body."

Theone was not finished. "Loving me has a high price. You must maintain your physical fitness because you will lead an arduous life. Also, your wit must be kept honed because you will need to be cunning and...smarter than your enemies. There will be enemies and you could have much to protect besides yourself."

"Yep, you, Babe. I'd give up my life to protect you."

"That will never be necessary."

"Lecture heeded. Now, enough talk, okay? Uh, don't I get to see you?"

Acquiescent, Theone removed her sweats.

Clothed, her figure appeared trim and modest, but naked, she had lush breasts with large, pale nipples, a soft, round belly and a profusion of pubic hair as unruly as that on her head and her brows. How did she disguise it? She was like...a stereotype Mother Nature! And why did it matter? He would adore her in any shape. Spider grabbed her.

Theone freely embraced him, reveling in the sensuality of his flesh, but she resisted his attempt to tip her on to the bed. "You can touch me," she said, "but I must be in contact with the earth when we join as one and the first time we will be in the wilderness."

He separated from her slightly and grinned. "Okay, okay. We can do other things. I'm carrying you to the shower."

The tub was short and the shower head low. With plenty of mutual rubbing, they took turns getting wet, then Spider braced Theone against the wall and began his kisses.

Like a dewy mushroom, he thought as his lips and hands caressed the smooth skin on her body, skin not marred by even the finest down. Theone did not make him think of bright flowers or pretty things, but of wet, green leaves; rich, soft loam; cold, clear mountain streams; pure, bracing air; sunny, windswept ocean beaches - basic, wild things.

"My nipples are hard," she murmured.

"Because they're trying to get my attention," Spider teased and descended on one.

Theone moaned and swayed into him.

Spider slid to his knees and buried his head between her legs. Her orgasm happened so fast and so forcefully that he was trapped by her contractions.

"Baby," he sputtered as he heaved for air, "you've been saving that for a long time." Spider looked at her face and her eyes stunned him. They were like rose quartz with white fissures. He had learned about crystals. Rose quartz was to attract and insure romantic love. Theone's Sexy Love Eyes. He stood up and brought her right hand to his groin.

"Just touch me a bit. You can't do anything wrong, and I'm so turned on, I'll go off with little trouble."

Theone laughed softly and pushed him around so that he was against the wall, then she fell to her knees.

Spider seized her head. "You don't have to do..." he felt like she had swallowed him! His knees went weak at the sensation and in seconds, he ejaculated.

"Uh, you've never done this before?" He gasped.

"No, but you told me I couldn't do anything wrong."

"Theone, you did everything incredibly, phenomenally! Who are you? Venus?"

"I am innocent physically, but I have a collective consciousness."

"...consciousness. I might fall into unconsciousness." Spider closed his eyes and let the shower spray pelt his chest.

She got to her feet and reached for a bar of soap to wash him. "That's why your past sexual experiences were crucial to prepare you and also why you must remain in peak condition. I can't be loved by any man, but a strong, seasoned one."

"Strong and seasoned, you got it, strong and seasoned, and I got it real bad."

She smiled at his dazed expression. "I love you, Gabriel, and thank Our Deity for the privilege."

"I believe the privilege is all mine, Theone."

When Theone and Spider re-appeared, Jasper and Pilar were still on the deck. Mag, Arela and Mike had joined them. Sensing alarm in their discussion, Theone led Spider outside.

Jasper stood. "We have some rather disturbing news which I hate to bring up under the circumstances," he gestured at Spider, "but he will have to understand how it is with you. The controversy is very real and growing."

"Has someone threatened her life?" Spider asked.

"Christians don't condone that sort of savage talk," Pilar said sarcastically, "despite their actions to contrary."

"They are the ones issuing ultimatums, but I expect Theone's opponents include more than Christians," Mike said.

"According to the press release, this is strictly on a volunteer basis, but a newly formed Christ Covenant has issued a directive," Jasper explained. "Those of the faith who will not renounce your Message in writing, Theone, and return to the worship of traditional Scripture, will be denied Holy Communion. They will not be welcome in their churches."

"Glenn Chandler is their elected spokesman," Mag said. She addressed Spider. "Chandler is Theone's sister's husband and he's an Inspiration of Grace minister."

"Son of a bitch," Spider growled without thinking.

Theone turned from her friends and gazed at the bottle-green lake. She raised her eyes to the mountains, then to the sky where cumulus clouds scudded by the sun. "And how can I change what humans with free will determine for the course of their lives?" She asked quietly.

"The media has been hounding us since before the book was available to the public. They want an interview with you, Theone," Jasper said. "Pick a newscaster and answer his or her questions. Clarify your stand. Let people see how well you handle yourself. Let a wide audience experience your sincerity with a one on one exchange with a respected journalist."

"That will change opinion?" Theone questioned without conviction.

Jasper sighed. "Not for those who are determined to hang on to the old patterns, but I guarantee that those who waver, they might just say 'phooey' to organized religion and be convinced that your Message is the valid one. It might serve to drown your critics or perhaps force a compromise."

"There isn't any compromise on The Message."

"We know that," Pilar soothed, "but humans, especially insecure, threatened ones, have a need to save face."

Theone turned to regard their anxious expressions and lingered on Spider's. "Who do you suggest, Jasper?"

"Someone who is close to impeccable, Rae Nolan. She is popular, yet serious, credible and unbiased. I think she would be fair and she's forcible enough not to be owned by this Christ Covenant. Is there a place you would like for it to take place?"

"On the Snake River in Idaho anywhere the weather permits and as soon as we can get there." She gazed at Spider. "It will be my last appearance for the public. If you're willing to travel a while more and don't mind the cold, I invite you to Paxton where Gabriel and I, Mike and Arela will be married legally by my uncle at Lake Femvivant."

Tears and congratulations interrupted Theone before she could finish her remarks. "Afterwards, Arela, Mike and Mag will return here. Gabriel and I will follow Jasper and Pilar to San Antonio to get my truck. We will be on our own in the future."

"Why?" Jasper cried.

"We are to stay in San Antonio?" Pilar wailed. "You need care and support!"

Theone stepped closer to Spider who put his arm around her. "It is my time now to be with this man Our Deity has sent to me. Your role is so important, Pilar. The way you handle business matters is the greatest gift. Jasper, your notes must be written up for Arela so that she has the Message and you must arrange translations for Ian to publish. Arela, Mike and Mag will be going to Europe and Asia." She paused to smile at Mag who wept. "I will contact you often. All of you. And I will never really leave you. You live The Message and every time you influence a soul, you draw closer to The Deity, closer to me."

They tried to smile at her to show respect for her wishes, but each realized sorrowfully that their time with her would soon be over. They were silent.

"Perhaps we could be off to Idaho in a day or so?" She asked gently.

"The Suburban is ready whenever," Mike replied hoarsely.

"I'm sure I can arrange the interview any time, any place, at any notice," Jasper added.

"Thank you," Theone said. "Gabriel and I are going into the mountains now to hike. The sun is glorious today. We'll be back to share the sunset with you."

⁂

Spider slowed the bike and drove to the tight shoulder on the steep, narrow road. He swore he'd heard Theone say, 'This is the right spot,' but that was impossible what with the insulating effect of their helmets and the rumble of the Twin V engine. The solid growth of trees he saw appeared to have no path through its underbrush.

Theone hopped off the Harley and walked to the edge of the forest.

Reluctantly, Spider kicked the parking stand and joined her. "It's remote up here, but is it really safe to leave the bike? We'll have a longer hike than we planned, if somebody hot wires our wheels..."

Two hawks shrieked their arrival and landed on either handlebar. The birds planted their feet squarely and bowed to them.

"No one will bother it," Theone said as she unlaced her sneakers and placed them with her helmet on the Harley's saddle.

Spooked by the hawks' presence, Spider mumbled as he removed his helmet, "Shit, I guess not, not with guards like that. Do our buddies have an army waiting in the branches to attack would-be felons?"

"Life isn't a movie about supernatural birds who are hostile towards humans," Theone kindly reproved, "but you must understand, Gabriel, that Our Deity has dominion over every creature. As Our Deity's Messenger, I am accorded respect from simple souls. This respect includes a concern for my welfare."

"It's the complex souls who vex you with their free will," he replied nervously. The hawks had vicious beaks and he swore, disapproval for him in their beady eyes.

"Yes, *human* souls. You needn't be afraid of the animals who are attracted to me, Gabriel. I told you last night that whether they are domestic or wild, they will never harm you."

"Sure, I believe you." He remained wary, though, because animals were not in his experience, outside a couple trips to the San Diego Zoo. Kizzie had refused to have pets; his stepmother was allergic to fur or dander. The places he had lived as an adult had not allowed them, not that having a pet fit in with his transient lifestyle. As far as nature was concerned, he had not paid any attention to it, other than to crush bugs who happened into his presence and only if they annoyed him like flies or mosquitoes or cockroaches around his food. Ones on walls or in corners minding their own business did not bother him.

Theone stepped between a shaggy pine and a bushy fern as if a well-defined trail waited. "There's a stream several miles from here with a grassy bed by it."

Grassy...bed? Spider forgot his uneasiness about animal familiarity and plunged after her. It did not occur to him as he squinted ahead that their dense, murky route was non-existent until Theone's bare feet trod the ground, making the hike for him much easier.

"It's like glass!" Spider exclaimed. "The water is the clearest I've ever seen and the sun makes it sparkle." He laughed. "I sound like a tourist bureau brochure."

Theone laughed with him. The scene by the shallow, rocky stream was idyllic. Birches shaded part of the bank where an unusual down of summer grass had not yet wilted. The temperature was cool, but the sun was warm and the wind had died down the moment they arrived. Animals galore had shadowed their hike, but demonstrated a rare restraint in seeking Theone's attention.

Spider gathered her into his arms. "I want to make love to you. Is this wilderness enough?"

She kissed him ardently, but backed away before he could get hold of her windbreaker.

"You have a button fly, not a zipper," she said as she undid his jeans.

Intent on her activity, Spider slurred, "It's easier on hair and flesh, but not faster."

Theone held his penis. "This is big," she pronounced, rolling it between her hands.

Spider gyrated to slough his leather jacket and his tee shirt, and his long hair tumbled free. "Uh, let go for a second so I can ditch my pants and boots."

"You won't get cold?"

"Babe, I'm so hot, I wouldn't get cold at the North Pole!"

She laughed and started to strip her jeans, but a rattlesnake could no longer exercise reserve. It whipped around her ankles.

"God!" Spider shrieked. "Check the tail! It's a rattler!"

His frantic outburst did not disturb the creatures observing their Mistress. Rather, the snake's boldness seemed to have a liberating effect. A fox showed in the clearing; a pair of mule deer wandered into sight; and a languid owl nudged away the row of birds perched on a tree limb overhead.

"Snakes are less evolved," Theone said smoothly, "so they are uninhibited compared to other species. Moreover, snakes possess a special affinity to a being like me which predates history." She spoke to the snake, "I acknowledge your tribute, now free me."

The rattler uncoiled in Spider's direction. He rapidly stepped backwards and went down on one hand when his foot landed in the stream.

"Please, Gabriel, the snake is benign."

As if to prove her remark, the rattler faded into the reeds. But trout attracted to Theone and her consort agitated the water close to Spider. Further intimidated, he clumsily sloshed out, his hair in his eyes.

"I'm not used to this," he said, sweeping back his hair. "I have to get used to the idea of it. You beguile these, these beasts that you talk to and they understand you!"

"People talk to their cats and dogs. The pet understands."

"A pet learns to obey orders. This is different. You actually communicate with things, undomesticated things." Spider buttoned his jeans and regarded her. "Does this talent of yours mean you can you read my thoughts?"

She smiled at him. "Only what I'm meant to hear. In human terms, Our Deity has made our relationship quite normal compared to other relationships I experience."

"Ha. Human terms. Normal." Spider ignored her charm and retrieved his shirt and jacket. "None of this is normal! In fact, I'm beginning to think I'm bewitched. You know, like you cast a spell on me. You speak of The Deity, but is that the one in Heaven or Hell?"

Theone repressed the tears behind her eyes and kept her expression serene, but her mind reeled. This is how humans' thoughtless words hurt others! No wonder humans broke The Deity's Rules. Thoughtless words triggered retaliatory action and she fathomed why wars broke out; she comprehended why murder and other atrocities were committed. It started with words *and like any human, her soul's shelter, her heart, felt deep pain.* Had she violated The Deity's Will in some manner and was this a reminder of who she was? Or was this merely a part of the experience she was meant to have? What point was there in sending her a companion who could not share the type of life she had to lead?

His fear and subsequent anger subsiding, Spider said, "I'm sorry, but I don't think I'm cut out for this, Theone. Nature just isn't my thing, and I can't imagine getting accustomed to...to reptiles or some woolly, ferocious mammal snuggling up as part of the regular bed scene." He looked at her compassionate face and almost capitulated. What had he done? She was a perfect being! He had been chosen, *the only one*, to love her intimately. And he did love her. But his fright had been real, and he could not foresee his feelings changing on this issue. Now, the resulting affront to his ego prevented him from extending a conciliatory gesture.

"It would be best to return, then," Theone said. "Will the hike back be okay for you?"

"Hiking I can handle," Spider said.

No creatures bothered them as Theone led their way to the motorcycle. The two hawks flapped off without ceremony just as the couple reached the road.

With anguish, Theone held on to his waist like he was a stranger just giving her a lift. No one was at the house when they arrived, and while he assembled his belongings, Theone went down to the lake. Spider did not say goodbye.

Growth involves difficult choices, My Child...because of their nature, humans have a tendency to pick the easy way, a choice that has little impact on growth...but a human's choice, specifically your consort's, will not be fully valid if you interfere...his will is powerful which is one reason why he was chosen...don't fret, My Child. He is not free of you...the love is there...the love binds him forever in this environment...

Theone heard The Deity's words - she had no choice like humans who could refuse a Divine Message - but the advice did not ease her sorrow over Spider's failure.

Her friends had gone to Grand Lake on errands. On return, Arela walked down to the lake to meditate and by chance found Theone seated on the stony bank, her feet being lapped by the cold waves.

"Hi, I didn't expect to see you so soon. Is Gabriel in the house?" Arela inquired.

Theone smiled at the woman whose faithful teaching would inspire thousands not privy to hear The Message directly from her. "Gabriel has some thinking to do and felt he needed solitude to sort it out."

Arela cleared enough rocks to sit on a level surface. Theone's expression was tranquil, but Arela was attuned to her mentor. She sensed her sadness. "Is he unsure of you?"

"He is unsure of the circumstances under which he must live if he joins me."

"Oh, Theone! How can this man be the right one?"

Theone gathered the silver chain from inside her shirt and held the moonstone in her palm for Arela's inspection. "As a child, this came to me from Our Deity."

"The profile is uncanny in its resemblance," Arela said. "It's a matter of trust, then. You must trust that Our Deity has control."

"Gabriel has the control, Arela. His will determines his direction."

"Do you believe he'll make the right choice?"

Theone linked arms with Arela and gazed at the nimbus clouds knotting in the eastern sky. "It was so sunny earlier," she said, "how quickly storms emerge in the mountains. It's wondrous to watch the change. Spider is an accomplished rider, but a torrential thundershower is dangerous, especially on a motorcycle. I hope he gets beyond the weather or is near shelter when the rain comes."

Her tone was neutral, but Arela could detect the omnipotence of The Deity in her words. She shivered.

Spider paid no regard to the altered sky or the increased wind. With his hair streaming freely, he rode the Harley at a reckless speed, spewing dirt and stones from the shoulder edge as he cut sloppily around the curves through the mountain passes which ranged west of Lake Latimer.

He believed unquestionably that Theone was an immortal being. He embraced The Message as legitimate and worthy. But he could not accept the role she claimed he had in her mission! So his soul would make a big stride if he became her consort. At what cost to his emotions? At what price to his manhood? He did not belong with her! He could not make that kind of commitment, no matter what it might mean to his soul's journey. He'd go at a slower pace. Reaching Peace would take him a while, probably a great while, but this was what he could deal with.

The rain burst in a fury, instantly obscuring the road. Spider eased the gas for the upcoming curve he expected, but unable to see it, he misjudged the grade and skidded. He had the skill to drive towards the inner lane, not the cliff edge, but an approaching vehicle was in the lane. Luckily, the driver in the four-wheeler was native to the area and accustomed to the weather. He ably avoided the motorcycle without losing control, but Spider saw a distinct red door loom within inches of him; shaking, he halted on the thin shoulder abutting a sheer boulder wall.

His teeth chattered more from nerves than from the drenching he was receiving. A minute ago, he could have been dead! Where was his soul? Not anywhere near where it should be if he hoped to advance beyond this phase of his journey. In reality, his soul had lost ground in this life because on balance, his choices had been...wrong ones.

He realized the rain had slackened and glancing up, noticed the sign for a town. Trembling, Spider decided it was time to get off the road. It was time to seek haven and recoup.

The motel room smelled moldy and was grungier than average for Spider, but he was too exhausted to care. He forced himself to drape his sopping clothes on the closet rod, then he took a hot shower. Climbing into the lumpy bed, he considered that it might have bugs, but bites would be proof that he was still alive. He fell asleep at once.

Hairy bristles against his cheek? Spider twitched. *Now a slimy bristle ...which was...a rough tongue?* He opened his eyes and gasped. *How had he gotten into this barren forest? In the middle of winter yet? Odd, he could see snow, but he did not feel cold.*

He did feel warmth like breath and focused. Silver eyes in a furry, silver face...a wolf's face right by his...but the wolf had its attention...on another wolf a foot away!

"I just want his hair," the wolf closest to him said.

"We should signal the pack...make a meal of him."

Spider shut tight his eyes. Take the damn hair, but leave my brain, he thought, leave my limbs and my liver.

"Just his hair. It would nicely improve the nest for our brood."

"You females are impractical!"

"You males are too contentious! We aren't hungry, and killing this human is unnecessary. Haven't we been hunted and slaughtered enough? They will track us, you can be sure. Now just shear off his hair."

"I suppose I am to do this without scratching his scalp?"

The female chuckled. "You're very good with your teeth. Do your best, Dear. Remember, Love Rules."

The male grumbled something Spider could not hear, but he could feel a tug at his hair...

Spider awoke on his side. He tried to turn over and discovered that his hair had gotten trapped under his shoulder which pulled if he moved. He laughed uneasily. The dream had been so real! But that's all it had been. A dream.

He fumbled for the lamp switch and found his watch on the nightstand. Five forty a.m. There had to be a barber shop in this town, and he was getting his hair cut.

Amy did not view herself as promiscuous, even if her stepfather, the preacher, accused that she was. *Former* stepfather. (Her mother had died last year from ovarian cancer.) She'd been to bed with five guys before her ex-husband, and only five guys since, two who were truck drivers that would not be back or would have forgotten her if they did. But she supposed the preacher had heard. Nobody blabbed loudly about who slept with who, but living in a small town like this one, everybody just seemed to know. God, it was because there just really wasn't anything else to do! Having sex at least made you feel something. She was twenty-four and pretty and had been curtailed too early from a fun life.

At her aunt's urging, she'd gone to beauticians' school in Boulder. If it had not been for Earl knocking her up on the front seat of his fancy truck, she would have stayed in Boulder instead of returning to this place to get married. Having Earl Jr. had kind of made her dependent on Earl Sr.'s child care support, though. Plus Earl Sr.'s father owned the cafe and a bunch of other property in town. His opinion carried weight and he had a soft spot for his only grandson. Also, her aunt leased space for her beauty parlor from her ex-father-in-law. Aunt Milly would not help Amy get away. Escaping with three year old Earl Jr., then, was not an option if Amy wanted to keep him.

Amy did not usually have to be here this early, but she had promised to tidy the beauty parlor this morning so that her aunt could run into Kremmling for supplies. She'd stuck a cranky Earl Jr. at her girl friend's. Since it was the middle of the week, there were no appointments until eleven and Amy figured she had time to loaf before she got to the cleaning. She settled into one of the empty chairs and raised the leg rest. The new issue of *"Flair"* magazine had come in the mail yesterday and she intended to lose herself in a fantasy of being a model in the Bahamas where the feature layout had been photographed.

At seven a.m., Spider left the motel and walked the short distance to a cafe to have breakfast. The waitress gave him directions to the beauty parlor which was a block up the street. He took a chance that it opened early.

Amy gaped at the handsome stranger. Where had this hunk come from? He reminded her of the male model in a fluorescent, bikini-style brief that she had just been drooling over!

"Can you cut my hair short?" Spider requested again. "It doesn't have to be styled."

"I sure can cut your hair," she blurted, "but why? It's gorgeous." You're gorgeous, she commented to herself.

The blonde was very attractive and her seductive tone indicated that she could be an easy conquest, but in a hick town, girls like her were married. Their husbands worked next door. Besides, he had to start improving his soul and presumably, empty couplings didn't qualify. Spider dismissed the notion.

"I'm ready for a change," he said. "Do you have time now?"

Amy bopped from the chair. "Come over to the sink so I can get my hands on you, uh, your hair. I should wash it first, okay?"

Following her, he checked her cute butt in the tight cutoffs and smiled. Living The Message did not mean giving up sex, he rationalized, on the contrary. Theone had said...Spider frowned. Before the Deity he'd made a serious promise to Theone. A promise he had meant...and still meant. But what about all those beasts? How could he be with her if he was afraid?

Spider's heart lurched as the significance of his dream hit him. Wolves weren't the only animals who liked hair for their nests. If his hair was short, he would be safe! Why had Theone not said that to him?

...Free will, Spider, you are a human with free will...

It wasn't rational; truthfully, it was an insane premise, but suddenly his fear was gone. So? Whatever worked to free him...he loved Theone and there would be no life for him without her.

Impatient to be finished and gone, Spider sat down in the chair that Amy indicated. "Just wet it," he suggested. "I'm really in a hurry."

"Why such a hurry? I get off at four today," Amy purred, "I'm single and available." She cranked back the chair, brushing his thigh in the process.

"I'm married," Spider said firmly.

"A lot of guys are," she countered as she massaged his neck.

Spider sat up abruptly, but kept his tone kind. "I'm VERY married. Can I just get a haircut?"

Amy sighed with frustration, but nodded. God, even strangers weren't decent in this town!

Stratus clouds shaded the sky, but the sun gleamed through regularly on Spider's return route. He had traveled quite a distance the previous day, and he was careful about the speed limit. It was late afternoon when he arrived at Arela's. Mike and Jasper were outside loading the Airstream for travel because the next morning, they were leaving for Theone's interview with Rae Nolan scheduled in five days at the Minidoka NWR in Southern Idaho.

Spider lifted off his helmet and smiled tentatively. Theone would have filled in her trusted friends on his defection.

"Theone is walking with Mag," Mike said in a mild tone. "They just left and might be a while."

"Do you mind if I just wait here on the steps?" Spider asked.

"You're always welcome, Gabriel," Jasper answered cordially.

In the kitchen, Arela and Pilar heard Spider's voice and paused from packing canned goods.

"I guess he made the right choice," Arela said.

"I knew he would return," Pilar stated with conviction. "There is an aura about him which he cannot extinguish. Gabriél, the angel, was a hero of God. This namesake's destiny is with our Theone."

An hour passed before Mag rounded the turn by Arela's property. Mike and Jasper had gone inside.

"Theone split off and took a lake route," she said to Spider. Giving him a wistful smile, she mounted the stairs and entered the kitchen.

Spider stood, then sat again. When Theone wanted to deal with him, she'd be here.

Theone could see the Harley by the Airstream as she climbed the slope. She checked the deck and located Spider on the steps at the front of the house, his head in his hands. Smiling, she increased her pace. It was going to be okay.

"What did you do to your hair?" She asked.

Spider startled. Theone's approach had been silent and suddenly she was before him. She smiled.

He smiled back. "Oh, I cut it off as befitting the husband of a goddess who doesn't want her animals to get tangled in it."

"It's uncombed and cowlicked and I like it."

"It's just a short, straight version of yours, Theone."

She ruffled the windblown black shock, and he caught her hand, kissing it.

"I'm sorry for what I said. I didn't mean any of it, and I'm sure I hurt you. Forgive me?"

"I learned something important from what happened. There is no blame," Theone said, "nothing to forgive."

Spider stood and hugged her. "Yes, there is," he whispered, "I was wrong, so wrong."

"Your soul knows," she murmured, "your soul recognizes your sincerity."

He kissed her deeply, then grinned at her. "The sun is low. Can I watch it set with you?"

"And when it rises in the morning?"

Spider winked at her. "Things that rise in the morning are very appealing."

She giggled at the implication.

His tone became serious. "I'll be there daily along with every critter in the area, but none of them will ever be as devoted as I will to you."

Theone rested her head against his chest and thanked The Deity for this human's special soul.

Mike grilled chicken and vegetables fajita-style for dinner; Mag prepared a red cabbage vinaigrette and spiced the pinto beans. Pilar steamed tortillas while Jasper concocted margaritas. It had grown chilly, but the group was accustomed to being in the elements, so Spider and Theone set the table on the deck to take advantage of the sensational sky. The meal was an occasion to celebrate Spider's return as much as it was an acknowledgment of passage. Theone had brought them together, changing their lives forever with The Message, and at her behest, their paths would soon diverge to inspire other lives with The Message.

Spider, in particular, enjoyed the sunset. Across the lake, a mist had nestled in between the mountain peaks, smearing their black shapes against a nickel-colored sky splotched with blue-gray clouds. Long after the sun's disappearance, a panorama of hazy cougars, lizards, grizzlies and other feral creatures drifted by. He lost count of the different animals who now simply kindled his interest, not dread.

"The waning moon is like a gold ark sailing on a celestial black sea," Spider said from Theone's pup tent where they lay on their stomachs in their inter-zipped sleeping bags looking out at the sky.

Theone kissed his neck. "What a lovely description."

"For the appreciation of the loveliest goddess." He nudged her shoulder so that he could reach her breast. Fondling it, he said, "I guess I lost my chance for that wilderness scene until we stop somewhere on our way tomorrow. Unless our present spot qualifies..."

"My period started a few hours ago."

He withdrew his hand. "How long does it last?"

"Five days, but we don't have to wait."

"Oh, yes we do." He kissed her. "When I enjoy it, I want you to enjoy it more. There's no rush."

Theone pressured him so that they were side by side, then she kissed him lustfully. "Lay on your back and I will love you the same way I did in our shower."

"Ah...no. Not tonight. When things can be more...mutual..." he chuckled at the memory, "and I'm rested enough to handle it...just do your magick for me so I can sleep."

"But you can do it yourself. Focus on a Glimpse of Peace like the stars or recall a moment spent in Peace like a walk by the ocean. Let go of the physical. Allow the spiritual to enter."

Spider gazed out to find a star in a black sky indistinguishable from the lake, but a rustling noise made him tense. Then a flash of familiar white stripes caused him to chuckle again. Just a skunk paying homage.

"She's right here, Buddy," Spider spoke to the night. "The doormat is always out for you and the rest of Nature's crew. That includes you less charming dudes, too." The desire throbbing in him lessened until it was replaced by a feeling of contentment. "I'm filled with Peace," he said, surprised.

"Peace comes in all forms and all degrees," Theone said. "The key is to remain open to it. Now hold me while we sleep."

They wrapped around each other and when the graying of dawn woke them, they were still in the same position.

Heedless of the stormy weather, Theone rode with Spider on his Harley during the trip to Minidoka NWR. Often she had him detour to Glimpse a wet Peace, but before sunset each of the nights they traveled, they found their companions. The sun would break free of its cloudy prison, and they would commune together in glorious sight of The Deity's daily Glimpse of Peace.

⸺

From inside a luxuriant motor coach, Rae Nolan stared irritably at the Snake River clogged with birds. Her research assistant had identified whistling swans and white pelicans congregated among the clustered, shifting ducks, geese and other game birds. Early in the century, a dam constructed across the river had created nearby Lake Walcott, and it had transformed a desert-like terrain into an inviting stop for waterfowl migrating the North-South route.

She considered that the area may have historical significance because of its path on the Oregon Trail; its designation by Theodore Roosevelt may make it one of the nation's oldest refuges, but in November, Minidoka National Wildlife Refuge was a clammy, bordering on frigid place to be outside. Dikes and marshes were not pretty sights to Rae. The steady vibration from the dam did not soothe. Furthermore, local accommodations were less than first rate. This crude swamp scene was a far cry from the beautiful homes and gardens of famous people which was Rae's standard interview setting. Yet Theone Jones was growing into THE NAME of the century or perhaps the millennium. Was she truly the Daughter of God? Rae alone of the media was going to have a chance to investigate the possibility first hand.

So pull on the ugly rubber boots over the thermal socks, wrap tightly in your environmentally correct fake furs, trust the waterproof makeup and eliminate the bitch in your attitude, Rae reminded herself. This exclusive interview was an incredible privilege and possibly the only one Theone Jones was ever going to grant. Summon your notable people skills and maximize the moment. The ratings *and Rae's popularity* were about to rank up there higher than the stars, human and celestial.

Kissing away Spider's objections, Theone allowed only Jasper to accompany her in the Suburban to meet Rae Nolan at a road-accessible river site where Theone had insisted that just essential electronic gear be used so as to not disturb the environment. Her friends were camped in the Airstream on Bureau of Reclamation land just below the dam. Courtesy of the network, they had a color television hook-up so that they could watch the interview.

"Are you nervous?" Jasper inquired anxiously.

She smiled at him. "No, should I be?"

"Rae's a real sharpie, yet civil. She can get things out of people, but she's not malicious about it. Too many of them are. It's that ratings' war they're always fighting. Rae's so entrenched that I guess she's above it."

Theone visualized the renowned news commentator who was in her early fifties. Reasonably attractive with exceptional hair, platinum blonde Rae had started her career fighting against the bimbo stereotype. She had cultivated a masculine timbre for appeal, but had refused to dye her natural hair color to fit an expected image and became a darling of feminists in the communications industry. But sheer ambition and a fortunate timing of opportunities, combined with an ability for disarming difficult subjects, had assured her long range success in her profession. It had not hurt to remain married to a powerful, high-profile Hollywood executive who owned substantial pieces of Lake Tahoe real estate.

"It won't make any difference, Jasper, how Rae treats me," Theone said. "I would say the same thing, regardless of who did the interview."

Jasper cleared his throat, then stuttered, "Her ques...questions mi...might be ve...very pointed. I'm su...sure she'll go af...ff...ter you on your...your views of...Christ...ianity."

"We're approaching the site. There are nine people hovering about besides Rae! But I'm pleased that they followed my request about minimizing the equipment, and I don't see any of those garish lights. See how relaxed the birds are? They aren't upset."

"Ra...Rae cou...could tr...try to...to..."

"Jasper, please trust me. You've been with me two years, and you still haven't learned not to worry about things! But I love you dearly. Now, get on back to the others." She opened the door, and the swell of greetings from the birds who had been anticipating her precluded any further conversation.

The news commentator and her crew had been observing the Suburban's approach, but they were distracted by the astonishing demonstration put on by the birds. Theone reached the people without notice and fixed on the creatures with a kind, firm look.

Silence.

Disconcerted, Rae re-directed her attention and gasped. Like a sprite, Theone had gotten right next to her!

Rae always demanded thirty minutes off camera with a subject prior to taping or live air. To break the ice, to ease a jittery subject, to get a feel for mood, to define the atmosphere - she was superstitious about extemporaneous interviews and a tête-à-tête, as she called it, gave her a means to gain control prior to the formal interview. Now, before it had even started, Rae felt on the defensive!

"They've had their say and won't disrupt us," Theone said without preliminaries, "you requested a private talk before your camera transmits. Shall we wander closer to this magnificent river so dense with a congregation of Our Deity's creatures? It is a Glimpse of Peace."

Uncharacteristically speechless, Rae nodded and glanced at Theone's flimsy silver jacket, brown twill skirt and bare feet. She had watched her and heard her and read the book. Several times on each count. She had been prepared in depth for what to expect so why did she feel such...school-girl wonder in this woman's presence? Get it together, Lady, Rae admonished herself. Get it going before you lose it like some ingenue!

"No tête-à-tête this time," Rae exclaimed. "This time we're just going to shoot." She signaled her producer. "No prelims. We're going straight on."

The producer gripped the earphones on his head and appeared stricken. In two minutes, they'd be live and had ready a script to do scenery and long shots of the two women while an out of view reporter discussed Theone's background. With commercials, it was timed to last thirty minutes. The interview slot was set for another thirty. "I can't just change the format!" He yelled. "The network will fry me!"

The sound technician, though, gestured and his assistant, a pessimistic, assertive fellow, dashed to Theone with a remote microphone while Rae's personal assistant rushed up to her boss to make sure her microphone was properly set.

Simultaneously, the photographer shouldered his equipment and spun around. He jogged to a position in front of the group preparing for broadcast and fiddled with his alignment controls.

Meanwhile, the sound assistant had looked into Theone's eyes and stood motionless. Theone held out her hand for the microphone and in so doing, she touched his hand. The young man's mouth gaped and his negative expression became euphoric.

Rae's makeup and hair assistants had arrived from the trailer, and she was too involved with adjusting her appearance to observe what had happened, but the director had joined the photographer. The director was already a believer in The Message and tears blurred her eyes as her co-worker docilely relinquished the microphone to Theone. The Messenger would need no instructions on attaching it correctly to her jacket. Theone smiled at the director to show accord.

By the time the photographer's assistant had gotten into place, the whole sequence of events had lasted no more than seconds. The assistant grinned at Rae and held up her thumb. The photographer focused on Rae and hit the start button.

"Rae Nolan here and today I am at Minidoka National Wildlife Refuge in Southern Idaho, at this time of year, a soggy, but vibrant spot teeming with migratory birds."

The director remembered her job. She yanked her attention from Theone and signaled for a camera sweep of the populated river before settling back on Rae. The photographer expanded the picture to include Theone in its transmission.

"With me witnessing this lush display of nature is Theone Jones, an ardent supporter of wildlife, and from the enthusiastic reaction of our feathered friends just moments ago, they are ardent supporters of her." Rae smiled at Theone, but did not connect with her eyes. Part of Rae's technique was to employ a sincere, earnest expression without actually focusing on her subject. It kept her thoughts organized, and she had learned quickly how distracting Theone could be.

She continued. "And there are plenty of humans - your term, Theone - who are ardent supporters as well. In a nutshell, you teach that for one's soul to advance, to progress towards an Ultimate Peace, a human has to be of modest, honest behavior and love others. If a human fails to act in such a manner, progress is halted or even regressed. Similar to Christianity, your message contains an elementary philosophy with potential for an optimistic result, yet with an irreconcilable difference. Christians believe that behavior has only a minor or no bearing on the soul's ascension to heaven. By virtue of acceptance of Jesus, Grace redeems you. You say no such thing is true." She paused and regarded Theone solemnly. "Such a controversy that has been unleashed! And how serious your foes have grown in forcing people to make a choice! Your own brother-in-law, Dr. Glenn Chandler, an Inspiration Of Grace pastor and a leading opponent, has issued a directive on behalf of the Christ Covenant. Communion will be denied to those who do not sign an allegiance to the creed as stated in the New Testament of the Bible. Well!" Rae chuckled huskily. Along with her hair, the throaty sound was a trademark. "Theone, I am giving you your forum today. Please, respond to this factious edict."

The camera zoomed in for a close-up of Theone, but she turned her head towards the river and her incandescent hair filled the lens before the photographer could zoom out. She spoke at the same time and her resonant voice came across disembodied.

"Forcing a resolution by involving an integral symbol of faith such as Christian Communion is a bitter judgment by its religious leaders. Judgment is not a choice for me and it is not a choice, either, for a human who truly desires Peace." Theone smiled fully and the photographer got a lock on her face. "Come," she invited. "The river is a Glimpse of Peace and summons us." Theone gracefully strode off.

Mesmerized by her, the photographer effortlessly kept pace and focus. Out of the picture, Rae scurried on the spongy ground to catch up.

"These religious leaders," Rae panted, "as a whole they profess that God called upon them directly and in some cases quite dramatically to guide others in faith. If what you're saying is true, then how can such a large group be so misguided?"

"Many are genuinely touched by Our Deity; unfortunately, just as many lack sincerity in their motives because a true leader of faith remains a humble teacher. Certain advanced souls are so well on the right path to Peace that in this environment, they are strongly motivated to teach, to share with others The Message that they themselves live by, but it is an incentive driven by the soul, not one for recognition or gain. Arela Pedersen who is with me, has such a soul."

"Arela Pedersen, a primary educator from Denver, and a recent convert," Rae detailed for the audience.

"Not recent," Theone said. "Arela's soul already followed The Message before she met me and understood Truth. My presence here is expressly to help every human recognize Truth and hopefully, The Message will steer their souls on the path to Peace."

"Yes, but what about Dr. Chandler and our current religious leaders?" Rae queried. "They are a viable entity that cannot be ignored. They control souls, as it were, by the power of their positions, and if they do not advocate your message, an irreparable schism may occur. The consequences..."

They had reached within several feet of the river and Theone bent to acknowledge a persistent pair of quacking mallards. She sighed gently. "The truth is, the greater the power one seeks and the greater the control one exerts over another, the less one's soul advances. Missionaries have good intentions, but it is pride to believe that their creed is the only path to Truth. Religions commonly set down dogma bolstered by explicit ritual. Weak souls are attracted to the definitive because they are in need of support on their journey, and self-motivated souls prey on their need. Organized religion also provides a stagnant place for complacent souls who neither retreat nor advance on their journey because they think belonging is all that is necessary; they take no risks. They ask no questions. But there is no right or wrong in this! Humans have free will. They make choices. For spiritual growth, though, for the soul to advance, the choice must be The Message; The Message must be lived. The consequences, then, are personal to each soul."

Watching with a leery eye the nearby throng of waterfowl, Rae remarked, "Throughout history, such consequences have caused wars."

"Yes, all too often it has been a human choice."

"Why do so many souls, as it were, choose this strife?"

"I cannot account for each soul's journey, but Our Deity has charted formidable obstacles in this environment. How can the soul advance if there isn't temptation? If there aren't choices? Because free will is part of human nature, Our Deity cannot prevent human destruction in this environment. There is no hope for change unless humans embrace The Message."

Rae smiled indulgently at the camera to convey the impression that this bit of Theone's doctrine was not shared by her. "Part of your appeal is that your ideas are sensible and insightful," she said to broach another direction, "yet your detractors scoff at your lack of education, at your simplistic demeanor. Comment?"

"You can study all you want, but if you don't live your faith, it's a waste of time. Faith does not have to be analyzed endlessly to be valid."

Rae glanced at her director to see how things were going and her expression was...beatific. What a ridiculously fatuous word, but somehow...her face...the photographer's assistant had a similar expression and the sound assistant had no business being this close to them, but he appeared...spiritually intoxicated? Confused, Rae forgot her control intentions and gazed at Theone's eyes.

Theone's eyes reflected Roger's dissolution! Roger, her husband of convenience, who liked to frolic with youth of either sex as long as their age did not exceed eighteen. Why did she stay married to such a reprobate? They weren't even friends! She stayed because she did not have to give anything to the relationship nor did he. Neither of them had emotional depth; self-interest consumed them. Their marriage offered a shield. Staying married kept others at bay. Perhaps professionally she had achieved the pinnacle, but what a waste she had made of her personal life!

Rae forgot the scenario that she and her production team had devised. Thoughts popped into her mind and she blurted them out. "Let's discuss specifics. The Ten Commandments. Any opinion?"

"The Ten Commandments were an attempt by Our Deity to clarify the guidelines for the Hebrews. Given the human propensity for aggression, they are good rules for every soul."

"How about the Lord's Prayer and the lessons of Jesus? Is there any truth at all in the forgiveness He promised?"

"The verbiage of the Lord's Prayer fits the historical moment, and I affirm The Message delivered by Jesus, but not the interpretation that has gone on since his departure. Forgiveness is part of growth, but should not be equated with instant salvation."

"Lord, Father, Son, Master - it is all masculine terminology. Our greatest prophets, the acknowledged representatives of the Divine, have been male. If a Goddess is so important, why did her worship disappear?"

"It has not. Until the past couple of decades, Her Worship has merely been forced to hide itself."

"In witchcraft?"

Theone smiled tolerantly. "In faiths harmonious to Nature and the Universe, the female essence flourishes beside the male essence."

"Whereby practitioners cast spells and consult means to see the future so as to influence it?"

"Prophesy is a gift granted to certain advanced souls, and for one so blessed, divination can be an accurate tool to help other souls who find it a comfort to have a map ahead of time. The moment the tarot is cast or the coins tossed or the runes are thrown for excess personal gain, though, the soul doing it loses ground."

"Perhaps so, but in general perception, the connotation is bogus," Rae said.

"Sadly true. Yet whether for good or bad purpose, magick is real."

"Are you recommending that people should practice good magic for their soul to advance?"

"Christian Communion is good magick," Theone said. "It is a ritualized spell performed to cleanse the soul and encourage a believer to aspire for Peace. Prayer, meditation, chants, incantations, charms - they are all means to reach Our Deity. For example, the energy in crystals and other natural elements can be channeled to heal spiritual pain, but this energy won't heal or make whole a failing body."

"Do you believe that drugs can be of a similar use?"

"Altering substances can enhance some souls' insight or they can ease a soul's bumpy path through physical illness, but in themselves these substances are detours on your journey. Drugs shackle progress because the mind muddles and the soul cannot choose clearly."

Rae took a moment to smile at the audience. "So with all these souls about taking journeys, does Our Deity continue to create new souls?"

"This issue isn't important," Theone said resolutely. "What is important is where your soul is at right now."

Rae raised her brows at the camera. "Mmm, I guess that question will have to be shelved. What about slavery and human rights. Shouldn't our goal be to strive for equality? Surely you will have a judgment on that!"

"Slavery is crushing and it is a progressive choice for those who seek an end to it, but each soul travels at a different pace. This isn't a judgment, but a fact."

"I see. Slavery, then, in your opinion, is a relational thing to soul." *And extremely controversial!* Rae savored viewers' indignation and the favorable effect on ratings. "What about suicide?" She inquired.

"Suicide cuts short a soul's journey, but does not finish it."

"Are souls ever lost?"

"Rarely."

"Which ones?"

"Atheists rank among those souls at the furthest point from Peace."

"Yet they still have a chance?"

"All souls, whatever level, are given choices."

"With the state of the soul of such maximum importance, surely you disapprove of the death penalty!"

"Some souls make great progress when their present physical self is terminated so harshly. It can be a growth experience."

"But certain humans are making a judgment which is detrimental to *their* souls!"

"Yes. Choices tend to be interactive."

Wow! Rae thought after the rapid exchange. Theone had a black-white sentiment on everything, but it jumped from liberal to conservative! She widened her eyes at the director as a sign to do a close-up of her as a 'touch base' with the audience, but got no response. The camcorder stayed riveted on Theone. A bit peeved, Rae said brusquely, "Death has been called the Great Equalizer. In other words, you can't take it with you. Comment?"

The assistant recognized Rae's displeasure and nudged the photographer. Instead of fixing on Rae, though, he broadened his focus to include both women.

"For the body, yes, but for the soul, physical death is a moment of truth and there is no equality about it. Particularly affected are those who profess spiritual values and have been taught Truth, yet have lived wicked lives. Let me assure you, in death these souls are on low levels of the progress scale. They recognized Truth and turned away from it."

"Have science and technology helped or hindered these matters of the soul?"

"Science and technology have made the soul's journey more difficult. Souls who have gained all they can from this environment have a right to pass from it. This gain may entail a life of a few hours or a century, but whatever age, keeping these souls alive beyond their need is injustice and a detour for those souls perpetuating it."

"Indeed! Hear that doctors!" Rae declared cheerfully. To hell with whom the photographer had in the shot, the greater picture was going to be the astronomical ratings. "Where does sex fit into this?" She sallied.

"All life is designed to procreate, but not in an abusive manner. The Message is clear about honesty. Rape is stealing, which is dishonest, and the soul of such a human is no better than an atheist."

Despite the penetrating barrage, Theone's demeanor remained composed and pleasant. Rae was thoroughly enjoying herself. "Souls must be born again and again to take the journey so apparently you are not an advocate of birth control," she said, "and God forbid abortion!"

"A soul unprepared to nurture another soul should not procreate," Theone said, "therefore, birth control is an absolute. Abortion is a choice of birth control, not an issue of right and wrong. Regulating it is a judgment.

"Originally, life was an issue of survival, but in today's advanced society, birth control should be given to every female at puberty for this very reason. Quantity is not the goal, but quality. The responsibility for a born soul is the greatest one a human undertakes and providing a nurturing environment advances the souls of both parent and child. A baby should not be conceived without that in mind. A soul can advance without experiencing parenthood, but successful parenting advances the soul greatly."

"Whew! You obviously do not advocate celibacy."

"Celibacy is a choice. It neither advances nor hinders the soul's progress."

"Are you suggesting that the soul of a holy man like the Pope doesn't advance?"

Theone shrugged. "The wealthy trappings of his office, the powerful position, the celibacy - I'm saying that on balance, his soul's journey will advance less than the destitute woman in a hovel who dies giving birth."

Rae laughed to dilute the import of the blasphemous remark. "How does this pertain to gays?"

"They are not celibate."

"But they don't procreate, mm? Does their sexual choice deter progress?"

"No, between consenting adults, human sexuality has little bearing on the soul."

"Uh, huh! Are there other environments?"

"Yes."

"And Peace is the ultimate one, like heaven or nirvana."

"Peace has been called many names."

"Does a soul ever reach Peace?"

"Oh, yes, and Our Deity rejoices."

"Theone, what level environment is Earth?"

"Be less concerned about the environment than the personal level of your soul's journey."

"Touché," Rae conceded. "You have an answer for every question."

"These answers have been available since the beginning of human existence. I am here to repeat them again because for too many in this environment, the answers have been obscured. From the creation of consciousness, Our Deity has been known to you. Gaia, Ishtar, Elohim, Allah - the faces of Our Deity are numerous. And you have been given directions to achieve Peace by many representatives of Our Deity, whether through conceptual god-form or the presence of an historic being. To name only a few, Brighid, Sophia, Ma'at, Devi, Eros, The Buddha, Mohammed and the greatest of these, Jesus! You have been availed Glimpses of Peace - a blooming garden, an ocean's tide, a painted desert, a leafy forest! Windows of Peace opened by great artists such as Michelangelo, Mozart and Picasso have left humans a legacy for inspiration. Other advancing souls have shared Peace through their exemplary behavior - Gandhi, Mother Teresa - this is inspiration, too. Humans are born with the finest vehicles to achieve Peace - the capacity to love and the ability to reason, yet on every life's road, there are detours, chuckholes and barricades. How you respond to these obstacles relates to your growth."

"In this environment, do souls, as a general rule, make progress?"

"Many souls do have journeys with progress, but others experience a mild decline in growth. A few have dramatic jumps or setbacks. There are exceptions either way, and they are usually striking."

Rae had recovered enough control not to stare into Theone's eyes, but she measured her with a shrewd look. "There is one final question, one uppermost on everyone's mind, supporters and foes alike. A question which could be judged as most important." She paused for climactic effect. "It is held by Christians that Jesus was the Son of God. Are you, then, claiming to be the Daughter?"

"Like you and other humans, I am of Our Deity."

"But you in particular," Rae persisted. "Are you a special soul? Perhaps one just meant for a singular journey or perhaps this journey is the last one for your soul? Unlike the rest of us, do you even have a soul?"

"I am here in this environment to deliver The Message. My soul's status is insignificant to any but myself and Our Deity, just as your own soul should be."

"Stop the hedging, Theone, and tell us...humans. Are you the Daughter of God?"

In a discordance of honking, a gaggle of Canadian geese rose from the river.

Theone raised her arms and spread wide her fingers. "Honor Our Deity!" She proclaimed in a voice heard clearly above the noise.

Every bird for a mile in either direction ascended in formation, and the cacophony was deafening.

Rae gawked stupidly and trembled while the cool-headed photographer panned from her to the river spectacle to Theone smiling sublimely.

Then, darkness. Birds blanketed the sky.

The water stilled. The air stilled.

Then, silence. Silence so profound that the camcorder picked up Rae's labored breathing. The photographer zoomed in for a close-up.

She swallowed and blinked several times as if unaware of where she was. The photographer took pity and settled solely on Theone who beckoned at the sky.

In a tremendous blitz, crushes of waterfowl returned to the slate-colored river still churned from recent occupancy. Theone laughed with gusto and with a final smile at the camera, started off in the direction of her companions' campsite.

The awed director did not need to instruct the photographer. His lens followed Theone who radiated from a bright light which had suddenly appeared in the gloom.

In Venice, California, Bobby stared malevolently at his new wide screen television broadcasting Theone's fading figure. The television, the white PVC furniture, the king-size futon and an un-crated state-of-the-art entertainment center in his newly leased apartment had been financed by

Yolenta and Tym with his promise that he not disappear again like he had. He didn't plan on it. Crude conditions and gadding through the countryside had been a temporary lapse in sanity. And he still could not believe how long he had abstained from sex just because Theone might have been inclined for a tumble.

Bobby clicked the TV remote. He was going to get even with Theone for toying with him and messing with his head, but precisely how had not occurred to him yet. It would, though, Bobby was positive.

Theone arrived at the Airstream, her eyes smoldering. Her companions charged around her, excited about the successful telecast with Rae Nolan, but she shook her head at them. "Gabriel!" She commanded. The others stepped back respectfully and he embraced her. She gazed into his eyes. "There is a lake in southeastern Oregon at Malheur NWR which fringes the Cascades. Please...take me."

Spider saw rosy quartz and he grinned at her double meaning. "What about our friends?"

She smiled happily. "They will drive parallel. The Glimpse of Peace at Malheur is a controlled environment, but it is an excellent testimony to humans' care for the wilderness."

The lake did not impress Spider. Theone had shown him phenomenal Glimpses of Peace - lush glens, spiring cliffs, waters so crystal blue that it hurt his eyes to look at them. But this spot had scanty vegetation and near it, stretches of white alkali flats; the lake or what seemed more like a pond was shallow and brackish. The area was part of the Pacific Flyway and there were ducks and shorebirds, but nothing like some of the splendid gatherings that he'd seen previously. At least no trees blocked the sun, he considered. The weather was crisp, and there would be little heat to warm his bare backside.

He walked from the water's edge to Theone who stood in a shoal acknowledging...he halted. Snails? Amazing.

She stepped from the water to a drier area, but it still looked pretty marshy to Spider.

"We won't be bothered here," Theone said and started undressing.

Test, Spider thought, another test. Disregard the weather and the ooze. This test had to be passed with a perfect score.

He unzipped his jacket and shucked his heavy wool sweater. Shivering, but dauntless, he unbuttoned his pants. Theone caught his hips before his jeans came down.

"Oh, Gabriel, leave them on."

His eyes ranged her nude, voluptuous body. "I'm just supposed to look?"

She giggled. "You won't be comfortable without clothes and I can't be in a sleeping bag." She tried to topple him.

"Heck, no!" He cried, planting his feet. "I'm getting naked exactly like you!"

Theone sighed while Spider used her for support and struggled with his laced boots. When his jeans fell to his ankles, though, she sank to the soft ground.

"Now, right, now, before you get too cold," she said, spreading her legs and arching her hips.

Laying across her, he mumbled, "Foreplay first. I'll hurt you, otherwise."

"You have goose bumps. NOW!"

"I DON'T WANT TO HURT YOU!"

They gazed at each other.

"Theone, I'm the expert here. It will probably be the only time it ever happens, but you don't get to call the shots on this one."

She grinned slyly. "Okay, Gabriel, but not too long. I don't need much."

"Sure you do," he muttered and kissed her. He'd pleasurably explored her body in detail just like she had explored his; they had both achieved some memorable ecstasy, but this time it was critical. This time it counted for the score, and he wanted his lovemaking to be fantastic for her.

At the consummation of their union, Spider forgot the temperature; he forgot his fear of causing her pain. He had always prided himself on his staying power, but he felt as if he was caught in a sensuous maelstrom and his control was nil. She got there, though, in a spectacular way. He could feel it almost better than his own swift climax.

"I finished as fast as I could to keep your discomfort at a minimum," he bluffed.

"Oh."

Spider got up on his elbows. "That isn't usually the case!"

Theone smiled broadly.

He shook his finger at her. "Next time you won't be smiling like that."

"Next time you'll know what to expect."

Abruptly, tears brimmed his eyes. "I love you, Theone. I love you and whatever makes you happy, I'll do."

"Then you're doing everything right because I'm very happy."

He grinned.

She pushed at him. "Get up and get dressed, Gabriel."
As Spider helped her rise, he noticed showy purple flowers where they had lain. "I didn't see those when we lay down. Of course, I wasn't paying attention to anything but you. It's peculiar at this time of year. What flowers bloom in November?"
Theone glanced at the cerulean sky. "None here. These are special irises fostered by our union."
"Did you happen to hear thunder?"
She laughed. "I hope you like the sound because you and I will be spending a lot of time doing this."
"Thank you, Goddess!" Spider yelled.
Jolted by his exclamation, a flock of ducks took off.
Theone pulled his sweater over his head. "If you must be gender specific, Gabriel, thank God who is the source of sexual attraction."
He kissed her hard. "I'm grateful to Our Deity for you."
"The feeling is mutual." Theone entered a shallow pool to wash the blood from between her thighs. No mud had clung to either of them.
Spider had his jeans ready to step into when he noticed the two wolves bellying towards them. Two silver ones like in his dream. Instinctively, he touched his nape and had an illogical, but soothing thought. The hair was gone so they weren't interested in him.
Theone sensed their presence and somewhat perplexed, turned. Wolves did not inhabit this area, but she stepped from the water to acknowledge their presence.
The wolves continued at an obeisant, but steady pace.
For an instant she was surprised; then, she smiled in understanding and stood still for them.
The wolves proceeded to lick her legs dry before backing away. They rose to height, howled and loped off.
"Do wolves always touch you like that?" Spider asked in astonishment.
Theone was introspective. "No, just snakes, although in these former Indian territories here in the West, wolves were revered, and they have shown me more familiarity than other creatures. Eagles might show similar behavior in the future. It's because I'm ripe now. Mature. I am a whole female whereas prior I was a maiden." She gave Spider a coy look. "Would you like me to lick you dry sometime?"
"Oh, Baby, sometime!" He hugged her. "Let me help you get dressed now."
"Tonight, we do this again," she said, "slower and in our sleeping bags."
"Maybe a couple of times again."
"Show off."

"Pushy dame."
They laughed like any contented lovers.

In the fortnight subsequent to the telecast, Jasper was implacable. Theone's performance with Rae Nolan had been triumphant and a tremendous surge in believers had resulted, but at the same time, the opposition had grown more vocal, more militant. She had been branded an evil dissident by the Christ Covenant which daily proclaimed with pride each new addition of support from conservative denominations. Formal liberal denomination support was patchy, but their abstention from the furor implied sanction.

To flame the controversy, three days ago in Chicago, a frail Edna Jones, braced by her granddaughter, Kristen Jones Chandler, her preeminent husband, Dr. Glenn Chandler, and her retired pastor, Reverend Kermit Reese, had entered the fray with a press conference. It was exceedingly grievous to go public with this information, she had stated, but the truth had to be known. The late Aaron Jones, her son and husband of Brigit Mane Jones Scougan, was not the biological father of Theone Jones; Brigit always claimed that she had no idea who the father was, but Edna had always believed that the Devil had spawned Theone.

Theone had forbidden Jasper to issue a statement and she had counseled her outraged mother to exercise restraint; in due time, the announcement backlashed. Believers in The Message asserted that the knowledge offered further proof that Theone's father was The Deity.

Kristen's publicity ploy was the last straw for Brigit. The sneaky stunt cinched their complete estrangement.

In Paxton, Sam expedited the construction of a high-grade security fence around his property. The buildings were already wire-alarmed and two Doberman-Rottweiler mixes were kept for pets as well as for protection; he had installed scramblers on the telephones. In the past, the media had shown an interest in Brigit, and Erik had been approached on campus for interviews about both his sisters, but reporters had not been obnoxious. Curiously, they showed an unusual respect for privacy, but, Sam decided, this would tip the balance. Besides, Theone was coming home to be married. Safety was a growing factor for her sake, too.

Near Rochester, Minnesota, Jasper pleaded once again with Theone to keep her ministry public to buoy the faithful and address her enemies, but she remained steadfast in her decision to fade from prominence.

"We will be in Paxton shortly to marry, then Gabriel and I are on our own," Theone said with forbearance to her companions who had gathered for supper. She stroked Spider's head in her lap. The day after their first lovemaking, he had come down with a flu virus. Fortunately, the weather had stabilized due to a high pressure front and Spider weakly agreed to let Mike, an excited neophyte, ride the Harley with Arela. Pilar and Mag had taken turns with Jasper driving the Suburban East to Wisconsin while in the Airstream, much to Spider's delight, Theone devoted herself to him - feeding him soup, massaging his sore muscles, reading to him, holding his hand. He was not accustomed to being nursed and had dragged out his recovery. (Theone was not fooled, but she was in love.)

Arela had listened enough to Jasper's objections. "Give me a chance," she said with intensity. "Theone's spirit envelops mine and I feel the right words ready to flow."

Mike clasped Arela's shoulder in support, and Pilar remarked, "An angel is with Arela, Jasper. I can see it."

Mag, who rarely offered any opinion, settled the issue. "Theone is Our Deity's Essence on Earth. There is no discussion here. We are to heed her decision."

Jasper lowered his eyes in surrender and let it go. After all, 'Arela' in Hebrew meant 'angel'.

Theone and her companions arrived in Paxton the week before Thanksgiving in the midst of the season's first snow flurries. After a day of visiting with the Scougans and a matured Erik, Mike and Arela took the Suburban to Ashburg. He hoped that by meeting Arela, his parents would accede to his lifestyle. They would return by Saturday for the scheduled weddings.

In addition to the master suite, Sam's sprawling house had four bedrooms and a den. Theone chose to sleep inside with Spider; Jasper, Pilar and Mag settled into the other available space. Brigit had spoken to Theone regularly, but she had not seen her since her initial departure for San Antonio. Yet a strong tie bound them. Being in her presence was joyful, but inessential to the closeness Brigit felt towards her Child of Peace. The accelerating news accounts of conflict over The Message distressed her, but Brigit had always believed it inevitable and had reconciled herself to what would be a tumultuous life for Theone. She had long anticipated meeting the disciples, as she viewed Theone's companions, but the inclusion of Gabriel, so quickly her daughter's lover, had thrown her off balance.

Watching him in earnest conversation with Sam by their living room fireplace, Brigit said to Theone, "He reminds me of Lyle, my fiance who died in Vietnam. And not just his handsome looks. He has a caring disposition."

At the dining table, Theone reached for another oatmeal cookie and dunked it in her milk. "Yes, Gabriel has a nurturing soul and will make a terrific father."

Brigit stared at her daughter. "Are you pregnant?"

Theone grinned. "Not yet, Mom."

"But you will be?"

"I presume I will be."

Brigit gripped her glass of milk. This was really unexpected. The Goddess would have a child? For what purpose? Instead of joy at having a grandchild that she might be in proximity to love, the idea filled her with foreboding.

Later in bed, Brigit mentioned her apprehension to Sam who half-listened. He was too amazed at Gabriel. Tonight the sense of familiarity about the young man had come back to him. He'd seen him before! Or rather, his eyes. Clever, affectionate, khaki brown eyes fringed with thick dark lashes. He'd seen Gabriel's eyes in Theone's when she had...helped him with his paralysis. Then, her words surfaced in his consciousness. *"You will share your technical knowledge with one who will prove more gifted than you, but who is undisciplined. Teaching self-control will be part of your role."* How did that figure? Gabriel had no deep interests other than Theone. Sam drifted to sleep. When it was time, Theone would let him know the connection.

CHAPTER FIFTEEN

Elliot

Both Becker sons were raw-boned with deeply grooved cheeks, jutting brows and wide-set cinder gray eyes like their father, Melvin. They shared in common an interest in hunting, and each boy at a young age developed expertise with high power rifles to kill the javelina, ugly suckers in Melvin's opinion, who inhabited the Beaver Creek area south of Sedona, their hometown.

The boys' personalities, though, and their relationship with Melvin were opposite. Elliot, the eldest, was obedient, prudent and in his father's eyes, weak like his mother, Delora. Donald, two years younger, was rebellious, selfish and in his father's eyes, a rugged individual like Melvin yearned to be. Melvin never had a chance to satisfy his wanderlust because Delora had gotten pregnant when she was sixteen and Melvin was nineteen.

Melvin's parents were farmers; his uncle owned a shoddy Indian jewelry shop in Sedona. Delora's part Hopi father was an occasional handyman and the family eked by. Marrying Delora was considered a social step downward by the Beckers, but she was affable and industrious. The uncle offered both of them jobs, and he used Delora's ethnic background as a selling point.

During the early sixties, his uncle died and Melvin inherited Becker's Jewelry Post. Sedona had a growing tourist industry and Melvin wanted to expand the store, to add better stock. Delora, who ran the business as well as he did, agreed. They enlarged the premises and their inventory, but distrusted the idea of hiring outside help. Instead, they made their young sons work in the store.

Elliot had a pleasant, talkative manner which made him a good salesman, but his shrewdness made him invaluable. To demand the best price, he reasoned that there had to be an apparent solidness to the silver-inlaid turquoise and coral. He also had a knack for picking jewelry pieces that sold. Melvin taught Elliot early the art of negotiation and always took him on the statewide buying trips to reservations. (Don referred to Elliot as the Opinionated Stodge. Elliot retaliated by calling his brother a lazy bum.)

Don liked cycles and speed for as long as the family could remember and at age eight, motorized his English racer. For his sixteenth birthday, Melvin finally bought him a Honda 250, the smallest model manufactured, although Delora swore he'd get himself killed. Itching to hang out with the biker gangs who rumbled through town, Don curbed his impatience. He hated hick Sedona more than he hated Becker's Jewelry Post, but to get out he had to have a decent bike and cash; he announced that in the future, he'd only work at the store if paid a wage. Otherwise, he was getting a real job.

Melvin considered the demand reasonable and started paying both sons the same wage. Elliot did the majority of the menial work of tidying and arranging the displays; Don was often late and frequently left early. Melvin's reprimands and threats to dock him did not faze Don, perhaps because he sensed that secretly, Melvin admired his spirit. Besides, Don overheard Melvin confess to Delora that Elliot handled things quite capably; Don just got in the way.

When Don graduated from high school in 1973, he went to Melvin with another demand. Sedona suffocated him and he deserved just once to see scenery other than desert, cactus and red rocks. It seemed logical to him to receive now what he'd get if Melvin and Delora dropped dead tomorrow.

Melvin was so surprised at Don's audacity that he had to laugh, but he also consented. Indian jewelry was the vogue and the store had prospered. Why should Don not have a chance while young to pursue his own dreams? Elliot would inherit the jewelry post someday, and with that promise, Melvin shut up his oldest son's objections to the agreement with Don. Then, Melvin sat down with his accountant, cashed in savings certificates and handed the sum to Don who promptly purchased a Heritage Softail Classic Harley-Davidson motorcycle customized with medallion gas caps, a screaming eagle motif on the bug screen and a fringed seat. Don left Sedona without regrets.

Soon after Don's departure, Elliot had a whirlwind courtship and a brief marriage with a tourist from Arkansas enamored of the red rocks more than she was of him. When she discovered the Grand Canyon, she left him for a Colorado River guide. The experience was bitter for socially awkward Elliot, but a friend cajoled him into a blind date which led to his second, successful marriage. Vivacious Heidi was an intelligent, but impractical woman from L.A. who had settled in Sedona hoping for success as an artist. Their opposite natures clicked. Her parents, who subsidized her, were elated to have Heidi find a stable chap willing to put up with her fanciful ideas.

Delora's Hopi genes surfaced in Elliot and Heidi's first daughter, Alana, born with the beauty of a stylized Indian maiden sprung to life from an oil painting on black velvet. Stunning Alana was nice, but dumb. Elliot labeled her a flake, similar to Heidi but without the brains. The rough Becker looks unfortunately manifested in their second daughter, Gina, but even as a toddler she showed signs of being very smart like her mother and astute like her father. Elliot pinned his hopes on this one taking over the store when she grew up. Their third daughter, pretty Sacha, had a winsome personality. This bubbly one was Elliot's favorite.

In the next decade, Becker's Jewelry Post's location on U.S. 89A, the main strip through expanding Sedona, insured visibility, thus a steady customer flow, but the market had glutted and the trendiness of Indian silver passed. Heidi's watercolors of the region's picturesque vistas had a tourist appeal, though, and the Beckers sold as many of her paintings as they did trinket jewelry. They were not rich, but they were comfortable; they got along together in the shop and as a family. The senior and junior Beckers felt that they had a good life. Then, in April, 1985, right after the bustle of the winter visitor season, Don returned to Sedona.

Don had not fared well. Every Christmas he would call his mother and report how great things were going, but in actuality, his life had amounted to nothing. For a lot of the years, he had ridden aimlessly around the country, attaching himself to whatever chapter of his biker gang, the Skulldiggers, lived in the area. He hit the rock concerts, did the drugs, added the tattoos, shared the mamas and rallied each August in Sturgis, South Dakota. By the time Don ran out of money in Elk City, Oklahoma, he was considered an old timer at age thirty. Other than a few jaded survivors like himself, current gang members averaged in their twenties. Original biker buddies had either overdosed, been slain or had dropped back into society. Since Don wanted to hang on to his valuable bike, he took the only job offered him, managing a self-laundromat used by local oil field workers. He had avoided getting hooked on heroin, but not bennies and reds, a nasty cycle of amphetamines and tranquilizers. The job did not pay enough to support the habit, so he started skimming from the coins he was trusted to empty from the machines. He was fired. Desperate for cash, Don traveled as far as Tulsa, sold his Harley and for a period lived on the considerable proceeds.

Depleted of cash again and strung out, he tried to rob a convenience mart with a toy pistol. However, the Vietnamese proprietor in the run-down neighborhood had experience with this kind of situation. His son sneaked up behind Don and clobbered him with a baseball bat. Beneath the checkout counter, his wife called the police on their cellular phone.

Since Don was a first-time offender, the judge remanded him to a state hospital rehabilitation program where he mastered his addiction. Upon release, he resolved to stay clean. But Don had no skills, and no mentionable work history. The best placement that could be found for him was in kitchen maintenance at a big cafeteria. Scrubbing stainless steel containers, swabbing floors and dumping trash ate away at his fortitude. A buzz from an upper would make it tolerable, he rationalized, and he wouldn't do a downer...sheer pride kept him straight.

He grew more tempted. Then, while scraping a salad bowl one night, a hint of silver stopped him. Like a bent fork, he thought, as he dug through the garbage. The bus help must have missed it during clearing. But the silver turned out to be a drop style earring set with quality turquoise. Don would know. He'd seen plenty of it in his youth. *His youth.* Memories overwhelmed him. On the annual call, Delora had been full of chat about store sales, the grandchildren, and the change in Sedona since word had gotten around about the vortexes in the area, alleged power points drawing universal energy. People were not only coming for scenery and the outlet mall these days, but to attune spiritually. A lot of New Age industry was moving in along side the artists and crafts people.

Sedona. He'd sworn he'd never return, but could it be any worse than the life he was leading now? He wouldn't ask for more than a temporary roof over his head, Don thought with swelling enthusiasm. He'd say that he'd been swindled by a trusted associate when he was very sick. He had not wanted to worry anyone, but now that he was well, he just needed a place until he could re-establish his contacts.

Don's haggard, ravaged face told the real story, so no one in the family was duped, but Melvin had missed his son. He not only welcomed Don, who vowed that his wanderlust had been satisfied, but Melvin sweetened the lure to stay when Don mentioned that he wanted to open a motorcycle repair shop. Melvin offered to finance it.

Elliot was furious. Don had received his inheritance. Why had he labored all these years? So that Don could come back and get some of HIS share? Melvin had no right to do this! But Elliot had been compliant too long. Melvin dismissed his eldest, assuming him as malleable as always. Delora understood Elliot's rage, but she too was grateful to have Don back. She agreed with Melvin. Heidi never quite related to anything worldly. Don was nice to her. Why was Elliot being stingy? They could afford to be nice to Don. Even his daughters seemed fascinated with the sudden appearance of an uncle filled with adventurous tales, and whose torso was tattooed with bizarre images like a dagger in a skull. Elliot repressed his rage, but he did not forget.

To his credit, Don settled down and supported himself. Fixing the bikes had been a necessity in a gang, and he knew his trade, but he had no ambition to earn more than he needed. Getting involved with Leslie, a biker's former old lady and cured morphine addict, smoothed his adjustment to sobriety. Leslie was determined to keep both Don and herself drug-free. She handled the repair shop's paperwork and soon shared the trailer Melvin bought for Don.

Four years passed. Elliot had stifled his resentment to the point where he could be civil to Don and enjoy family functions again.

Mid-week, early August, 1989, Don and Leslie offered to take the three nieces to Slide Rock, a popular swimming spot, where channels carved in the tiered, sandstone ledges along Oak Creek formed natural slides. Elliot had no objection. He'd taught the girls to swim himself and Sacha at five had more sense than Alana at twelve. State park employees monitored the bacteria level at Slide Rock and occasionally issued warnings to which no one paid much attention. The creek ran swiftly and cleaned itself. Weekends, Phoenicians invaded the area, but during the week it was not too crowded.

The next morning after the outing, Sacha failed to rouse. Alana attempted to get her up and Sacha awoke irritable. Her neck was stiff, and she complained of having a headache and feeling hot. Her fever was high, but Heidi was not concerned. Gina had just recuperated from a cold, and Sacha had probably gotten the virus. Heidi gave her baby-dose acetaminophen. At lunch time, Heidi emerged from her studio, found her two oldest watching TV and remembered to check Sacha. Sacha was having a seizure, and Heidi fainted at the sight of her daughter shuddering convulsively, her eyes rolled back in their sockets. Alana stood by crying while Gina called 911, then the store for her father.

Paramedics recognized the symptoms and got Sacha to the hospital in Cottonwood where the emergency room doctor ordered an x-ray and a lumbar puncture, a tap of the spinal fluid at the source of the infection, in order to identify the organism or virus causing Sacha's meningitis. The doctor isolated her as a precaution that she was contagious, then checked the family for symptoms. Sacha was administered penicillin until culture results would indicate which course of treatment would be most effective.

Sacha got worse. The bacteria was a virulent strain; her brain and spinal cord were further inflamed and the meningitis did not seem to be responding to the antibiotic. Then, an observant nurse noticed the rash on her chest. Sacha showed an allergy to the penicillin, complicating an already grave condition. She was switched to less effective sulfa.

Elliot's resentment towards Don re-surfaced and exploded. Bacteria! Slide Rock was full of bacteria! Don was responsible for this! The family was too distraught to refute the irrational accusation, and Don left the hospital angry at the blame.

The Beckers had no religious affiliation, but their next door neighbor was an active member of Calvary IOG Church. She organized a prayer vigil for the sweet child liked by everybody, and asked the minister for pastoral care to call on the family huddled miserably in the waiting room.

Sacha's heart arrested, but she was revived by the medical team. Elliot's anguish had already prompted bouts of vomiting and diarrhea; he was desperate to try anything to save his favorite child's life, including a personal petition to God. Inspired by the compassionate IOG minister, he went to the hospital chapel. On his knees, Elliot vowed that if God saved Sacha's life, he would become a devout Christian. He and his family would be in church every Sunday. He would tithe. He would believe and live accordingly. If he had to, he would even forgive his damned brother if God would just spare Sacha.

Several hours later, Sacha's delirium abated and her temperature dropped. The doctors were cautiously optimistic - she might be deaf, she might suffer from nerve paralysis - but Elliot knew she would recover fully. God had performed a miracle to prove to Elliot that his faith was justified. Now, he had to make good on his end of the deal.

Dr. Glenn Chandler baptized Elliot, Heidi and Alana in the central courtyard's rock garden pool when they became members at Calvary IOG Church. Along with their younger girls, Gina and Sacha, who regained her entire health, the Beckers absorbed themselves in Bible study and church activities. Elliot's conversion turned him into a zealot, and he had no difficulty living up to his end of the bargain with God except for his negative feelings towards Don; he did not relate Dr. Chandler's insightful sermon on the Prodigal Son to his own situation. Instead, he repressed his rage into a pious condescension for his heathen brother who lived in sin. For his part, Don was relieved about Sacha's recovery, but he never blamed himself and doubted that God had anything to do with the incident, either.

A few months later, Delora's facial melanoma and rapid death shook the family, but not Elliot's faith. His mother's time was at hand; she did not suffer unduly; and most significantly, at the end, she accepted Jesus. It was God's Will.

God's Will? Melvin, Don and Leslie concurred. Cancer was terminal and God could care less.

At Delora's funeral at Calvary IOG, Melvin met Judith Hutchins. Maybe God's divine intervention led him to Jesus Christ but in his heart, Melvin viewed his conversion as a matter of romance rather than faith. He did not admit it to anyone, though, including cynical Don.

Judith

From earliest recollection, Judith Cole could find things. Whether it was her mother's antique thimble or her assistant postmaster father's reading glasses or her brother's teddy bear, Judith had only to concentrate a second before sending the seeker to the exact spot.

As she got older and her circle expanded beyond her family, her reputation grew. At her IOG church in Point Elizabeth, a small, affluent community strung with marshes on the southern coast of Maine, the minister claimed that Judith's gift came from the presence of the Holy Spirit. People accepted the stamp of approval and Judith gave freely of her gift to whomever sought her assistance. She never viewed herself as peculiar, but the attention did make her somewhat imperious.

When she was fifteen, a detective in East Portland aiding in the search for an escaped killer from New York City heard about Judith from his sister who lived in Point Elizabeth. They had tried every conventional method; why not extrasensory perception? Judith touched one of the man's shoes lost in the escape and concentrated. She visualized Old Orchard Beach, a wide shore south of Point Elizabeth and a popular tourist spot. The pier had been built up with shops and restaurants and the town had an amusement park. He'd been working the Rockets ride, she said, but had moved on south to Portsmouth, New Hampshire. On a lucky fluke, police picked him up on a speeding charge in a stolen car just outside Portsmouth. Judith's accuracy made her a minor celebrity, but she was not interested in being known for such a trait. Her main ambition was to get married and have children, yet the boys she knew were aware of her ability. She was not exactly a freak, but they treated her differently. She could tell it affected their feelings towards her.

College in Portland broadened her personal sphere, but being a local campus, it gave her faint hope that there was a fellow who had not heard of her. Yet August "Augie" Hutchins had not.

Augie's dad ran a second-rate flea market in Saco. His fondest dream was for his son to rise above his plain beginnings, and Augie did not disappoint him. Augie dedicated himself to earning a scholarship and entered college with the ambition to become a stockbroker. Judith was in his French class, and he was impressed with the fact that she was from Point Elizabeth because his father would be impressed. Personally, he found her reddish brown hair, soft complexion and large bosom attractive. Skinny Augie had a nerdy appearance - from a prominent Adam's apple to horn rimmed glasses to thin hair to a pocket protector in his short sleeved white shirt. But when Judith mentioned that she was the one who could find things, Augie drew a blank. She was impressed with him.

The Coles were less than thrilled with Augie, but Judith was adamant about her feelings, and her mother, accustomed to her bossy daughter, convinced Judith's father that Augie did have potential. Upon graduation, they were married at the Coles' church and moved to Boston where Augie, set with a business degree, had accepted a job with a large investment firm.

The years of stress brought on by the need to excel caught up to Augie, though, and when their baby died from a heart defect a week after birth, he developed severe asthma. Boston or any coastal region would be bad for his condition and doctors recommended an arid climate. A grieving Judith found the suggestion appealing. A new location was just what she needed to recover from her loss, and no one would know about her gift, either, which as an adult she had come to view as a burden. Total strangers would contact her with all sorts of bizarre requests, none of whom cared a whit about her as a person. Augie was frightened of the change and of what precisely he could do to earn a living, but not being able to breath frightened him more. They moved to Phoenix, Arizona.

Phoenix in the late fifties was a provincial town, but the dry desert air was ideal for pulmonary health problems. A medical industry was well established and Augie accepted the first job he was offered as the bookkeeper-office manager for a newly licensed general practitioner.

The doctor's practice grew and with it, Augie's position; the Hutchins bought a better quality tract house in East Phoenix. In their travels around the state, they liked Sedona and purchased a new cottage built on an acre lot with a view of Chimney Rock. Life was pleasant and prosperous marred by one failure. Eleven years passed before Judith got pregnant again. The pregnancy was difficult and labor severe, but the baby, Ginger, born in 1969, was perfect. Both Augie and Judith doted on their daughter who by kindergarten, was annoyingly spoiled. They defined Ginger's behavior as precocious and Judith decided that public schools were not good enough. She would home school. Judith had a degree in education and adhered to state proficiency requirements, but Ginger's isolation and unhealthy ties to her parents intensified her fractious conduct. When she reached eight years of age, Augie's employer, the doctor, urged them to put Ginger in school, if just to aid in her social development.

Ginger hated the discipline imposed by a classroom and resented any attention not focused solely on her. She had behavior problems; she had academic problems; she gravitated to the worst group of kids. Judith and Augie spent the next six, agonizing years trying to get Ginger to adjust.

Her freshman year in high school, Ginger and three others were returning to Phoenix from a party in the desert. They were standing in the flat bed of a truck driven by a drunken companion who smashed into a canal embankment. Ginger was killed.

Inconsolable, Judith started spending more time in tranquil Sedona. Calvary IOG Church was on the way to their cottage and passing it got her to thinking. She had no purpose in her existence, no anchor to life. In her youth, she had enjoyed going to church. Perhaps she should just stop in some Sunday for services.

Dr. Guthrie, the minister who preached the day she attended, had a marvelous sermon that seemed meant specifically for her. He talked about gifts and whether or not a person viewed them as precious or trifling, God treasured them. Judith re-affirmed her faith and proudly announced during introductions that unusual as it may sound, she had a knack for finding things. Inanimate or animate, it was her gift to help others. She joined the women's organization, volunteered for service projects and soon got to be friends with Tawi Shinkawa who recognized a valuable asset when she met one.

In Phoenix, Judith's absence appeared permanent to Augie and he found solace in one of the women hired for front office help at the doctor's. He considered his affair serious and had Judith served with divorce papers. She was not surprised. They had been informally separated since Ginger's death. As long as she got the cottage and enough financial support to insure her lifestyle, Augie was free. Yet before papers could be filed, Augie found an odd bruise on his chest that would not heal. He was diagnosed with aggressive lung cancer, given three months to live, and his new girl friend left him. Judith summoned her Christian charity, stuck with Augie to the end, and as solitary beneficiary of a half million dollar insurance policy, she became a rich widow just barely into middle age.

Judith had been alone for six years when she met Melvin while serving refreshments to guests in the fellowship hall after his wife's funeral. Both had lost their spouses to cancer; neither ever cared to live anywhere but Sedona; they had nothing but praise for Calvary IOG, the finest church in the area. Despite a disparity in culture and education, they found enough important things in common and began keeping company.

CHAPTER SIXTEEN

Seated at the small, floor-bolted Formica table, Spider watched his wife straighten the bedding on the loft in the camper shell. He knew she slept inside because of him. He was willing to brave biting winter nights in the tent, but Theone would not hear of it. She walked shorter distances, hiked less arduous trails, and considered his stamina before she led him into any rough terrain. He argued that he was in peak condition; he was perfectly capable of keeping up, but she would just smile in her gentle, glorious way and do as she intended. Spider could not love her enough. Had it only been three months since they'd wed?

The day they exchanged formal vows, the woods, the frozen lake, even the beach's dun-colored sand had shimmered like it had been crystal-plated. A storm the previous night had laced the Lake Femvivant area with ice.

Lake Femvivant. To the indigenous Chippewa Indians, the water body was sacred because they believed that the Woman of Spirit lived in it. Theone had remarked that the name 'Femvivant' was a corruption of the French words *femme* (woman) and *vivant* (alive), the language of the men who had first explored the region. Spider figured it fit with Theone, especially after she told him that Brigit had been at the lakeshore when she received The Deity's blessing of conception.

At the bed loft, Theone turned, regarded Spider with serene, mint-green eyes, then started putting away the breakfast dishes that he had washed and left on the drain board. Her habit for neatness was greater than his, but he was learning; he was learning *a lot* of things.

Like courteous communication. The majority of his life he had spent in a solitary stupor or he had imparted only what was necessary to be left alone; now, he had to share his feelings from the deepest, wholehearted confessions to the mundane such as what to have for supper. He had to trust. He had to admit vulnerability before he could truly understand the meaning of love and with it, friendship. Theone was his first best friend, his only real friend ever, and he believed that she would be the sole one for life.

Learning about her physical world was another thing, and he found her knowledge of Nature fascinating. Tree, herb, flower, insect, snake, bird, whatever - Theone knew each species and was patiently teaching him to distinguish. He could classify the different clouds and what they forecast. He knew on any given day the phase of the moon.

He had run across every quirk in human nature, but Theone explained to him the whys for behavior and with understanding, he developed compassion. Perhaps recognizing that an inferiority complex motivated a bully was common to others, but Spider had never bothered to think on it.

Now, he did. And throughout his education, he got to know intimately the Goddess that The Deity had deigned him worthy of loving.

Theone's changing eyes fascinated him. He could interpret her mood based on the color. Gray indicated the dreamy, psychic state she attained when she read a soul, although he understood that the recipient got a personal view of someone important to him or her spiritually - positive or negative. (The only eyes he ever saw were hers because, he assumed, she was the one most important to him.) Shades of blue revealed empathy and personified the spiritual healing in her touch whereas shades of green meant that she was happy; violet became prominent when she communed with The Deity. Varying brown hues disclosed to him her degree of sadness such as when they witnessed a Glimpse of Peace and found human litter. Amber indicated a reaction to injustice and was as close to indignation as she got. Rosy irises were reserved for sexual excitement. He had asked her what color her eyes were actually. She had answered, clear like windows, but few saw them that way. She had shown him, and through the panes, Spider had seen a vivid rainbow.

Her golden brown hair also fascinated him. It seemed to absorb natural light, thus giving off its own glow. Her hair did not soak from rain; water rolled off it similar to a duck's down or a retriever's fur, yet she could wash it. Like last night in a stream, he'd washed her wavy locks himself.

Spider paused in his musing on Theone and looked outside the camper's window at the drizzle. The weather had been like this the day they left Paxton. Following a teary farewell with Theone's family and Arela, Mike and Mag, who were flying to Denver, they had traveled with Pilar and Jasper to San Antonio. Theone's old Ford truck had just needed minor maintenance before being serviceable. Spider had stored his Harley in the truck's place in Jasper's coach house which had been converted to a garage.

Another teary farewell ensued with Pilar and Jasper as he and Theone departed for the East. She wished to meet his mother and father, which made little sense to Spider. His parents were like aliens to him.

In sunny Miami, he'd been amazed that Kizzie *was not* amazed that he had been chosen as consort for The Mother as she referred to Theone. She made the remarkable comment that years ago, around the depressing time of her divorce, she had dreamed of a divine cherub with silver eyes and awakened believing in its significance for the future! Kizzie had read Jasper's book and seen the telecasts, particularly the one with Rae Nolan. She had already accepted The Message and associated with a growing group of others who had, too. Real estates sales were not so important, anymore, but her volunteer work was. Through donations of time and money, she supported Education-Independence-YES!, a self-help program for single teenage mothers.

Kizzie had embraced Spider, and when Theone took her hands, she cried. She stated reverently that she had been favored by The Deity through her son's bond and that being in Theone's presence was the high point in her life. Spider left his mother with a thoroughly altered perspective.

In snowy Boston, Adriano had been aloof to Spider's sudden appearance with a wife until he looked into Theone's eyes. Spider had no idea whose image he saw, but anxiety, repentance, then ecstasy reflected in rapid sequence. With unprecedented humility, Adriano had dropped to his knees on the cold concrete floor of his warehouse and begged for Theone's blessing. Next, he begged for Spider's forgiveness!

Theone interrupted Spider's deliberations on his parents.

"Shall we get going?" She suggested. "I'd like to be at Delta NWR by tonight."

"Yes, Dear," Spider jested in a monotone. "You were the one who kept the day from starting with your playing around. Imagine, we're legally married and sex hasn't lost any of its fun." He hugged her. "In fact, it just gets better."

She giggled.

Spider gave her an affectionate kiss.

Thus far, the media had not discovered their marriage. Presumably, Uncle Patrick, the judge, had done some sophisticated shuffling to obscure the public record of their license. Gabriel Giovetti's identity had remained anonymous, too, although reports circulated that a striking man, not the renowned Jasper Stroud or Mike Zimmer, was presently Theone's singular traveling companion. Spider hoped it stayed that way. The Christ Covenant via Glenn Chandler had issued statements condemning what they perceived as lewd behavior if indeed Ms. Jones co-habitated with someone. Other factions had expressed similar disapproval through the media. Spider hated to think about the politicians already taking sides to please voters. Despite the First Amendment, enough control might be attained in government and laws enacted...yet Theone showed no interest in defending herself against any of the opposition's challenges. She had other things to do like visiting Glimpses of Peace such as the one of marsh, bayous and ponds to which they currently headed. Theone had commented that the proliferation of birds was staggering at this NWR located in southeastern Louisiana where the mouth of the Mississippi River mixed its fresh waters with the salty ones of the Gulf of Mexico. (To Spider, each swamp had more birds than the last one, but he bet none would ever top the bizarre varieties found in the Everglades.)

Theone's main preoccupation, though, remained all the weary souls that needed healing. Aside from her devotion to Spider, she cared most about touching souls, which she did everywhere. There were humans who did not respond, but more did than not, and Spider never failed to observe with renewed awe a person's spiritual transformation. He could spend his life contented in this vagabond existence, loving her and witnessing her sacred work.

On a wider scale, news accounts indicated that in Western Europe Arela was winning converts to The Message, but she had also received death threats in Italy and France. Naively, Spider had inquired if Arela had a translator with her to clarify her speeches. Theone had smiled sadly. The Deity had gifted Arela with a master knowledge of language. Her words fostered no misconceptions.

He wondered about countries such as India, ones in the former U.S.S.R., those in Asia and on the continent of Africa. Would Arela even be granted a visa to cross the border? What about the Islamic nations? If she got in, how safe would she be? Mike and Mag had no means to protect her.

But The Deity did, Theone had gently reminded a troubled Spider. Arela had been endowed with certain divine privileges, a certain immunity...for a while. Relieved, Spider had not registered Theone's qualification.

Theone understood what Spider in his absolute trust could not. Arela would succeed outside the United States as much as she, Theone, had succeeded inside. Numerous souls *were* living The Message and by so doing, others *were* being convinced, but in general, her coming had been a failure because it had occurred too late. The Christian establishment's rabid resistance to The Message attested to the fact. In earlier ages, humans had lived intertwined with Nature; thus, they were cognizant of The Deity's Laws. Today, an influential number of humans had gotten sidetracked by their material strides; they were too enamored of their own self-importance for The Message to have a lasting, universal effect.

She realized for responsive souls it was good that her influence continued to grow, but danger was a coexisting factor. Recently the Christ Covenant had labeled her the 'She-Evil', and she had difficulty tempering Gabriel's anger when he heard it or read it. He had also been subject to attacks and referred to as 'The Companion'; his tall, dark, attractive looks alluded to as a clever disguise by the Devil. She sensed that her enemies had moved beyond words in their attempts to quell her. They were trying to track her movements, and she felt that if they caught up to her, they would eliminate her like other representatives of The Message had been, but an end in this environment was not what troubled Theone. She comprehended what humans had not. THIS time The Deity had run out of patience. The Deity had already concluded that free will was a failure and if she was destroyed, the results for humankind might be catastrophic...

Her elusiveness was necessary to carry on the work that she had been foreordained to do and so far, The Deity had given her rein on this issue, but it did not help that her absence from public view, combined with human nature's romanticism, was building her into a legend. Interpretation was resulting. Incredulous, Spider had read to her that a group of followers now revered coyotes. They had established an alarming practice of trapping and caging them for pets because the leader had witnessed a coyote bowing to Theone at one of her appearances!

Theone despaired. Why could souls not embrace The Message and not her as the Messenger? Why did humans have to establish rituals centered on a being such as herself? Why were people so in need of complications?

Humans could just not grasp that in spite of their evolution, ultimately, it was The Deity who controlled the environment. The Message simply was the exclusive direction for their soul to have a productive stay, and the result of their choices was their only destiny.

Heather Meyer, part time college student, part time bartender, rolled away from Bobby Lon's nude body and found her glasses so she could focus on the small television he had in his bedroom. A special bulletin had flashed. Famed IOG minister, Dr. Glenn Chandler, was currently speaking at the sports stadium in L.A. and outside the gates, a disturbance was in progress. The commentator stated that allegedly unarmed protesters demanding respect for Theone Jones had been attacked by opposition allegedly wielding small clubs. As soon as they had their remote connection, viewers would have a live report.

"Boy, that's getting to be common," Heather said.

"Riots in L.A.? It's been a fact for decades," Bobby said in a bored tone as he scratched his crotch. The spermicidal jelly she had used for birth control irritated his genitals.

"Racial and gang riots, not religious. No matter how much that preacher denounces the violence he sparks, I think he secretly condones it. Have you ever listened to him? He claims in this syrupy baritone that Christians have God on their side and no believer has to stoop to such base tactics to triumph over the She-Evil. The fights are staged by her supporters which is Satan's way. Personally, I'd bet on those crazy militia types sprouting up all over who boast ultra-conservative theologies as the more likely instigators." Horrified, Heather watched as the camera panned on a muscular man shoving a tall woman to the ground. "God!" She cried. "Where are the police?"

Bobby pressed the power off on the channel changer.

Heather looked at him indignantly. "Why did you do that?"

"Because I don't care about it. I know Theone Jones and I'm tired of hearing about her."

"You know her?" She said skeptically. "You really know her? You've spoken to her?"

Bobby snorted as an affirmative response. He had thought his time with Theone would remain a burning issue because of the way she had treated him, but other than a few facts, he was having trouble recalling details, including how long he had spent with her. It ranged about half a year, give or take a month. Since he had not been able to access any drugs during his stay, he could not understand why everything had gotten so vague, and it was not like they had done anything exciting to jam his memory. Day after day, their travels had been through the same dull scenery.

For months now, pro or con, you could not avoid hearing about Theone on the news. Supposedly she had a dark companion traveling with her now, and one of the things Bobby did remember was the guy who had shown up with the pizza. He had deduced angrily that her present pal had to be one and the same. The other thing he remembered was a fluke. The first week after he had joined the group, Pilar had been writing checks. Bobby had been helping her stuff and stamp the envelopes, one of which had a pre-address for the motor vehicles department in Wisconsin. He'd asked about it and Pilar mentioned that Theone had a truck which she kept stored in San Antonio. The tags were expiring, and the application for renewal was past due because the mail could not keep up with them. An hour later while filing in Pilar's metal storage box, he had taken the carbon copy of the license form and forgotten it until just yesterday when he had discovered it during transfer of id's to a new wallet. Useless information...

Heather grabbed at him. "Tell me how you know her! I've seen her on TV, but when I tried to get close at one of her appearances, the crowd was too great! Is she really as fantastic as she seems?"

"Are you a She-Evil supporter?" He inquired in a nasty voice.

Heather drew away from him. "I wouldn't have taken you for a detractor, Bobby. You seem so...shallow about things and Theone Jones' philosophy is a pretty harmless creed that even you could relate to."

"Yeah, well, I lived with her. She's not the way she appears." He yawned. "You should go. I gotta get some sleep."

Heather had already left the futon and was pulling on her shorts. Initially, she had found Bobby to be very attractive. He had also seemed rather sweet during banter with him at the sports bar where she worked and he frequented. Their date had been fun and the sex fine, although he had balked at putting on the condom she offered him and youthfully philosophical, she had not pushed it. She would not bother with him again, though. Anybody who so much as gave lip service to a fundamentalist stance

- in her mind, an anti-woman attitude - was not a person Heather wished to waste time on.

The next evening after a rushed Happy Hour, Heather and the other bartender scheduled with her were taking advantage of the lull. A game or sporting event was always being broadcast, but tonight no major draw packed in a crushing crowd. While Heather did a cursory inventory of the stock, her co-worker leisurely re-organized glassware. Heather mentioned her date with Bobby, and they got into a discussion about him because the other girl had gone out with him once, too. They agreed that basically he was a jerk. The exchange led Heather to remarking that Bobby claimed he knew Theone Jones, which they dismissed as part of his jerk mentality. Why would a public figure like Theone Jones bother with someone as petty as Bobby Lon?

In the booth closest to the bar, Stewart Austin, sworn soldier of God and recruited Christ Covenant agent, sipped his club soda and listened carefully to the conversation. He did not approve of drinking or scantily dressed female bar employees and would never have come into such an establishment if it had not been for a tip. Bobby With No Last Name had yakked to others around Venice about an affiliation with the Jones woman, but the only solid lead Stewart had received was one referring to Bobby's appearances at the V Grill. His persistence had paid off.

Bobby squinted disagreeably at the stranger. "You're in my sun, man," he complained. The blue eyed, golden blond dressed in tee shirt and jeans had a California look, but he wasn't from around Venice. For one thing, in a town big on buff, tan bodies, this guy was thickset and pale. Moreover, if he had any savvy about beach code, he would never block a sunbather's rays.

"I'm sorry," Stewart said. He moved to Bobby's side and squatted. "I guess I'm so excited about meeting someone who I've heard actually knows Theone Jones!"

Bobby sighed in disgust. "Who's spreading that around? That bimbo bartender at V Grill?"

"You don't really know Theone Jones, then," Stewart replied.

"Yes, I do or did, but she's no big deal. All this fuss? Believe me, she's a zero. Like you'd expect magic spells or feats of wonder or a couple miracles. Nothing. She wanders around nature, the wilder the better. It's a drag."

"There's a lot of nature. Where does she like particularly?"

Bobby rolled to his stomach. "Everywhere. She doesn't stop moving."

Stewart already knew that and stood up. He had wasted enough time in this degenerate town pursuing this dissolute, colored liberal, precisely the kind of permissive loser that was tearing apart the moral fiber of America. His boasting about the She-Evil was false.

"I met the guy she fucks," Bobby said, "some greasy, black-leathered dude on a Harley which sure says a lot about her mentality to be attracted to a biker. They're off riding into one of her infernal sunsets."

Stewart lost his limited patience. "I'd say you know her less than most people," he spat, "she and her companion travel in an old truck."

Bobby turned over and sat up. "Yeah, I bet that old truck is a 1981 half ton green Ford pickup. I have a copy of the owner registration. I think I happen to know quite a lot."

Stewart's eyes gleamed dangerously behind his mirror sunglasses, but his expression was indifferent. No witness had been able to recall anything precise about the truck aside from its being old! "Why would you have something like that?" He asked casually.

"Because I took it when I was living with her."

Stewart squatted again and spoke in a confidential tone. "If that registration is legitimate, it could be very valuable to certain parties. Of course, it would have to be verified."

"I don't need money, man."

"Everybody needs something," Stewart countered.

"I'd like to see the bitch suffer."

"What did she do to you?"

"None of your goddamn business."

Stewart quickly grew conciliatory. "Oh, we could arrange to make her pay for whatever it was, if we could just find her."

Bobby shrugged. "I'll meet you at Wilson's Office Supply around...four o'clock tomorrow and you can make a copy." He grinned. "It's a souvenir and she is kinda famous. Someday, I might be, too, because I did live with her and it's sort of proof."

"Yes, thank you and I promise to keep you informed of the results of our deal," Stewart answered pleasantly, but authentic or not, he was already planning a different scenario for obtaining Bobby's document.

Several unseasonably hot days passed before the landlord knocked on Bobby's door to collect the rent which he had overlooked paying. Bobby had never been late on purpose, but he was forgetful. The landlord usually had to ask for the money which Bobby promptly paid.

Bobby's van was in the parking lot, but the neighbors had not seen him. That was not unusual, either. He had an independent source of income and did his own thing, occasionally involving a bender or prolonged high.

Gaining no response, the landlord tried the door as in the past and found it open. This time, however, a stench gagged him and he backed out swiftly, but not before a fast scan of the living room revealed that it had been ransacked. Robbery, he thought as he vomited on the stoop, and somewhere in there, hapless Bobby must have caught the guy by surprise. The landlord had been in Vietnam's jungles and the heated smell of dead, rotting flesh was unforgettable.

∽

In San Antonio, Theone and Spider enjoyed the Vernal Equinox with Jasper and Pilar before they took off again on the Harley which Jasper had arranged to have fitted with luggage boxes. Their route took them straight up the center of Texas and across the Panhandle into northern New Mexico where ancient Indian ruins fascinated Spider. Theone indulged his interest, and in a zigzag pattern they visited Pueblo and Anasazi sites.

They stopped briefly in the northwest corner of the state at the bleak Bisti Wilderness, distinct for its fossilized remains of plants and animals, then entered Utah. At Zion, Cedar Breaks, and Bryce Canyon, they glimpsed the Peace wrought in imposing rock formations tinted by minerals to hues of lavender, green, pink and red.

From these regions of geologic marvels, they rode north. They hit more than one late season blizzard, but Spider rode with confidence that The Deity shielded them from harm. At night, he teased Theone that she was better than a space heater because no matter how cold the temperature dropped, the tent was always cozy. South of Provo, Utah, they changed their path to the west and traveled steadily through Nevada on U.S. Highway 6 which fed into 395 at Bishop, California. From this point they angled south towards the coast.

At Malibu they accessed Highway 1, the route parallel to the Pacific Ocean, and went north. April 3, 1994, they arrived in Big Sur. It was Easter Sunday. The Moon had waxed past the first quarter.

On the road's shoulder towering above the ocean, Spider studied a steep, narrow path posted with a prominent NO TRESPASSING sign. Up or down, could his bike take the incline without flipping? A glance at the darkening sky further increased his reluctance. The sandy dirt would turn to mud. They would be stuck in the cove below until it dried which could be days if a storm front hung on.

"Let's not do it," he said.

"Your bike will make it," Theone replied, "I'll drive."

He gaped at her in astonishment. "You don't know how! You've never shown any interest to learn..." Her eyes were bright amber, a sign of displeasure. If she said she could do it, then who was he to question? She was the Goddess. "Uh, okay," he answered and climbed on behind her. But he was hanging on tight. He was human with very scrapable skin and breakable bones.

The clamorous surf out roared the Harley's gnarly descent to the wedge of beach sheltered from the sea by onyx boulders except for a several yard wide opening for the tide. A strong wind pummeled them and hard spray battered them, but Theone easily reached the bottom where the atmosphere was suddenly calm.

The tipsy pattern of sandpipers and the pronged stamp of seagulls marked the shore near the tide-mark, but no birds were in the vicinity. Spider considered evidence of their presence unusual because these species preferred to live around people, and there were no humans for miles.

He crouched to the ground. Black silt edged smooth ripples in the sand which sparkled as if dusted with gold glitter. Inconceivably, it was warm, dry and soft to touch. He looked at Theone watching him.

Her eyes were like rose quartz.

To heck with the pending storm, he tore off his clothes.

Theone did the same and forced him down on his back.

"I am in control," she ordered. "It is my scene."

Spider relaxed and opened up for her.

She mounted him.

Lightning blazed, and thunder cracked or Theone screamed. Maybe both, Spider thought, and in ear piercing volume.

The wind whipped into a mini tornado centered over them, but no sand particles stung him.

He saw constellations, luminous and fiery, in orbit around them.

The sun came so near that he felt the flames from its hot gasses sear his forehead.

The moon appeared, a gigantic, silvery sphere, bathing him in a healing froth which then cradled him in dreamy suspension.

He somersaulted through the change of seasons. Winter's stark extremes softened to Spring's pastels which melted into the verdant hues of Summer before deepening into Autumn's rich palette.

As if transported into space, he viewed the Earth spin in a kaleidoscope of wispy clouds, bright speckled greens, loamy browns and dazzling blues.

Spider ejaculated and cried out in ecstasy. Future lovemaking could never surpass this zenith!

Theone arched her body and gazed skyward, her silent affirmation of triumph bittersweet.

CHAPTER SEVENTEEN

Elliot Becker was mightily concerned. His personal shepherd and divine counselor here on earth, Dr. Chandler, was distressed. Each sermon he had preached in the past months, his distress had increased. Now, on national TV, broadcast right here from the new studio built adjacent to the church, its transmitter beaming off the scenic mesa by the sanctuary, the good preacher's distress had reached epidemic proportions. And it all had to do with that Theone Jones. The She-Evil was luring noble people away from Jesus; she was seducing them with lies about the most wonderful gift God could ever bestow - Grace.

What could he do? What did he possibly have that he could offer to Dr. Chandler which might be of help in this terrible battle with Satan's ill-gotten off-spring?

Elliot would make an appointment to see Mr. Ulrich. From what he had seen and heard at church, the man was almost as saintly as Dr. Chandler.

The moment his office door closed on his visitor's departure, Vaughn Ulrich chuckled jubilantly. God be praised! Right in his own backyard! Elliot Becker was an answer to prayer. Manipulated properly, the fanatic, *who also happened to reveal that he was a crack shot with a high-power rifle*, would be the perfect candidate to handle certain matters which Vaughn's grave associates had determined as the only alternative. It had been agreed unanimously that only a lone person of indubitable zeal, but with no militia affiliation, could be the one responsible. It was the only way to control the situation and prevent the deed from boomeranging. Yet finding such a unique person had remained an unsettled issue. Now, if someone could just pinpoint Theone Jones' location, they could set up a concrete plan of action!

It should be simple to achieve. A brigade of Christ Covenant agents was on the road actively searching for her. The Scougan house near Paxton had been staked as had Stroud's San Antonio residence. A field agent kept checking the Zimmer family home; one watched for her appearance at Eloise O'Hennessey's and another at the Pedersen woman's place on Lake Latimer. Recently, they had gotten a lucky break - a truck's license number registered to Brigit Jones which seemed to confirm reports that the daughter traveled in such a vehicle, although conflicting information continued to be received on the She-Evil's mode of transportation. Some asserted that she and her companion traveled on a motorcycle. Either means, they had police informants in touch with their agents and plenty of sympathizers everywhere in the country, yet there was no pattern to her appearances and no recollection by witnesses of her next destination. Would anybody ever attain solid evidence of her presence before she disappeared again? She seemed to have the knack to vanish at will.

Another trick of Satan's, Vaughn decided. All the more reason that they could not cease their hunt. The longer the She-Evil was allowed to live, the more people would be deluded by her false message and the harder it would be to steer folks back to The Savior.

Vaughn loosened his diamond-studded bolo tie and sighed. Eliminating the woman would be just a start on the eradication of mutated, misguided beliefs that would have to take place before Christians could lead back the brainwashed, wayward flock and rest easy again. (Non-Christians were heathens in Vaughn's view and damned to eternity by their conscious rejection of Jesus. No one *in their right mind* who knew about Grace, chose any other path but The Cross.) Yes, Christians would have their work cut out for them, but they had Glenn Chandler, THE Defender of the Trinity, THE Spiritual Head for the Righteous. Glenn was a leader so charismatic that while other ministries floundered financially in the wake of Theone Jones, the incensed, enthralled faithful kept Calvary IOG richly solvent. Calvary approached megachurch status, and outside of Phoenix and one church in Tucson, it had the largest membership in the state.

They had to find Theone Jones! She had not preached in public for months, but her presence was reported continually by folks claiming to have been touched by her. These conversions to Satan's fallacies *had to cease*, Vaughn thought ruthlessly, but how?

He'd talk things over with Tawi, truly a man's perfect helpmate. Since his marriage, his most successful endeavors were the result of incorporating her valuable perspective with his own.

⤳

From California's northern coast Theone and Spider rode inland, trailing the arrival of Spring through the Sierra Nevadas. Leaving the motorcycle under the watchful eye of a raptor - Spider suspected that the hawks and eagles drew celestial straws for the privilege - he and Theone would hike and climb one remote peak after another. But they were never alone.

Squirrels, gophers, mice, chipmunks, marmots - rodents galore scampered in their path, and rowdy birds greeted them. Snakes would undulate beside them. Theone would stand in a stream and golden trout would clog the water. Deer and bighorn sheep were also bold in their attention. As they passed through their territory, coyotes and mountain lions approached with dignity.

Spider's education of Nature continued. Theone described the belts of mountainside vegetation as life zones, so named for their ecological resemblance to a continental region. Groves of live oaks, full of foliage, melded with the prickly chaparral of the grassy Upper Sonoran zone. Fushia-colored filaree, graceful lacepod, violets, miner's lettuce, owl clover, golden-fluted poppies, purple-tipped five-spots, gossamer fiesta flowers, flamboyant farewell-to-spring - Spider savored the brief life of the tiny, vivid blossoms whose fragile appearance belied their hardiness.

The sight of ponderosa pine marked entrance into the Transition Zone where the perfume of the wildflower, mountain misery, scented the air, and the slopes abounded with mustang clover, larkspur, helianthella, mariposa lilies, cow parsnip, lupine, shooting stars and cranesbill geraniums, a scarlet-striped flower which Spider especially liked. Snow lingered in the Canadian Zone, home to red fir and lodgepole pine. Theone explained that other than the chunky red snow plant, flowers such as the corn lily would not appear for another month.

Red heather edged the melting snow in the Hudsonian Zone. Indian paintbrush sprouted here, and on wet ridges, growth of sierra stonecrop and western roseroot could be detected. Whitebark pine survived along the timber line, their branches molded by the harsh elements to cling grotesquely to the rocks in their upward growth.

At each pinnacle, the Arctic-Alpine Zone, Theone and Spider would stand naked among the massive rocks and hardy yellow columbine. In the clear light and braced against the eternal wind, they always celebrated The Deity's Presence.

From these summits, they descended into an arid land ranged with sage brush and stretches of salt flats. Spider had crossed Nevada and Death Valley when he had originally ridden to the coast from his discharge point in Virginia. He had not liked it then or any better now.

They entered Arizona on the west side rather than the north. Spider expressed surprise. They were missing the Grand Canyon, touted as one of the Great Wonders of the World! His awakened sensitivity pleased Theone and she agreed that Grand Canyon was a wondrous Glimpse of Peace, but it was too human a place for her, overcrowded and popular. Their journey would take them through the Hulalapai Mountains and the Prescott National Forest, perhaps not as staggering a Glimpse, but assuredly, just as wondrous.

It made no difference to Spider. Just being with her satisfied his needs.

The Harley backfired and lost speed.

"Shit," Spider muttered. Compression had fallen, causing the power down. He was only a mediocre mechanic, but there was no mistaking when a ring had blown on a piston. Oil sprayed out of the exhaust pipe, fouling the air. That would not bode well with Theone who took personally any sort of pollution. He left the road, braked and looked over his shoulder. Theone had an internal map, and Spider never questioned her directions or their destination.

"Are we near anywhere, Babe?" He inquired.

Theone tightened her hold on his waist and closed her eyes. They were in the midst of Oak Creek Canyon. She knew The Deity's intent. The Deity's Will was hers, and she did not challenge it, but Spider was human and she loved him. Would their time together be enough to sustain him through the future he faced?

"We are just north of Sedona," she answered. "There will be a shop for you to take the bike."

"Sedona? Well, I guess we were headed there, anyway, huh?"

She assumed he meant Glenn Chandler and some sort of showdown. "I will not confront anyone," she said.

"Confront? Is that what you call it when you enlighten a soul? I saw a TV special on Sedona's power points. Are we here to re-energize our spirits? Which one are we hiking to? Bell Rock? The Airport Mesa? Or some obscure place known only to you?"

"You mean the vortexes!" Theone exclaimed. She often tried to second guess him, but Spider consistently surprised her, and she liked it, not always knowing his thoughts.

Spider pulled off his helmet and rubbed his damp, disheveled hair which he insisted Theone cut regularly. "Are vortexes too New Age for your interest?"

"Power points give some a focus for their soul, but you do not need a special place to re-vitalize with The Deity's Energy. Peace is everywhere if you simply seek it."

He sensed that she withheld something. "Okay, a vortex isn't the draw. Are we here for a reason?"

Theone hid her sadness and said cheerfully, "We're here to fix your bike."

Spider slapped his forehead and winced. Theone had found a weed which she had crushed for its juices to relieve the sting, but the crescent-shaped burn, the curious result of their fantastic interlude on the Big Sur beach, had not fully healed yet. The white scar of a waning moon would be small, but obvious. "Your sister lives here!" He uttered. "God, are you supposed to see her?"

"No."

"But this is enemy territory! Look, we can go on to the next town. I don't like coughing out oil, but..."

"We'll stop in Sedona. No Chandler will be aware of my presence." She smiled at him.

Theone could be a regular wizard with that dazzler...in spite of his misgivings, Spider gunned the bike.

Don Becker admired the stranger's chrome-gilt Harley Electra Glide. No fancy-pants turquoise or yellow paint job on this classic FL hog with its fork-mounted fairing and imposing 1340cc V-twin. The company emblem on a maroon gas tank was the only concession to color and decoration. Just clean, mean lines. This was a serious owner, and Don had a lot of respect for the man who possessed such a superior machine.

"This here FL's a beaut. You at Daytona Beach in '82 or '3?" Don queried. "How 'bout Sturgis same years?"

Spider had been in high school in the early 80's and shook his head in a friendly manner. Bikers were their own breed - instant bonds forged among owners - but he had not attended rallies, including the two most famous in Florida and South Dakota. Riding a Harley evoked a certain image that before he met Theone had seemed important, but he had never been much for the lifestyle. Now, the motorcycle served as a convenient form of travel through wilderness settings.

"Mine's parked over there." Don pointed at a chopped Shovelhead FLH, a Harley model circa the mid-seventies, its black gas tank customized with a macabre skull. "Well, it'll be a pleasure to do a ring job on this hog," he said. "Course it'll take me a day to break it down and replace 'em. I'll even buff the chrome. Sure seen some serious exposure to the elements, eh? You and your old lady can catch a beer yonder, and if you wanna shack up, there's a motel by it. It's our kinda joint, not one of them upscale places." He pointed at a tavern down the street.

Spider smiled apologetically at Theone, but she had her attention on the smudgy window of the shop. He followed her eyes to Leslie who was staring, her expression faintly puzzled. The woman doesn't see The Message, he thought with relief; they did not need to leave any reminders that they had been in Sedona.

Theone walked towards the open door and went inside.

"Does the pop machine work?" Spider asked Don who was wheeling his bike into the garage.

"Yeah, but if I was you, I'd get a beer or three. There ain't much else doin' in Sedona 'less you like to shop souvenir shit or them artsy fartsy things."

"I'm waiting for my lady," Spider said.

Don winked knowingly. "Who's one foxy babe."

"Yep, she is."

"Have we met?" Leslie demanded the moment Theone entered the dim, messy interior.
"Not that I remember," Theone replied.
"Sure, we have! What's your name?"
"Theone Jones."
"Your name is sure familiar. If we haven't ridden with the same guys, then we rallied somewhere. I wouldn't forget somebody like you." Leslie wagged her finger at Theone. "You were probably freaked out."
Theone's silver chain hung with the moonstone suddenly sparked.
"Say, is that doodad electrified?" Leslie peered at the necklace. "Ah, it's just a white stone. The silver must a zapped off the mirror behind me." She caught Spider out of the corner of her eye by the pop machine, swiveled her head and wolf-whistled. "Whoa! That is some dude you're cruisin' with, Honey. I'd swap spit with him, any day."
"May I use your bathroom?" Theone asked pleasantly.
"It's a pit."
"When you have to go..."
Leslie chortled and thumbed at a dirty door.

Tears filled Theone's eyes as she slipped off the silver chain. She had worn the moonstone since finding it that dawn more than a decade ago. This special cabochon, this beloved gift from The Deity which had Gabriel's profile etched so distinctly, was to be left here. Theone tenderly twisted it about the grungy pipe connecting the sink to the wall, arranging the stone so that it was hidden from casual view.

Neither slept well the night they spent in the Sedona motel. Too many people around, Spider said, or the negative energy of fundamentalists. Theone gently reminded him not to judge. He noticed at once that her moonstone was gone, but she carefully soothed his concern with the remark that she had the real man. The image was not necessary, anymore.
They camped the next night near Prescott in an aleppo pine forest where a mild, but steady rain sent them to bed early. On their stomachs inside their sleeping bags, they looked out of the tent at a parade of squirrels and mice, ignoring the weather for Theone's recognition.
"Are you tired of our diet?" Theone wondered.
"No," Spider said and kissed her cheek. The Steady Steak Man Himself had certainly changed! His wife gathered edibles such as nuts and berries from the environment, but their staples were purchased cans of soup, milk, beans, jerky, bread and dried fruit - easy fare to carry and fix with the simple cooking tools they packed. It was not the best nutrition-wise, but

Theone made him compensate. Every morning, he had to take a multiple vitamin. Spider rated their meals the best he had ever eaten.

"Does our primitive lifestyle get tiresome?"

"No." He nuzzled her nose. They did not live totally natural like animals - Theone had a grainy, biodegradable paper for body waste functions - but he did not require frills for physical comfort.

"We should do laundry again."

"Okay," he said, rubbing the stubble on his jaw. They regularly rinsed their few clothes and cleaned themselves in the rivers and lakes discovered in their travels, but spared the soap. Either they were inured to body odor or more likely it was not offensive because Theone always made contact with humans. She wore some kind of organic fiber sanitary pads, though, which she washed and re-used.

"Did the bike repair drain our funds?"

"I charged it."

Theone chuckled. "It's funny how that pleases Pilar."

"She told me it was like getting a postcard from us when the bill comes. The same goes for those rare wires we send to request money. You'd think we never called! Of everyone you care about, Pilar has the hardest time not being close."

"She is just the most vocal. We'll see them shortly. We're returning to San Antonio to get the truck."

"Let's do it in a few months," he replied. "You want to hit the Badlands and go east to the Great Lakes Region. Does that maybe include a swing by Paxton? It's the beginning of summer and the best time to be riding a bike!"

"I'm going to have a baby in December, Gabriel."

He rolled Theone on her back and leaned over her. "It's about time I hit the target. I sure try often enough!" Actually, he had been expecting her announcement since the first time they had made love months ago, but doubted if his sperm would serve any purpose in the conception.

She did not giggle at his teasing. "It is *your* baby."

Spider stared at her. "You mean...human?"

Now Theone laughed. "Half-human."

"Well, that's what I meant..." Tears choked him. "Mine? That's...the best gift..."

"Being a father, nurturing our child, is your soul's opportunity to achieve its greatest advance."

"I thought loving you was it."

"And the child is the result of your love."

He kissed her softly. "I won't fail because I'll have you to guide me the whole way."

"My Beloved," Theone answered, "you will always have the part of me that is important to count on, but you will succeed because of the compassionate, caring man that you are."

He wiped at his eyes. "Does this mean we can't have sex?"

"Oh, Gabriel! More than ever. Being pregnant..." she pushed him off, pinned him on his back, then straddled him. "...makes me feel sexier than ever!"

"Are you sure this isn't Peace?"

"Just a Glimpse."

"Is there sex in Peace?"

"Hush, Gabriel, and kiss me."

⌒

This time on their passage through New Mexico, Theone and Spider traveled the southern route. Near Alamogordo at White Sands National Monument, they gloried in the full moon illuminating the wind-lashed gypsum dunes which drifted like warm, powdery snow.

Spider wanted to see Carlsbad Caverns whose only appeal to Theone was the huge colony of bats that left en mass each evening for their meal. Joining other visitors, Spider entered what appeared like a yawning mouth in a rock face and descended into the immense, natural cavity. Theone spent the time exploring the barren surroundings which animated with snakes and lizards alerted to her presence. At sunset, they relished the sight of the flat, elongated horizon flamed pink beneath a clear, blanched sky.

In San Antonio, Theone docilely permitted Pilar to mother her for a few days. This friend had a palpable bond with The Deity and like Brigit, Pilar suffered a feeling of foreboding for Theone. Spider wondered, but made no comment when she did not inform Pilar or Jasper about the baby.

With the motorcycle swapped for the truck, they headed out again straight north to the Dakotas. In southern Kansas, a preschool boy wandered to their dusty roadside picnic table, and Theone's touch inspired his timid mother to leave her abusive marriage. At a small grocery store in central Nebraska, Theone deeply touched the soul of a wild, young man with some accurate and scary remarks about his future if he did not straighten his path.

They traveled the northern prairies into Minnesota where they traced the flow of the Great Lakes - Superior, Michigan, Huron, Erie, Ontario - a route which took them to upstate New York. Uncertain as to the reach of the Christ Covenant, Spider cautiously remained within the U.S. border and in returning to the Midwest, he drove south by way of Pennsylvania, Ohio, Indiana, Illinois and into Wisconsin.

Throughout the summer and fall, Theone tirelessly sought to reach souls and continued to acknowledge the wildlife, yet as the baby grew, Spider sensed an increasing urgency in her. She no longer lingered at any Glimpse of Peace. After a brief communion, she wished to be on her way to the next place as if there would not be enough time to experience everything.

He was not disturbed by her hurry, though. Because her pregnancy, like her voluptuous figure, was only hinted unless she was naked, Spider kept reminding himself that emotional changes were as normal as obvious physical ones. Theone may be a Goddess and radiant in her pregnancy, but she was still entitled to her whims.

CHAPTER EIGHTEEN

The first hard frost in Sedona occurred in early November. Leslie relied on a space heater to keep the shop warm, but they closed over the weekend so that Don could go hunting with Melvin and Elliot.

Monday morning, Leslie used the bathroom and found the toilet would not flush. No water ran in the sink faucet, either, and she bent to check around the pipes. Discovering Theone's necklace made her forget to call the plumber for an hour.

Leslie

Sharing king size beds was the standard in the Daniels household because the family had nine siblings, two or less years a part, and never enough bedrooms in the places they rented. Leslie had two older brothers and three older sisters; two younger sisters and one brother. Plus her mother provided child care for several toddlers to supplement her father's sales income. Leslie was not sure what he sold, but they moved a lot between Utah and Arizona. There was always a better job offer from a fellow Mormon or so her mother vaguely claimed. Before each move she would say, consider our blessed forefather, Brigham Young, who led the faithful safely through the wilderness to Salt Lake. Leslie could never relate to the comparison, but did not pursue clarification.

The Daniels' marriage sacraments had been performed in the Temple at Salt Lake City which meant that their vows would not terminate at death; the marriage had been bound for eternity. As good Mormons, they believed a multitude of souls existed, searching for a bodily home, and it was their godly duty to provide as many 'homes' for these lost wanderers as they were capable, so that they would have the opportunity to be enlightened to the faith. Leslie grasped what that meant. A big family. An over-crowded house. Limited everything, including parental attention.

They subsisted mostly on bread. Homemade, whole grain. The house always smelled like yeast, a delicious aroma ordinarily, but one Leslie hated for its constancy. She would dream about the bland, fluffy white bread like she saw on TV. The Daniels children were encouraged to make friends at school, their faith irrelevant, and to be polite to their friends' parents so that they could freeload whenever possible. Their mother pressured them to take along brothers and sisters, and to wheedle whatever they could because the world outside their denomination was fair game. They were taught that non-believers were non-people and the only divine judgment that could be made against a Mormon was if that Mormon harmed in any way another Mormon.

Money was scarce, yet at a cost to the household's budget, the Daniels tithed, mandatory for upstanding Mormons. But Mormons believed strongly in helping each other, too, and church attendance was a must to insure that help. The Daniels received plenty of used items. Leslie dreamed of owning a tee shirt that did not have stains.

Communication limited to a superficial level was an unaddressed family predicament. Leslie's parents stood by their Mormon platitudes; she and her siblings disagreed, but did not confide in one another. Unbeknownst to the others, then, because it would be a sinful admission, the Daniels youth shared a fervent desire to get away from home as soon as possible. And not one grew up with any desire to have children.

Despite the close age ranges and disorderly living conditions, the Daniels enjoyed good health and were lithe, attractive people like their parents. They had glossy brown hair, excellent teeth and dark blue eyes.

The superior-attitude religious philosophy combined with the fine appearances, however, turned a number of Leslie's siblings into arrogant adults. Both older brothers got into gangs. One was blinded during retaliation in a drive by shooting; the other went to prison for statutory rape. A sister was murdered by the L.A. drug dealer that she thought she could control. Another stabbed her husband during an argument.

Leslie's escape came in the form of a palm tree trimmer whose chief diversion was his biker gang chaptered in Phoenix. Besides recreational purposes, the gang dealt drugs for a collective income, but each member also held a low skill job. When he was around, Quif lived with his mother in a trailer in Apache Junction where he kept a thirty year old, rust-eaten truck, a climbing belt, spiked boots and saws. When necessary, he scrounged buddies to assist him.

The Daniels currently lived in Mesa and Leslie was a senior in high school, but close to nineteen. Frequent moving and crowded, noisy living quarters had not been conducive to earning high grades. All of the Daniels had been held back at some stage of their education and none aspired to college.

The day Quif trimmed the two palms in the front yard of the Daniels' rental, Leslie was off for Veteran's Day. She had a line job at a fast food restaurant, but had called in sick and was sunbathing in the backyard.

The racket of Quif's truck in the alley startled Leslie. Quif had not lost any front teeth yet, but already his tattoos were liberal. The sight of the bare-chested, exotically decorated man with a blond pony tail and chains hanging off his filthy jeans fascinated Leslie. She wandered over to the fence.

Leslie's ill-fitting bathing suit forced her breasts to spill from the bodice, and Quif paused in unloading the palm fronds to cast an appreciative eye on her cleavage and long legs. The renter was holding payment and he had told the owner that he would haul away the refuse. He prepared to lie that he would be back later to pick up the debris.

But it never occurred to Leslie that Quif might be doing something sneaky. She was curious about him and drawn to his rough appearance. Dating Mormons was a restriction that at first hobbled Daniels youth; in Leslie's case, she had been involved with the same insipid boy since freshman year. Tobacco, liquor and drugs were strictly forbidden to Mormons, and sex was a sacred act inside marriage. They had not been daring enough to indulge in the three vices because they had no means of getting them, but they had done everything sexually, except have intercourse. Leslie was too petrified of becoming pregnant and her boy friend was too intimidated by her fear to push for it.

Pretty Leslie's friendliness prompted Quif to ask her to go for a ride on his bike. That evening, she bundled up and met him on Main Street, Mesa's original business strip a couple of blocks from the house. They rode out to the desert and Quif introduced Leslie to beer. This sequence repeated twice before Quif swore on the safety of condoms and Leslie succumbed. Her surrender was greater than her virginity, though. From his long, streaked blond hair to the lewd serpent tattoo twining his back, everything about Quif was so different, so exciting. She understood now why her brothers and sisters had done what they had done. They'd had no life growing up! They'd had to catch up, to experiment, TO LIVE! In her romantic daydreams about Quif, she forgot about the consequences that her siblings had paid for living on the edge.

Their desert dates continued for several weeks before Leslie's old boy friend got exasperated at her unwillingness to see him and followed her. He informed her parents.

Meanwhile, Quif had built enough of a cash reserve and was ready to split again. The emotional eruption at the Daniels coincided neatly with his plan to take Leslie with him. He'd gotten fond of her singular devotion, enjoyed the regular sex, and he would get status for bringing a foxy old lady into the gang, presently gearing to leave town. Quif had already mentioned the idea and Leslie had been enthusiastic.

The next time she was scheduled to work, she wore several layers of clothes to her job, hoping Quif would stop by so she'd never have to go home again. He'd been hanging around the gas station next door for just that reason, and the moment her father's car disappeared on the street, Quif was at the restaurant. Leslie waited until her break and sneaked away.

Quif and Leslie joined up with the gang partying in Wickenburg, then headed west to California. The travelers lived on the Southern Coast through the winter, crashing at the homes of buddies or sleeping by the roadside.

Leslie's wholesome school girl image transformed as she tanned permanently from the sun and her jeans frayed. Quif bought her a black, fringed leather vest and boots. He paid for her shoulder tattoos. At swap meets shopping with the other old ladies, she found snug tube tops and colorful bandannas for her hair. Lean, tawny Leslie developed into a tough beauty.

Quif also got her fixed with birth control pills which relieved Leslie immensely. Prevention was better than an abortion, she reasoned. A soul searching for a bodily home just wouldn't find a welcoming egg swimming in her tubes. In case there was any truth in Mormonism, though, snuffing a soul might be a critical error.

Drugs and booze were daily fare for the gang. Leslie rarely imbibed alcohol because of Mormon indoctrination, but she believed naively in her rationale for what she ingested of drugs - if she felt in control, it wouldn't hook her.

Grass made her cough. Bennies made her eyes tingle and her teeth ping. So did snorting cocaine, plus her nose ran which was gross. Mormonism had too thoroughly ingrained in her the peril of needles and addiction; therefore, Leslie wouldn't touch heroin, but the cough medicine Quif gave her when the grass choked her had codeine. Medicine couldn't harm you. Mixing red devils, blue heaven and yellow jackets sedated her sometimes in a scary way, but the pills went down easy. Quif suggested she try morphine. It was used as a medicine and came in pill form. (He neglected to tell her that morphine in a converted form was heroin.) Leslie tried it. She enjoyed the euphoric effect which could be produced with one drug without burning her nose or throat and without sticking a sharp needle in a vein.

In early spring, they returned to Apache Junction. Quif's mother liked Leslie who was polite to the older woman just as she had been raised to treat a potential benefactor. His mother was a social security recipient vicariously living in her TV soap operas, but a busybody, too, who knew everybody in the trailer court, an advantage for Leslie. She heard that a cafe in Chandler needed another counter waitress and got the job on the neighbor's referral. At the same time, Quif canvassed the East Valley lining up palm trimming jobs. Leslie tried her old phone number, but it had been disconnected. Back to Utah once more, she figured, mildly angry. She'd had a rapport with her immediately younger sister, Jessica. It would have been nice to tell her that she was okay.

The pattern of travel and occasional work was not very different from her nomadic childhood so Leslie easily adapted to Quif's routine. In some ways, his mother's trailer became her first real home; it was more of a permanent dwelling than Leslie had ever experienced in her youth.

Quif considered himself a lucky son-of-a-gun for having found Leslie because other bikers never failed to check out his compliant, stunning companion with envy. Also, his old lady was faithful, despite his own sporadic straying.

During the raunchier rallies, Leslie's highs did not dim her awareness of Quif's infidelities, but objections had not been voiced in the Daniels household. Life went smoothest if you just accepted things, and she was not about to change the pattern now. Besides, Quif made sure that she had a steady supply of morphine to which she grew heavily addicted. Morphine was an emetic and often she vomited from taking too much. The narcotic was also a depressant and she cried easily. But Leslie never got close to finding out what withdrawal might entail because at the slightest tremor or feeling of irritation, she had her fix ready to swallow.

Leslie and Quif remained together for over five years. Their breakup, though, was not by choice. The gang was riding south from Flagstaff and had just passed through Sedona on their way to Phoenix. A heavy rain slicked the road and obscured visibility. Quif, accustomed to driving drunk or high, had maneuvered through worse situations, but somebody's novice cousin had joined them in Flagstaff. The novice cousin was from Cottonwood, the next town on their route, and eager to get home to brag about his experience with a real biker gang. When a redneck trucker taunted them with horn blasts, the novice cousin startled and lost control, taking out three bikes with him in a tangle of metal, hot motors and limbs. Arizona did not have a helmet law, but Leslie was wearing hers because of the rain. It saved her from being a fatality as she tumbled off, but Quif's spiked Kaiser helmet made no difference. He stayed put while his Harley plowed into another, and the bikes exploded.

Leslie was clothed in leather, minimizing her surface battering, but she suffered multiple fractures and internal injuries. Notice of her addiction to morphine was delayed until doctors reduced her access to the painkillers administered during her healing. She spent eighteen months convalescing at the expense of the trucking company whose driver's behavior had been witnessed by a gleeful personal injury lawyer from Phoenix. A stunned gang member who had escaped the carnage received the lawyer's card before the state highway patrol arrived.

Apart from a generous cash settlement, the accident had additional benefits. Leslie's sister, Jessica, had discovered that God did have a more lucrative side than any Mormon worship had ever brought a Daniels. Curious about the New Age atmosphere in Sedona, she moved there upon high school graduation, and a newly declared spiritualist hired her to be his administrative assistant. His idea was to conduct seminars for those seeking attunement with Sedona's vortexes. Blending meditation, lectures, vegetarian meals and hikes to the power points, his business rapidly flourished.

Jessica readily accepted her thirtyish employer's philosophy. South Red Rock Country had two vistas; one the most famous, Bell Rock, was noted for its bolts of energy emitting into the universe. The other ran in spurts along Schnebly Hill Road. West Red Rock Country had several power points - Airport Ridge where emotions kindled; Cathedral Rock in Red Rock Crossing which had a tranquil effect on emotions; and Boynton Canyon, a spot that sparked the memory of previous lives. In Oak Creek Canyon, north of Sedona, Indian Gardens grounded a person and generated peaceful feelings.

Her enthusiasm paid off professionally and personally. The spiritualist soon married Jessica and made her his partner.

Jessica and everybody in a fifty mile radius heard details about the accident which killed five bikers and severely injured seven. Leslie's identity was taken from her expired driver's license still tucked inside her shredded jacket.

The sisters' reunion influenced Leslie's recovery more than Jessica's religious ardor. Quif and the gang had been her whole family. Jessica offered a convenient substitute for Leslie's mass loss, and settling in Sedona seemed the next logical step.

For Jessica's sake, Leslie tried to get into vortex worship, as she viewed the spiritualist's business, but she had been spoiled by the ease of motorcycles which could go almost anywhere. Traipsing around on foot took effort. Since she had the settlement money for a livelihood, she worked in their office answering phones just to keep busy and for further convenience, she rented one of the cottages on their estate overseeing Oak Creek.

Drugs and her harsh experiences on the road had aged Leslie, but she retained a definite appeal to a certain type of man. One day while on lunch break, she spied Don Becker's Harley parked near the retreat center office. Don admired Leslie admiring his bike, and like her relationship with Quif, the one with Don was instantaneous.

⁌

Judith Hutchins did not have much use for Leslie Daniels, whom she considered crass, or for flaky Heidi Becker, Elliot's wife, but she was crazy about their girls and spoiled them like a grandmother would. In return, Alana, Gina and Sacha adored Judith. To share in their holidays, then, Judith always invited Melvin, Elliot's family, and Don and Leslie to her residence for dinner. Since neither Heidi or Leslie could cook well and Judith did, acceptance was unanimous.

In Judith's spacious living room, Elliot glanced around at the fireplace, the vaulted ceiling and the multiple level, double hung windows. Her southwest decor reminded him of the desert, bleached and arid, but the architectural design was contemporary with a Swiss chalet influence.

The room curved past a compact, galley-style kitchen which faced the dining room at the back of the cottage. Sniffing at the scent of turkey, Elliot walked to the sliding doors near the dining table and stepped out on to an angled deck.

He looked at the eaves. Judith's cottage had only two bedrooms, but the second floor also had a loft and there were two full baths; the upstairs one had a laundry alcove. The cottage was pricey real estate, Elliot assessed, plus up the ante for the marvelous view. But he did not begrudge her. Judith was a devout Christian and deserving of her good fortune. She made Melvin happy and she was very kind to his kids.

"Hey, Elliot," Leslie greeted as she joined him on the deck.

He turned and nodded coolly at his brother's whore...girl friend. (Heidi always chastised him for his un-Christian name-calling.) Their raucous motorcycle arrival had motivated him to step outside to avoid them.

"It's just one gorgeous view after another here in Sedona," Leslie said. "You get kinda used to it and don't really notice."

"God's love for us is unconditional, but surely you vex Him," Elliot said. "Why don't you two quit living in sin and get married?"

"Sin is something bad and like what we got feels so good. Marriage might wreck it." Unlike Quif, Don was loyal to her. If she pushed it, he would marry her, but Don liked kids and Leslie did not want to take a chance on him wanting one if they were wed. The legalities weren't worth it. She should tell Elliot to fuck off, but Leslie got tremendous pleasure from baiting the sanctimonious ass. It seemed a just reward for having had Mormon guilt forced on her as a youth.

Elliot sputtered, "Good? Your unsanctioned union is bad because it's against God's Law. What's bad will be eternal! What's bad is your soul roasting in Hell!"

Leslie shrugged. "I was raised to believe that when you got married, it was an eternal deal. God, that's pretty scary if you make a mistake. That's what's bad."

"Don't take Our Lord's Name in vain."

Heidi opened the door and sighed. "I've painted the breathtaking scene of Chimney Rock three times from this deck and feel inspired to capture it again." She smiled at Leslie whose free-spirit lifestyle, silver-threaded hair and jaded expression intrigued her. Heidi had tried to paint Leslie, but she had been unable to render the woman as she envisioned. "That's a new necklace, isn't it? I'm drawn to it."

Leslie lifted Theone's moonstone so that Heidi could see it better. "So am I. A customer lost it in the shop bathroom and I just can't take it off."

"You are guilty of stealing and you should return it!" Elliot said.

"Couldn't. She and her fellow were just passing through. God, he was a good-lookin' dude! She seemed so familiar to me and her name, Theone, rang a bell, but I couldn't place her. Don said the same thing about her."

"You will refrain from uttering The Lord's Name in vain around my daughters!"

"Imagine that!" Heidi said. "There are two women who have that name. I'd never heard of it before Theone Jones."

"That was her name," Leslie replied.

Elliot forgot his indignation at Leslie's breaking of the Third Commandment. "*Theone Jones* was at Don's shop?"

Leslie enunciated loudly, "You're over forty, Elliot! Your hearing must be goin'. Yeah, some woman named Theone Jones was at Don's shop."

"Thank you, Sweet Jesus!" He cried. "Now? Is she in town now?"

"Nope, it was last summer. I just found her necklace when the pipes froze up the weekend you fellows were off shootin' at elk."

His zealous expression crumpled in frustration. "Mr. Ulrich would have been so grateful. For months, he has been trying to help Dr. Chandler find the She-Evil."

"Oh, Dr. Chandler is on the rampage," Heidi informed Leslie in an awed tone as she pivoted for the sliding door. She was very impressed that Leslie had been involved in an encounter with the She-Evil and had survived. Leslie, though, had survived living with drug addict-rapists and had recovered from a serious accident. Perhaps she was better prepared than most to resist the She-Evil. Still...Heidi could not wait to tell the others.

~

In the church's main fellowship hall where the men's maintenance committee constructed booths for the annual Christmas Bazaar, Tawi Ulrich delicately clamped the mouthpiece on her cellular phone. How convenient that Vaughn was in his office - she did not have to wait to share the good news.

Judith was one of God's gifts, Tawi thought as she walked briskly across the central courtyard. Theone Jones had actually been in Sedona and Judith had one of her possessions! An intimate possession - a crystal pendant. It had taken Judith several hours yesterday with her fullest concentration to feel any inkling, but she had been positive of the accuracy of her reading. She continued to strive for a detailed impression.

The Lord had clearly indicated just whose side He was on, Tawi considered righteously, because her husband's prayers were about to be answered. Theone Jones could be found.

⸺

"...Amen." Vaughn opened his eyes at the conclusion of his prayer and warmly regarded Elliot seated by him on the black nubuck leather sofa in his office. "Thank you for responding so promptly to my request to see you."
"I'm honored to think you might need me, Sir."
"Need you? God needs all of us to carry on His Work among the wicked. But you, Elliot." Vaughn smiled. "How blessed you are! He has chosen you to be His Special Servant, My Friend. It is an esteem not many of us are granted and in such an active, positive way. Heaven will reward you."

Elliot lowered his head submissively and twiddled with one of the down filled pillows covered in fabric of a Zuni design. "Mr. Ulrich, Our Lord saved the life of my little girl to convince me to be faithful to the Cross. Whatever I can do to repay this tremendous debt will never be too great an undertaking."

Vaughn's benevolent expression masked his exultant feelings. Elliot was like the clay God used to fashion Adam! His control over the man was consummate, even greater than his influence on Glenn. (In matters of theology, Vaughn graciously conceded to the clergy, and Glenn earned his respect as master of The Word.) Vaughn needed to caution Elliot, though, that there were conditions to his service. Crucial conditions.

He leaned forward, templed his fingers under his chin and appeared to study the fresh flowers which Tawi replenished daily. The geometric, cut-crystal vase containing the mums was ultra modern, but most of his office furnishings reflected Tawi's current interest in the Arts and Crafts Period. His desk was her prize - a Stickley original. The desk also concealed a sophisticated monitoring system recording the immediate conversation by way of remote microphone. The instrument resembled a fountain pen similar to the one Vaughn used, and he had the device clipped inside his shirt pocket.

Elliot shifted nervously in the silence, but kept mute. Vaughn Ulrich was one of the anointed to do God's Work and the man overwhelmed him.

Vaughn sneaked a glance at his Rolex and let Elliot stew a full minute. With simpletons like Becker, his directions would have better impact if the man was first allowed to anticipate. He found that it worked to help the Becker types to focus solely on the instructions, and they would be less likely to botch them up. Taping the conversation was insurance because words could be shuffled into other meanings if instructions were still botched.

"Elliot..."

"Yes!" He bobbed clumsily.

Vaughn patted Elliot's clenched, knobby hands. "God needs for you to do something very serious to save the Faith. Something that might be miscontrued as being illegal, but we answer to a Higher Power, don't we? Our souls are what matters to God whose forgiveness will be foregone."

"Yes, Sir."

"God wouldn't be asking this of you if it wasn't a last resort solution for stopping a desperate scourge."

"I understand, Sir."

"Good." Vaughn stood up and walked to his window which overlooked one of the several meditative gardens maintained by his father-in-law. Presently, the area lay uncultivated for the short winter months.

"I have heard from a colleague in the field. Your father's dear friend, Judith - God blesses her sacred gift - has guided him to the She-Evil's location. Theone Jones has returned home to Paxton, Wisconsin, and fortunately, seems to be settling in for a spell. But to take advantage of the situation, we should act fast just in case she changes her mind. It is becoming extremely urgent to resolve this matter." Vaughn would not apprise Elliot of the obvious reason for Theone Jones' extended stay in one place. Agents had corroborated the identity of the truck, but despite sophisticated tele-photo equipment, they had not been able to identify unequivocally the She-Evil. A woman at the house looked to be in a state of advanced pregnancy, though, and Vaughn had deduced that it must be Theone Jones. But even if she was not the pregnant woman, the idea that she might be in a state of advanced pregnancy might make Elliot balk at the deed. To Vaughn, it was all the more justification for the situation to be resolved BEFORE she spawned another one of her kind. He shuddered at the possible abomination.

"I will do anything to help!" Elliot cried. He stood up, took several paces and knelt awkwardly in front of Vaughn. "Please, what are your wishes?"

"First, do you accept full responsibility for your actions?"

Elliot looked puzzled. "I won't shirk from my duty."

"You will plan your strategy secretly so that no one else will have to lie if they are questioned. Given the remote possibility that you are apprehended, you must not implicate anyone else. You must swear that you acted alone. If you attempt to involve others, they will deny it and they will have airtight alibis. I realize how harsh this sounds, but we cannot jeopardize those who would lead us back to The Light. We need them, God *needs them* in their roles just as much as He needs you in your role."

"I'd be a scapegoat, but, if needs be, I'll take complete responsibility."

"I find 'hero' and 'martyr' apropos. Remember, this is what God wants and any sacrifice on your part assures you instant redemption."

Elliot's face brightened, then grew morose. "What of my family? My precious little girls? I can't just leave them to...to fend for themselves. My wife is rather...uh, she needs to be...supervised."

Vaughn placed his hands on Elliot's head as if in benediction. "The Lord will provide for them because you will please Him vastly. By association with you, your girls and your wife will be esteemed among mankind for destroying the She-Evil." His tone softened. "And if your physical life does have to end to ensure success of your mission - and that is not a given - well, Sir, I guarantee, your spirit will ascend directly to the Right Hand of God. There will be a magnificent welcome in Heaven for you!"

"Yes, mission. It is my mission and I'll do it," Elliot whispered. "In the name of Our Savior, I'll do it."

"There is no time to mull, then," Vaughn said, his tone respectful, "go forth knowing that you go with God, My Dear, Dear Friend in Christ and shortly, you will be contacted with details. Stand, now, and I will close our time with a word of thanks for your mission."

His head bowed, Elliot could not see Vaughn's satisfied smile as he prayed.

⤙

In the barren woods by partially frozen Lake Femvivant, Theone ceased walking. Spider glanced about to see what creature she had attracted. Small mammals, including mink, always appeared here as did deer and fox.

"The bald eagle in the young maple," Theone said.

"He's out of his element, isn't he? How did he get through these tight trees with his wing span? And the guy is a month late for the fall migration."

"*She* and *her* mate, who is hidden in those twisted oak branches, are the last of the gathering that takes place at Necedah NWR which is southeast of here."

"South East?" Spider ribbed her. "Did they hang around on the off chance of meeting you?"

As if comprehending, the eagle transferred to a closer branch.

"Yes," she said nonchalantly. "Stand back from me."

He took a couple paces and watched.

She braced herself. The eagle landed on her left shoulder and rubbed its big, hooked beak on her cheek before returning to the branch.

"Okay, brace yourself for the male," she advised.
"What?" Spider jerked his sight at the oak.
"Go ahead!"
"Shit," he mumbled. This was a first. He'd had more than one bow to him, but animals did not want to touch him. Had his short hair finally lost its good luck charm? Fortunately, he was wearing his leather jacket. The talons on these raptors were awesome.

Suddenly, a surfeit of brown feathers blocked his vision as the eagle swooped to his shoulder. The thing had to weight ten pounds. How did Theone handle this so effortlessly? He screwed his eyes shut, trying not to cringe.

"Gabriel," Theone chastised, "relax."

The eagle took off almost the moment it landed, though. Spider sighed with relief.

"You were just honored very highly," she said.
"If you say so."

Theone laughed gently, then yawned.

"Are you getting tired?" Spider asked. They were several miles from the Scougans' house.

"Gabriel, we should return, but not because I need to rest. The garage called to say they've finished fixing the hydraulic lift on Sam's van. Erik is working every day, so I told Mom that I'd drive her into Paxton."

"You stay home. It's Christmas Eve and a million people will be in town trying to finish up their shopping. I'll take Brigit in."

"The Moon was in the first quarter last night. I must go with you." She patted her swollen abdomen which towards the end of November had suddenly manifested in her outward appearance. The occurrence had coincided with their arrival in Paxton. "The baby has dropped. It will be soon now."

"I'm not ready," he replied glumly.

"Oh, you are! You'll be fine." She hugged him for encouragement.

"Sure, I will." He kissed her forehead to hide his worried expression.

Spider had spent the past eight and half months since her announcement reading books on every baby subject from colic to diaper rash, but he had memorized the most important one, *"Being Prepared for the Unthinkable: Procedures for An Emergency Childbirth"*. Regardless, he continued to carry the worn paperback on his person at all times along with his Navy knife and a small spool of thick string because in his situation, it was thinkable and expected. He knew it was his job to deliver their baby. Theone had promised repeatedly that The Deity would direct him, but he could not muster the faith to trust that a spiritual hand would be so readily available.

Elliot Becker had done his work expeditiously and thoroughly. Despite being the Christmas season and a busy time for the shop, he told Heidi and Melvin that he had a hunch. He was going on an extensive buying trip to the reservations in the Reno, Nevada area and might just do a little skiing while he was there. As strange as it seemed, his intuition about merchandise was always sound; also, several winters ago he had started skiing in order to accompany the girls and had taken a liking to it. They were reassured by his promise to be home for the holidays.

Minneapolis was closer to Paxton, but Elliot had flown into Chicago's O'Hare, a larger city airport, and perhaps a less likely place for someone to remember him. He had used his smarts about purchasing a weapon in Madison, too. Hunting whitetail deer up North with a high power rifle was confined to a brief period around Thanksgiving, but rabbits, squirrels, partridge, ruffled grouse - small game remained in season. Game hunted with a shotgun. To cloak what he planned as his real purchase, a 30-30 lever action Winchester rifle, Elliot bought a shotgun and an assortment of shells with different size shot. Shot was only good at a distance of 15-20 feet. For accuracy and the capability to take out a human, he would have to have slugs, and he was limited to a maximum distance of forty yards. A high power rifle was a necessity. By chance he looked over a display of used rifles and discovered an old Springfield M1A Standard with two 5-round box magazines and a variable power scope. Except for a heavier trigger pull, the Springfield M1A Standard had the same specifications as the Springfield M1A match rifle, one still used by target shooters in high power competition. The rifle was in excellent condition and surely here for him as a sign from God. He told the gun store owner it was a sentimental buy because the rifle reminded him of his target shooting days. The owner probably figured the real reason was he intended to poach a deer, but Elliot counted on the man being a hunter and sympathetic about gaming restrictions.

His recreational vehicle, the rental paid in cash, had four-wheel drive and was fully self-contained. It bothered him that he had to provide detailed identification in each transaction, but trusted God that somehow who he was would not be traced.

Elliot had been advised that they had been unable to fix on Theone's exact spot, but a field agent watching Scougans' had provided a list of vehicles in and out of the secured grounds, one of which matched the description of the camper truck witnesses had stated Theone Jones drove. Motor vehicle records had confirmed that a Brigit Jones held title to the truck. It was reasonable to Elliot, then, to assume that the Scougans were hiding the She-Evil.

He went straight through Paxton without stopping and entered the state park, heading for the northern boundary. (The park employee did not seem to find it unusual that he purchased a week's camping permit, and he decided that the presence of other hardy campers was a sign from God that his actions would go undetected.) The field agent had provided compass coordinates along with a detailed description of Brigit, but Elliot could not get a close enough position from the state woods to set up an effective stakeout. He doubled back and on a drop in the landscape he found a dense forest site close to the road which led to the Scougans'.

For three days he sat in his camouflage thermal-wear. With binoculars ready and only a 2-quart thermos of canned stew to nourish him, he waited, hopeful that the She-Evil would pass by. The hike to his vehicle camped next to an interior park road was more than a mile, but zeal for his mission helped sustain him.

The sight of a green truck alerted Elliot whose hope on the fourth day had begun to dwindle. He sharpened his focus on the windshield and scanned the occupants. Dr. Chandler had likened The Companion's reported dark looks to the Devil who would appear seductively handsome. The man driving the truck fit the image and next to him...was a woman...a sudden brightness blurred his view. He closed his eyes which hurt. There's no sun to cause a reflection, Elliot thought, baffled. He inched the binoculars to the person seated by the passenger window and cautiously opened his eyes. His heart hammered.

He had stared enough at the She-Evil's mother's picture to have memorized the woman's pretty features, and no mistake, this woman was Brigit Jones. Elliot tried again to see the center person, but the same brightness flared. This was the She-Evil, he was certain. Satan had provided her with an diabolic shield and it served as further proof that he had found the one he sought to destroy. *The one that God had requested for him to destroy...*

The truck passed by his position, but Elliot had dropped his binoculars. Grinning, he watched the vehicle until it was out of sight. They would be back, and he would be ready.

Stratus clouds, low, gray layers guaranteeing snow, had plastered the sky when Spider, Theone and Brigit had departed for Paxton to get the van. Now, as the two vehicles left Highway 27 from town for the two lane county road to Lake Femvivant and home, the guarantee was paying off.

The temperature had dropped and sleet washed the deserted road, freezing when it hit the blacktop.

Spider eased the gas to widen the gap between him and the van in which he had insisted Theone ride with her mother. Unlike her truck with just its lap belts, the van had shoulder harnesses attached. No sense increasing the possibility of sliding into them, he thought, or into one of the trees which grew so close to the road. The fork to the lake lay ahead. He blamed his heightened anxiety on the pending birth of their child.

In expectation of their return, Elliot had left his tree shelter and flattened himself behind the road-bank. He spied the van approaching, glanced at the truck following it at approximately 200 yards and settled his binoculars on the van.

The driver of the van was the Brigit Jones woman and the passenger... the light, the hurtful light. His adrenaline coursing, Elliot dropped his binoculars and grabbed for his rifle. They had picked up the van from somewhere and it really excited him. The She-Evil and the One who Spawned the She-Evil were *together*. By themselves. It was a sign from the Almighty! Elliot murmured a quick prayer of thanks with a entreaty to God to steady his hand and got the van in his sights, narrowing it to the front right tire. During the past hour, he had re-considered shooting the woman outright as he had intended originally. The light obscuring her made focus impossible and if he missed a vital organ, he might not get a second opportunity. Security around her would be alerted. He might be caught, too. The gas tank was a sure shot to explode the truck, but it was on the wrong side to be facing him on the return trip. Now, he didn't have time to check the gas tank's location on the van. But Elliot had already figured if he instantly deflated the tires, with the steep downgrade of the road a vehicle would careen into the trees, causing fatal injury to the passengers. Also, it would settle the nagging feeling that he had about the Sixth Commandment, Thou Shalt Not Kill. If God truly meant for Theone Jones to die, then He would make sure she did. If not, Elliot's conscience would be clear.

With conviction, he fired two shots at the right front tire and at once fired two more at the right rear tire. The heavy explosions of torn, thick rubber jarred the still air as the passenger side of the van plunged to its metal wheel rims.

Brigit panicked. Twisting the steering wheel left, then right, she locked the brakes. Instead of crashing into the trees, the van skidded across the blacktop and pitched up the incline next to the road. Sparks lit the murky sleet as the van lurched on to the passenger side and flipped to its roof. The flat metal surface on the ice-slicked road quickened the van's speed and achieving a lethal spin, the vehicle slid on the road's downgrade directly towards Elliot's position.

He could not move! He'd been serious about his pledge to Mr. Ulrich, but he had not really meant to get himself killed! Yet he could not move! His fingers were numb, his feet - his whole body was numb!

Horrified, Elliot watched as the van whirled closer, front, side, rear, side...like some grotesque roulette game. He absurdly wondered how he should place his bet. Which point would strike?

The driver's side hit him. Odd, he thought, as the van rammed into the trees with him in their midst, Brigit's upside down face was not distorted with fear. Her expression was tranquil, and she smiled at him with joy.

Elliot's eyes bugged with comprehension. *What had he done?* In the finite second between life and death, he glimpsed a vision of the future in which his soul spiraled downward from a welcoming radiance to a dismal abyss. Hell? That wasn't the promise! That wasn't God's Will...

But God's Will had no bearing on what he had done. *Humans' did.*

With a sick clarity Elliot realized that he had made a very bad choice by ignoring The Deity's Message. Theone Jones *had been* speaking The Truth, and now, now, his soul's next journey would be starting from the deepest, darkest pits.

⸻

"Theone?"

"Yes, Mom."

"I had this wonderful dream. My grandparents were in it, and Lyle and Aaron. They were greeting me as if...as if I was coming home..."

"You are coming home."

"But my mother and father were in it, too, and Erik, an older Erik with a beard. He told me how happy he was to be working at the NWR in Necedah. And Kristen was kind. We weren't alienated, anymore, and I got to see the grandchildren. Kimberlee has Aaron's eyes."

"Our Deity is allowing you to say 'goodbye'."

"Sam was in the dream, too, but in a quite...melancholic way...others were to a lesser extent. But they were all loving and conveyed understanding. I felt okay to leave them because they were still on their journeys, but mine was ending now."

"Your soul is reaching Peace."

"Do you see the rainbow over the lake? The water is azure! And the sky is so brilliantly clear. How can that be? Why...there are lotus! I can smell their sweet scent! Lotus at Lake Femvivant in the winter? ...But not our pale yellow variety...*white* lotus like those depicted in ancient Egyptian art!"

"Lotus in Peace. It has been your final journey, Brigit. Your soul has reached Peace."

"Oh, Theone," she sighed in ecstasy, "Glimpses are nothing compared to this! It's incredibly better than you ever described."

⁓

"Please, Deity, no!" Spider cried and hit the gas pedal of the truck to gain on the overturned van, but he knew there was little he could do until the vehicle stopped. "Not the trees! Stop before the trees! It's too dense, there's no chance..." he yelled as he followed the van's collision path with the forest.

The crash echoed and re-echoed in the stillness as sheet metal ripped and splintered hardwood exploded.

Spider realized how fast he was going and pumped the brake to avoid leaving the solidness of the road. The truck swerved to a halt on the graveled shoulder, and he wrenched the gear to park. Slipping on the icy ground, he made his way to the van, entangled in broken trees.

The passenger side faced him. Airbags had been optional the year the van had been manufactured, and Sam had not ordered them. Relief made Spider feel guilty because under the circumstances, the way the van had hit, little likelihood existed that Brigit, on the driver's side, remained alive.

Spider approached the upside-down vehicle and looked in anxiously where a window had been.

Gravity pushed Theone to the roof, but her seat belt had kept her fairly stationary. She was able to turn her head to him.

"I'll get you out!" He shouted.

She nodded with difficulty.

The door handle had been ripped off on the van's initial spill, though, and he would not be able to pry the door with his bare hands. He could not pull her through the window frame, either, because she was too pregnant.

"Reach inside," Theone whispered. "The door will open...if you try from the inside."

Spider ignored the sharp edge ripping at his jacket as he groped for the interior handle. He lifted and felt the door release, but the door was bent. If he let go of the release to yank at the door, the latch might re-catch.

Theone's hand closed over his wrist. "Move back. I can brace it... enough."

His fear eased as he readied to open the door. She did not seem to be hurt badly. Shoving upward on the damaged metal, Spider could see none on Theone, but blood coated what was left of the mangled interior. All he could recognize of Brigit was her hand dangling close to Theone's suspended hips.

"Grip my shoulders...while I release...the seat belt," she said, "help me."

"Is Brigit gone?"

"Yes, but you can tell...Sam and Erik it was instantaneous. She didn't suffer."

"You can tell them."

"Gabriel, I must...get out of here. Labor has started."

"Labor? Theone! I can't deliver a baby here!"

"We have time for you...to get me out and into...the truck."

"And?"

Her crooked smile was patient. "You're taking me to...the lakeshore."

Spider clenched her shoulders to support her weight while she released the seat belt mechanism. "We are going to the house and calling an ambulance," he informed her.

Theone said no more as she concentrated on helping him ease her sideways and on to the ground. He hugged her awkwardly.

"You'll have to carry me," she advised, "I'm too weak and can't walk."

"Are your legs hurt?"

"Carry me to the truck, Gabriel, and drive me to the lake."

"Theone, you need medical care and I don't give a shit..."

"Do as I tell you, please."

Spider breathed raggedly and he muttered incoherently, but he followed her instructions.

By the time they reached the beach, the sleet had stopped, but the sky remained heavy. Unmindful of the weather, Theone ordered Spider to lay her on the sand and remove her clothes.

"It's damn cold!"

"I don't get cold! Please, My Beloved, the baby is crowning. You must do as I say, then bend my knees. I can't do it myself because there is no feeling."

Spider reluctantly obeyed her directions.

"Hold your hands ready," she gasped, "the baby is coming."

Black hair like mine, Spider noticed of the slick head emerging, and a long body. He gripped the slippery infant and turned it to see the pubis.

Spider grinned in spite of his fear. A girl. A girl who looked like him except...the infant had opened her eyes and was staring at him...solemnly. She had her mother's eyes. Theone's wise, magickal eyes, but somehow Spider did not get the impression that their child would seek to reach souls. Maybe the time for reaching souls had passed...

"Waaaa. Waaaa."

"I haven't smacked her butt yet," Spider joked. His part in the delivery had not been the least bit difficult.

"Cut and tie the cord," Theone murmured, "then place Ansonia at my breast."

"An-sone-ya," he repeated softly as he formed their daughter's umbilicus. "She is Ansonia."

Theone gazed at the sky and a gentle rain began to fall, cleansing her and the baby who suckled. When the rain ceased, she instructed, "Now, swaddle her, Gabriel, in my skirt, then my windbreaker. She will be fine."

"I forgot blankets! I'm getting blankets from the camper!" He exclaimed and tried to rise. The truck had been left a tenth mile back at the end of the service road.

"The truck is gone."

"Who took the truck?"

Theone's voice rose. "Gabriel, there isn't time for this! You must take Ansonia to the house and keep her presence...not concealed, but low key. She is to grow up here without others besides you, Sam, Erik and Mag being aware of her real identity. Uncle Patrick will be an ally, but you won't be required to give him an explanation. You will need to inform Jasper and Pilar in person for legal reasons, but it isn't crucial yet." She nuzzled the baby's dark, downy head. "The day will come soon enough when the world will be apprised of who Ansonia is. Gather close your daughter and protect her."

Spider felt an emotional rip in his chest as he lifted the baby and laid her on her mother's skirt. "What about you?" He uttered. "Where will you be?"

Her expression was compassionate. "My work is over," she said gently. "I have to leave this environment."

"You said you'd stay with me as long as I needed you! I need you, Theone!" Tears streamed his cheeks as he wrapped Ansonia.

"Not your soul. Your soul is strong."

"My soul? What about my heart? What about...my life?"

"It will be about raising Ansonia and utilizing your genius finally in a productive way. Gabriel, my love will never leave you."

"No, it ends for us." He laid Ansonia by Theone's shoulder and slumped next to her.

"As a constant physical presence I must leave you, but I will remain a part of your spirit."

Sobbing, Spider pressed against her with intensity.

Ansonia gurgled.

He choked back his tears and regarded their daughter.

"When Ansonia's soul is strong enough to continue on its journey without your guidance," Theone said faintly, "your journey will end, Gabriel. You will reach Peace."

He hiccuped and breathed deeply in an attempt to steady his voice. "I know what you teach about soulmates, but is there...is there any chance, maybe as a special favor from Our Deity, that...that you'll be there when I arrive?"

She smiled, but some of the glory had faded. "I am returning to Peace. Therefore, one day we will be in the same place again for always."

"Okay, okay," he said. "I can go on if I know that some day..."

"Wear this until Ansonia reaches puberty. It will help to protect you." Theone's clenched left hand was upright under her breast. She opened her palm to reveal her emerald ring. "Give it to her with my stones which you will also safeguard for her."

He clasped her fingers to take the ring, and they felt like they were loosing substance! Disconcerted, Spider mentally catalogued the citrine, the aquamarine, the jet and the amber. "The stones zipped in your jacket."

"Yes." Theone gazed at the sky again, and a sudden beam of silvery gold permeated the murk. "My time is here."

Spider looked at the light, then at Theone. She appeared ethereal. "Oh, no. Not yet! I can't let you go so quickly..."

"Take Ansonia in your arms, My Beloved, and close your eyes. Remember, I am always going to be a part of you. Always..."

"No, no, no..." he whispered, but long ago he had accepted what loving Theone meant. It was unconditional and his commitment infinite. He picked up the baby and buried his face in Theone's jacket framing Ansonia's head.

A powerful, but peaceful presence enveloped Spider.

Welcome to Peace, Child, a melodious feminine voice exclaimed. *We are so pleased with you!*

But not with humans, a rich masculine voice declared. *Humans have failed us for the unequivocally LAST TIME...*

Theone's voice interrupted with her customary vibrancy. "Oh, certain ones, yes, but so many have listened to The Message! They will share it with others who in turn will tell still more. Truth will succeed this time! It won't be necessary for Ansonia..."

Your purity of Us, Child, rightly blinds you as intended. Ansonia is half human...as intended. Her purpose...

Spider strained to continue hearing the dialogue, but it had tapered off into the lapping sounds of the lake.

Ansonia snuffled.

Warily, he opened his eyes to check her and was amazed to find full sunlight. The incandescence seemed to caress the baby and she was...

smiling. Gas, he concluded with confidence. Absorbing the information in those child care books was about to pay off because he was it. Father AND mother...

Spider stared wistfully at the drying sand, then patted the deteriorating impression where Theone had lain. He would mourn her for the rest of his life, yet life would go on because his promise would be kept. He would live The Message as best he could and in so doing, try to be the best example he could for Ansonia.

Tears blurred his vision, but he spoke with some of his usual humor. "So, Kid. We gotta get you secured at the Scougan compound. Lucky you. You're gonna be surrounded by doting men since your grandma is gone, too..." Spider's voice cracked. Sam, Erik, himself - Ansonia would be raised by grieving men.

Theone's emerald on his left pinkie finger twinkled, and he realized as reluctant as he may feel about letting go of the last contact with her, they had to leave. On dry ground, it was a good distance to run and he was bound to hit a lot of mud from the sleet. Possibly the accident had not been reported yet, and he hoped he could be in time to notify Sam about Brigit before the police did. Theone's death...disappearance would not be explained. Her evanescent, obscure actions in the past year had already rooted her in myth; only a trusted few were aware of his name. But it was not something he had to worry about because the story would weave in a way that The Deity intended. Spider's trust in his destiny was absolute.

He started to rise, but a movement at his peripheral vision caused him to freeze. A gray wolf sauntered towards them!

Automatically, he felt his head. Theone had just cut his hair again. But there weren't any wolves in this region! What the hell was going on?

The wolf drew closer, then cocked its head playfully.

Silver eyes like in his dream, Spider thought, silver eyes like the two who had touched Theone after the first time they had made love. This wolf was of the same type and here to pay Ansonia homage. He had no doubts, either, that the animal was female, and held up his daughter so that she could see her. The wolf crouched in obeisance.

Spider watched Ansonia's face and her expression was...poised. An hour old and already she seemed...to comprehend who she was. She seemed...to expect the reverence as her due...

He got an inkling of the future. Unlike Theone, Ansonia's nature would not be kind or merciful. Half her nature was human...Ansonia had been born to command, not offer haven, and it would be on her terms.

CHAPTER NINETEEN

Brigit's death profoundly stunned Kristen. As if bodily ill, she went to bed and stayed there for days, ignoring her anxious family and friends. Her mother loved children and Kristen had thought that by cutting her off from G.J. and Kimberlee, she was helping God teach Brigit a lesson about faith. She had assumed there was plenty of time to reconcile with her mother which would happen when Brigit eventually recognized that the only way to immortal happiness was through belief in Christ.

The announcement by authorities that the late Elliot Becker, a member of Cavalry IOG, was the one responsible for Brigit's terrible accident hurled Kristen out of her insentient state. *A Believer from her own church had murdered her mother?* Incensed, she demanded to talk with Glenn.

"Explain to me how God could have allowed this to happen!"

Glenn nodded earnestly. He was so relieved that his wife's torpor had lifted! Anger he could handle, but Kristen's depression scared him. It reminded him of Nancy, a failing that he had kept firmly repressed for years.

"Darling, God can't control a sick person. This Elliot Becker was crazy!"

"Did you know him?"

"No," he replied sincerely. He purposely did not remember anyone unimportant. When Vaughn reminded him that he had baptized Elliot, he had drawn a blank, even after viewing the man's picture in the church directory.

"How could anyone who has heard you preach like you do be...be so twisted as to...to break a Commandment? You tell people to fight against Theone's falsehoods, but no matter if the Devil spawned her, you've *never* condoned physical violence to achieve it! We pray and we set an example! Did this, this lunatic think by killing my mother he would sabotage Theone?"

"Krissy, I have already denounced Becker's vile act as irrational and have explicitly established that no genuine Christian had any part in what he did. The only weapon we need is the Power of God through the teachings in the Bible. This man has hurt The Faithful with his unthinkable crime against another person, regardless of where she stood in her faith."

"Are you suggesting that my mother didn't go to Heaven?" Kristen's voice was shrill. This was her deepest fear and Glenn had just hinted that it might be valid!

He took her hand and kissed it. "No, Darling. I'm positive Brigit asked for forgiveness in her final moments. Grace was bestowed as it always is."

"I'm positive, too," Kristen said, mollified. She started to weep. "Oh, she never saw Kimberlee."

Glenn leaned forward and kissed her cheek. "Brigit watches her from Heaven."

She sniffed and put her arms around his neck. "Has Theone done anything in public since Mother died?"

"Not a word as usual. Your stepfather held some sort of private memorial service at their home. Whether she was there, no one knows."

Kristen nudged him and sat up. "We will have our own very open service. You will eulogize Brigit and talk about how she found Jesus again and that God Himself greeted her because of what a good person she was!"

Glenn grinned in agreement. He'd do anything, ANYTHING, to get Kristen restored to her normal, perky self. The Christ Covenant had swiftly set in motion an effective public relations campaign to distance him and themselves from Elliot Becker, including an astute Christian outreach of forgiveness and assistance to the Becker family. A personal gesture on behalf of Brigit, however, would serve to dispel further the inevitable negativity that had been thrown on his ministry. Or, an even better way to take advantage of the situation might be just to turn it against Theone, implying that she had cast an evil spell on Becker in an attempt to discredit Glenn's IOG church. It could very well be true, Glenn rationalized. Many of the Faithful judged Theone as a demonic witch, and it would take little to plant the idea that she was capable of such an atrocity as killing her own mother. Her supporters were often vocal, but weak since she as their leader never defended her position. And if Theone was finally goaded to respond, the damage to her credibility would still be heavy.

Fact or not, Glen was confident Vaughn would applaud the idea. Whatever it took to foster the Faith his friend supported because Christianity was the Only True Way to God. The vital issue was that ultimately, Theone Jones and her kind would be vanquished, thereby chalking up another defeat for Satan.

Up the road from the Chandlers, Vaughn Ulrich sat in his study also pondering Theone Jones, but he was not considering damage control. The flak would die down because IOG supported the Right Faith and God was Their Master. Rather, Vaughn dealt with frustration. Somehow, the She-Evil had slipped through their net during the lull in surveillance! Agents had infiltrated Paxton for over a year, but direct orders in early December had vacated them from the Lake Femvivant area and additional instructions had been sent for them to stay away during the accident, then murder investigation. As a result none of them had witnessed the event or had any contact with the assassin. Exactly the way Vaughn intended; however, it had also allowed Theone Jones a freedom of movement. The visitors to the Scougan compound had not been monitored, and apparently, she had sneaked out in her truck because The She-Evil had been reported active in other areas of the country. No mention was made of any infant or the Companion, though. She traveled alone these days.

The baby, Vaughn kept thinking grimly, what about the imp-offspring? Real or imagined? Was it simply a Satan inspired tactic to confuse him? The unresolved situation bothered Vaughn tremendously, but since he could not control it, he forced away its priority. He would just accelerate pursuit of the She-Evil and pray that soon all of what she comprised would be obliterated.

EPILOGUE

Indifferent to the snow pile soaking his jeans, Spider stood in the courtyard, staring at the first full moon since Theone had left him. He remained in the same bedroom that he had shared with her, one on the north side of Sam's house which had a sliding door to Brigit's cherished garden. The location, next door to Ansonia's nursery, currently offered a view of the moon in every phase, but tonight he had felt compelled to go outside despite the cold and heavy drifts.

Spider was intrigued by the sight. Moisture in the atmosphere had formed ice crystals around the moon, and some sort of turbulence had shaped the crystals into a heart. Like a celestial valentine, he mused, except his special girl was gone from his life.

Although, Theone sightings and those claiming to be touched by her continued. Spider would smile pensively at the news reports, not entirely convinced that it wasn't true. In his mind, he envisioned Theone as having graduated to superior angel status, qualified to travel with ease between the spiritual and corporal dimensions. And had not Jesus done the same kind of thing by visiting his disciples after his ascension?

Spider swallowed hard on the thickness in his throat. He was going to cry again if he dwelled too long on Theone and forced himself to think about the joy in his life - Ansonia. He did not have any comparison, but she seemed exceptionally alert for an infant - her clear eyes always studied him - and she was unusually strong - her neck needed scant support. Ansonia acted very smart about drinking from her bottle, staying motionless as he clumsily bathed and diapered her, and she seldom fussed. Of course, he hovered. Sam and Erik were almost as bad. But with Brigit and Theone both gone simultaneously, the baby had served to ground them in the sudden chaos of their lives and had given them a common cause on which to focus for recovery. Neither Sam nor Erik found strange Spider's explanation of Theone's departure and without question, they had sworn to keep secret Ansonia's divine parentage.

Spider gazed at the moon, recalling the many times he had savored the celebration with Theone, and shut his eyes. How he missed her! He ached to share the details of Ansonia's growth, but felt too silly to talk to the sky about it. Sure, Theone would hear him, but he was afraid if he started vocalizing, he'd babble and breakdown and he could not bear to feel so unhappy, not when he was struggling so arduously to adjust...

"You're cold, Gabriel. You know better than to be outside like this wearing only a sweatshirt."

He said automatically. "I can count on you to generate heat, Theone. Why should I bother getting a coat?"

"Because you need to be more responsible now. I see you've finally tired of shaving altogether, but a beard suits you. Your hair has silvered! And it's as unruly as ever. Who's cutting it? Sam?"

Spider opened his mouth, then furrowed his brow. This grief was bad and his self-imposed quarantine from the world beyond Scougan's was affecting his sanity. He'd started hallucinating and having a conversation with the air.

"I have more substance than air," Theone said.

He slit his eyes and squinted.

Silhouetted against the moon...Theone in a white caftan? He knew she'd become an angel, but where were her wings?

She smiled at him. Her best, most captivating smile. "I don't need wings, My Beloved."

"I've lost it," he murmured, blinking. *But she seemed real.*

"I am real," she said. "During the hours of the full moon between sunset and sunrise, Our Deity has granted that you will benefit from my presence."

"Real? Can I touch you?"

She laughed flirtatiously. "Gabriel Giovetti, was there ever a time you could resist?"

Spider took a deep step and ended up on his knees in the snow. "Even if Sam has to call the loony bin in the morning, I'm going for this one totally," he uttered.

"You're not losing your mind," she said, laughing as he managed to reach her position and tentatively squeeze her arms. "My remarks about the depth of our love swayed Our Deity. Being a goddess has its advantages."

"*Every* month?"

"Yes. Let's go inside, but leave open the sliding door. While I'm here the moon's position must be aligned with my physical presence; sky conditions permitting, its glow must bathe me, and no one else can be aware."

"The door is always open, anyway. I guess I got used to it." He grinned and shivered.

"Inside!"

"I still sleep in our bags zipped together on top of the bed," Spider said as he hugged her.

Theone glided over the snow, lifting him with her and bringing them to their feet on the hardwood floor of the room. "Change your pants," she ordered.

"I'll just take them off..."

She laughed.

Spider kissed her hesitantly, then with exuberance and sighed. "I have so much to tell you about Ansonia!"

She knew exactly how their daughter fared, but she smiled to encourage him. "Mention to Sam and Erik that you dreamed about Brigit. It was a peaceful dream and you felt her love for them."

"I will. They've had a bad time."

"Be their strength."

"I can now! Theone, I've been playing with one of Sam's computers. I used to be pretty good at games, and I have this idea about writing one. Sam says he'll teach me C, a programming language..."

Theone nodded. She was cognizant of this situation, too, but Spider had no one else with whom to share his feelings and his isolation could affect Ansonia's development. Hence, for the child's sake, and ultimately, humanity's, it was important that her father have a confidante. The Deity had thus determined for Theone to return at intervals in her human guise.

Yet it was not difficult for Theone to leave the Wonder of Peace and be with Spider again. On Earth, in Peace - whatever the environment - she would cherish this soul for eternity.

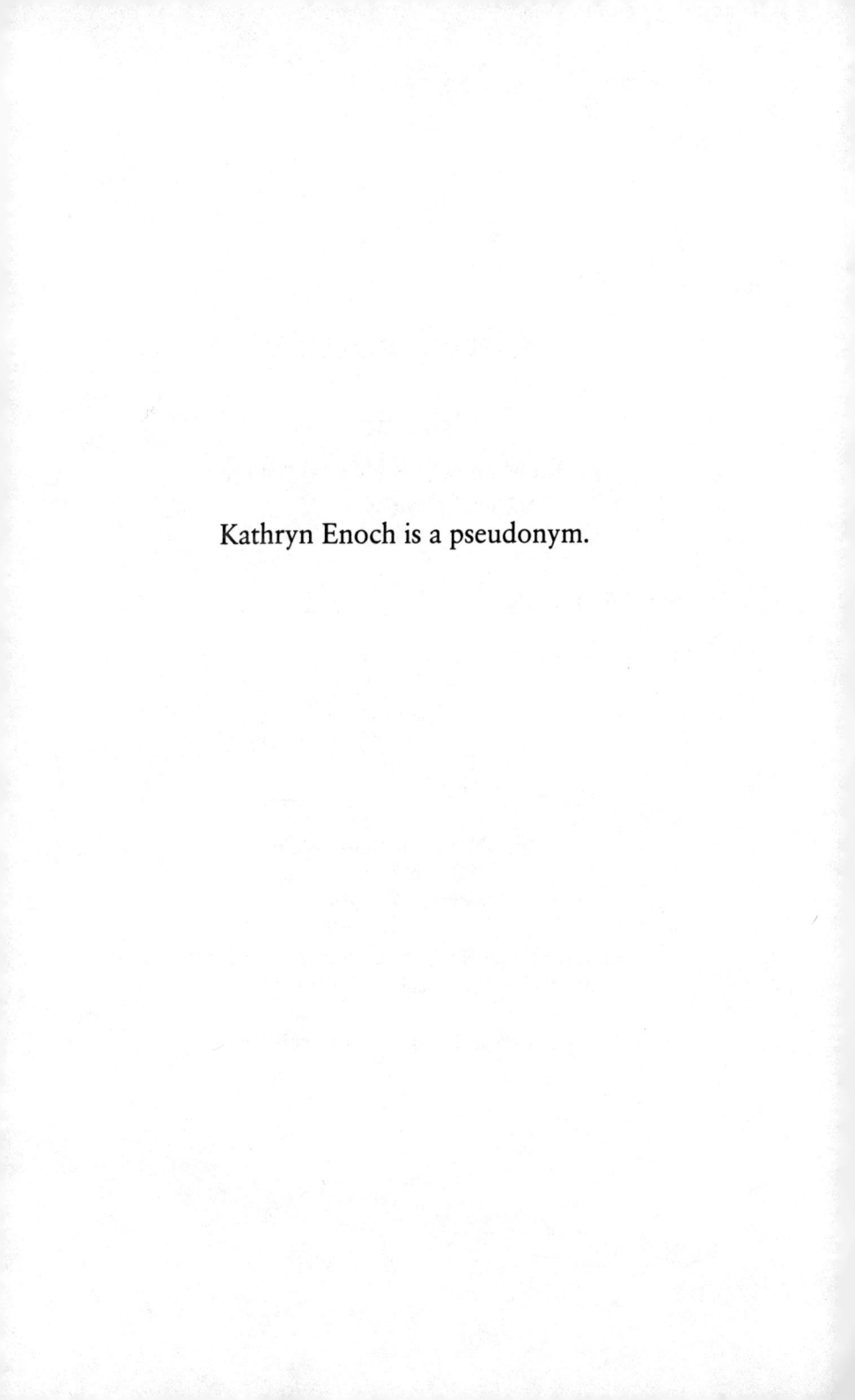

Kathryn Enoch is a pseudonym.

Order Form

Theone
The Old Message, A New Messenger
by Kathryn Enoch

___ copies @ $12.00 $ _____.__

\+ $4.50 **each** shipping & handling $ _____.__

Arizona residents add sales tax (.84¢ per book) $ _____.__

Total Enclosed $ _____.__

Rowan Press, Inc.
PO Box 80346
Phoenix, AZ 85060

credit card sales through internet book vendors
or check with your local book store

contact Rowan Press, Inc. for dealer prices